FANNY
The American Kemble

FANNY
The American Kemble

Fanny Kemble, by Thomas Sully
Philadelphia 1834
By kind permission of Mrs. Robert Nigel Brunt.

FANNY
The American Kemble

Her Journals and Unpublished Letters

Edited With Annotations

by

Fanny Kemble Wister

Tallahassee
1972

Printed for the South Pass Press

by Rose Printing Company, Inc., Tallahassee, Florida

94165

For

Gertrude and John C. Wister

Preface

This manuscript is an editing of Fanny Kemble's *Records of a Girlhood,* her *American Journal* published in 1835, and new material from unpublished letters to and from Fanny Kemble, and comments by Mrs. Stokes. The unpublished letters are:

All letters to George and Cecilia Combe, and the June 28, 1830 letter to Miss Cox from Glasgow: Manuscripts in the National Library of Scotland, Edinburg.

All letters to Kate Sedgwick Minot and Mrs. Charles Sedgwick: Manuscripts in the library of the Historical Society of Massachusetts.

All letters to Sarah Paine Perkins (Mrs. Henry Cleveland) and letter to Mrs. Follen: Manuscripts in the New York Public Library, Manuscript Division, Berg Collection.

Letter to Mrs. Joshua Francis Fisher: Manuscript in the library of the Historical Society of Pennsylvania.

Letters from Pierce Butler to John Cadwalader and the Sidney George Fisher Diary: *The Pennsylvania Magazine,* published by the Historical Society of Pennsylvania.

Names filed in the blanks of Fanny Kemble's *Journal,* published in 1835 by Fanny Kemble, date undetermined, and paragraphs in her handwriting stitched into the same volume with information regarding Mr. Hodgkinson and Francis Henry Fitzhardinge Berkeley: Manuscript given by Mrs. Frederick R. Hazard of Syracuse to the Brandon Matthews Dramatic Museum, now in the Columbia University Library.

Letter from Henry James to Sarah B. Wister, 1893: Manuscript in the Owen Wister Collection in the Library of Congress and never published.

Letters to Fanny Kemble from Sir Thomas Lawrence, 1829; letters to Fanny Kemble from the Reverend William E. Channing, 1833; letter to Fanny Kemble from Edward John Trelawney, 1834; and letter from Edward Everett, 1843: manuscripts in possession of the estate of Owen Wister.

Acknowledgements

The author wishes to thank the following for permission to use the letters from Fanny Kemble and other materials in their collections:

Mrs. Langdon T. Marvin for lending the copy of the Butler vs. Butler divorce, and a copy of the "Conditions";

Columbia University Libraries for permission to quote from the annotated copy of Fanny Kemble's 1835 *Journal* in the Brander Matthews Dramatic Museum;

the Harvard College Library for permission to use the letter to Samuel Gray Ward;

the Henry W. and Albert A. Berg Collection, the New York Public Library, and the Astor, Lenox and Tilden Foundations for permission to use the letters to Mrs. Sarah Perkins Cleveland and to Mrs. Elizabeth Lee Cabot Follen;

the Historical Society of Pennsylvania for permission to use the copy of the James Schott *Statement* in their possession, and the letter to Mrs. Joshua Francis Fisher;

the Massachusetts Historical Society for permission to use the letters to the Sedgwick and Minot families;

the National Library of Scotland for permission to quote the letter to Miss Cox and all letters to George and Cecilia Combe;

Nicholas B. Wainwright for permission to quote from his edition of the Sidney George Fisher diary.

All previously unpublished materials not specifically acknowledged are in the possession of the estate of the late Owen Wister. The letter from Henry James to Sarah B. Wister, 1893, is in the Owen Wister Collection in the Library of Congress.

The author also wishes to thank Mrs. Edmund R. Purves for introducing her to the late Mr. Ellery Sedgwick who told her the

ix

anecdote used in the opening sentence of this book; Mr. George N. Kates who typed the original Fanny Kemble letters in the possession of various institutions and helped her select the ones she uses; Mrs. Burt T. Sheldon, who put her wonderful collection of Kembliana at the author's disposal and who told her of the annotated copy of the 1835 *Journal* in the possession of the Columbia University Libraries; Miss Sally Smith, who gave the author first editions of the *Journal of a Residence on a Georgian Plantation* and the 1835 *Journal* which provided the excerpts used in this book; Mr. John C. Furnas, who told her of the Kemble letters in the Library of Scotland; Mrs. H. Hayes Aikens, who typed the manuscript; Miss Marice Bezdek, who helped proofread the text; and Mr. Julian D. Mason Jr. for giving this book its title.

Works by Fanny Kemble

Kemble, Frances Ann. *Far Away and Long Ago*. New York: Holt, 1889.

Butler, Frances Anne. *Journal*. Philadelphia: Carey, Lea & Blanchard, 1835. 2 Vols.

Kemble, Frances Anne. *Journal of a Residence on a Georgian Plantation in 1838–1839*. New York: Harper & Brothers, Publishers, 1863.

Butler, Frances Anne. *Poems*. Philadelphia: John Penington, 1844.

Kemble, Frances Anne. *Poems*. London: Richard Bentley & Son, 1883.

Kemble, Frances Ann. *Records of a Girlhood*. 2nd ed. New York: Henry Holt and Company, 1879.
————. *Records of Later Life*. New York: Henry Holt and Company, 1882.

Butler, Mrs., late Fanny Kemble. *Year of Consolation*. 2 Vols. Hartford: Silas Andrus & Son, 1851.

Works About Fanny Kemble
and Her Life

Armstrong, Margaret. *Fanny Kemble: A Passionate Victorian.* New York: The Macmillan Company, 1938.

Boaden, James. *Memoirs of Mrs. Siddons.* London: 1827.

—————. *Memoirs of the Life of John Philip Kemble.* 2 Vols. in 1. Philadelphia: Robert H. Small, 1825.

"Butler vs. Butler," *The Pennsylvania Magazine* LXXIX (1955), 101–108.

[Butler, Pierce]. *Mr. Butler's Statement.* [Privately printed; n.d.]

Campbell, Thomas. *Life of Mrs. Siddons.* New York: Harper & Brothers, 1834.

[Fisher, Sidney George]. *A Philadelphia Perspective: The Diary of Sidney George Fisher Covering the Years 1834–1871,* ed. Nicholas B. Wainwright. Philadelphia: The Historical Society of Pennsylvania, 1967.

Gibbs, Henry. *Affectionately Yours, Fanny.* London: Jarrolds Ltd., n.d.

Geffen, Elizabeth M. *Philadelphia Unitarianism 1796–1861.* Philadephia: University of Pennsylvania Press, c. 1961.

Greville, Charles C. F. *The Greville Diary,* ed. Philip W. Wilson. London: Heinemann, 1927.

Grills, Rosalie. *Trelawney.* London: Constable & Co., 1950.

[Hone, Philip A.] *The Diary of Philip A. Hone,* ed. Allan Nevins. New York: Dodd Mead & Co., 1927.

Howe, M. A. DeWitt. "Young Fanny Kemble as Seen in an Old Diary," *The Atlantic Monthly,* December, 1944. pp. 97–102.

James, Henry. "Frances Anne Kemble," *Essays in London and Elsewhere*. New York: Harper & Brothers Publishers, 1893.

Nolan, J. Bennett, *Annals of the Penn Square, Reading*. Philadelphia: University of Pennsylvania Press, 1933.

Parsons, Mrs. Clement. *The Incomparable Siddons*. London: Methuen & Co., 1909.

Poe, Edgar Allan. [A review of Fanny Kemble's 1835 *Journal*], *The Southern Literary Messenger,* as quoted by Margaret Armstrong, *Fanny Kemble: A Passionate Victorian*. New York: The Macmillan Company, 1938.

Ritchie, Lady. *From Friend to Friend*. New York: E. P. Dutton and Company, 1920.

[Sedgwick, Catherine M.] *Life and Letters of Catherine M. Sedgwick,* ed. Mary C. Dewey. New York: Harper, 1871.

Sherwin, Oscar. *Uncorking Old Sherry: The Life and Times of Richard Brinsley Sheridan*. New York: Twayne Publishers Inc., c. 1960.

Schott, James W., Jr. *Statement.* Baltimore: [Privately printed, July 29, 1844].

Sumner, Charles. *Memoirs and Letters,* ed. E. R. Pierce. 4 Vols. London: Low, 1878–1894.

Thackeray, William Makepeace. The letters and private papers of William Makepeace Thackeray; Collected and edited by Gordon N. Ray. Cambridge, Mass.: Harvard University Press, 1946.

Watson, Amelia M. *Memories of Fanny Kemble*. [Typescript in possession of Owen Wister estate, n.d.]

Wyndham, Henry Saxe. *The Annals of Covent Garden Theatre From 1732 to 1897*. 2 Vols. London: Chatto & Windus, 1906.

Contents

Illustrations

CHAPTER I

Fanny Kemble

"Young man, don't imagine that you know anything about Shakespeare until there are patches on your trousers from kneeling before Mrs. Kemble." Thus spoke Henry Dwight Sedgwick of Boston to his son in the 1850's, and hundreds of others shared his admiration. Fanny Kemble, born in England, was then reading Shakespeare in public in cities of the Eastern seaboard of America. She was in middle life, but as a girl she had won instant fame as an actress on both sides of the Atlantic. Despite her great success, she left the stage at the age of twenty-four for domestic obscurity in the United States. After ten years her marriage failed, and she had emerged to hold for twenty years, and in two hemispheres, an undisputed place in her second profession. In addition to her proved abilities as an actress and reader, she had a third talent: she was a writer. Publishers were eager for whatever flowed from her copious, lively pen, and all her books sold well. Necessity imposed these three careers. She had to earn her living.

Fanny Kemble wrote plays, essays, one novel, and five journals. Only the journals have stood the test of time. It is as an autobiographer that she achieves lasting stature. Her first journal, "A Residence in America," met with enthusiasm and also censure. With many a tart comment on the manners and customs of the new world, she delightfully recorded what she saw and did while touring as a star during 1832–34. Three burlesques of it were published, the highest compliment that can be paid to a book, but gauche young America was stung by the Journal, and many who had enjoyed her acting turned against her. Most newspapers attacked it; only a few magazines saw its merits. After more than one hundred years, "A

1

Residence in America" is of rare historic value, and shows her to be a skilled diarist.

Thirty years after writing "A Residence in America" she published "A Residence on a Georgian Plantation," her vehement, vivid account of her life as the wife of a slave holder. Unlike "Uncle Tom's Cabin," it is not melodramatic, describes no floggings, and has many lyric passages about nature. Establishing her as an abolitionist, it struck a blow for the anti-slavery cause. In its field "A Residence on a Georgian Plantation" is unrivalled. Sixteen years later she published "Records of a Girlhood," an endearing, personal story of her often sensational early years, adding valuable eyewitness accounts to many significant events in social and theatrical London. As Henry James said, these Journals "form together one of the most animated autobiographies in the language." Now that her unpublished letters have been transcribed Fanny Kemble can be seen as a complex woman whose varied gifts and moral fibre made it mandatory that she magnificently fulfill several roles in life. Marriage was not one of them. The bitter failure of her marriage marred and scarred her but did not quench her spirit.

Fanny Kemble belongs to no category and bears no resemblance to the well-known women of her day or of today. She was not a devourer of men like many an actress or woman author, nor was she a spinster like many a lady reformer. She had abundant talents and dominant vitality. Her character had many aspects and many facets; her life was crowded, arduous, and mostly unhappy. She had a quick tongue, was headstrong, uncontrolled, and would not be ruled by her husband, who was a dullard unaware of her genius, and who eventually hated her. There were those who could not tolerate her. Her neighbors in the South despised her, realizing that she was a menace to them and helping to undo their lives. Thackeray wrote of her, "Have learned to admire but not endure Mrs. Kemble," though as a young man he and Tennyson were in love with her when she first played Juliet. But most people were drawn to her and enthralled by her; she had many dear friends. They had seen her accept fame casually and not be self-impressed, rise beyond misfortune with the courage of a lioness; they basked in the warmth of her heart, felt her great compassion, were dazzled by her formidable intellect, and honored her integrity. They upheld her through the years. Many of them were in the usual pursuits of life; others were in the world of letters and music. For two generations and in two hemispheres they valued her friendship. Sir Walter Scott, Browning, Longfellow, Henry James, Mendelssohn, and Franz Liszt were among them. Knowing great men was in the Kemble tradition.

Fanny Kemble was the youngest member of the Kemble family of actors, renowned for three generations in Great Britain. She had gone on the stage at nineteen, with no experience, at the request of her parents in an endeavour to save from sale by its creditors The Theatre Royal Covent Garden, London. Her father, Charles Kemble, was owner-actor-manager of Covent Garden. The immense success of his daughter earned thirteen thousand pounds for the Theatre in her first season, 1829, paid off the most pressing debts and staved off disaster. Cheering throngs had crowded Covent Garden when she starred and demanded many curtain calls. Her father then led her to the footlights, and she curtseyed to thunderous applause. King William IV and Queen Adelaide made an official appearance to see her. As a young celebrity she was found charming, graceful, apt in conversation, and with opinions that she expressed freely. She was accepted in the social and literary glitter of London while mastering and acting eight roles in her first season in Covent Garden. After three arduous years in leading roles, with her father always in the cast, the Kembles came to the United States to tour. Fanny met with huge acclaim, but in America it was she and not her father who received critical praise and filled the theatres. In Boston the Harvard students walked in droves from Cambridge to see her act, mobbed the stage door, took the horses out of the shafts, and pulled the carriage to the hotel.

As an actress Fanny Kemble was the least and the last of her famous family whose lives are enmeshed in British theatrical history. From Drury Lane and Covent Garden their names have rung down the years. They sat for their portraits to

Reynolds, Gainsborough, and Lawrence. John Philip Kemble, her uncle, consulted Dr. Johnson about his Shakespearean roles. Her aunt, Mrs. Siddons, who ranks as the greatest actress of the English stage, was entertained by Dr. Johnson and had Edmund Burke to dinner; Boswell wrote of her. The Kembles were lionized and sought after in titled circles. "Saw Kemble last night in 'Coriolanus'," wrote Lord Byron of John Philip. "He was glorious."

Though Fanny Kemble was like her family in many ways, she was also different from them in other ways. She had the Kemble resonant voice and faultless articulation, the half-Greek, half-Roman nose, the splendid dark eyes and dark hair, and best of all, their clearly defined symmetrical eyebrows which are seen in all portraits of all Kembles. She was shorter, plumper, and not as handsome as were Mrs. Siddons, John Philip, and her father. She was not commanding and thunderous on the stage as was Mrs. Siddons; nor did she have the range and power for Lady Macbeth and Queen Katherine that her aunt had, though she played both parts. She lacked the polish and discipline of her father both in life and on the stage. Like her father and uncle she was educated in France. She wrote plays as her uncle, father, and mother had, selling a drama in blank verse for four hundred and fifty pounds when she was twenty. Though as an actress she does not compare with her illustrious family, as her life progressed, she achieved fame in spheres beyond their talents.

Like all actors, the Kembles' lives were governed by the need of success in the theatre; they knew nothing else, and they cared for nothing else. Mrs. Siddons, John Philip, and Charles had all worked their way from the provinces to Drury Lane and Covent Garden. Mrs. Siddons and John Philip had reached the summit of their profession and were able to leave the stage and live in comfort. But Charles, who was not as great as they, had fallen onto evil days and want. Fanny was born into the world her family had achieved, but in which they could never be more than invited guests, as they had no title, no great fortune, no vast country estate. They could offer nothing but their beauty, their industry, their arresting theatrical gift, and they were valued for themselves. One more attribute set them apart. It was written of them, "by the purity of their lives, the Kembles elevated the British stage." Fanny enjoyed this world and could only stay in it by her continued success. She had never wanted to be an actress and had not daydreamed of being a second Mrs. Siddons when, with three weeks of instruction by her mother, she set foot on a stage for the first time. She soon learned that unlike her family, acting could never be for her the essence of existence, and she never overcame a dislike for her profession. Her family accepted as a matter of course that she should become the galley slave of Covent Garden in their last attempt to save themselves from ruin. Her glowing youth, inherited theatrical ability, teeming strength and willingness made it possible for Charles to continue as owner-manager. It was a tremendous good fortune for the Kembles to have a daughter who overnight became the darling of the London stage.

What would the future hold for such a girl? How long would she be the support of her family? What kind of a man would she marry? Surely she would not marry an actor and stay on the stage as Mrs. Siddons had. What kind of a man would provide for her the world of social swish and creative vigor in which she had grown up during the reign of George IV and which now in her own right accepted her? If she left the theatre, would she stay in that world? Would she find a husband with the means and position to furnish the background in which she could still shine? Would he have a light hand on the reins in the day of the subjugation of women and accept her headstrong ways and rejoice in her talents? At nineteen only one of her talents was apparent, but it could be seen that she would not play second fiddle to anyone. And so it was her destiny not to succeed in marriage. Least of all would it be possible for her to be the meek, hearthside companion in a not-too-long-ago colony of a limited, grudging man.

The first Kemble that is known in Fanny's lineage is Roger, her grandfather. Full blown and as a strolling player he is spoken of by contemporary biographers as the founder of the family. At that time in England strolling players, actors who

wandered from town to town giving crude theatrical performances with makeshift scenery, were regarded with contempt
and scorn, on a social level with gypsies. They were subject
to arrest without a warrant, hooted out of villages, and often
stoned. There are no tombstones for Roger's parents, and no
parish christening records of them. Nor does he ever speak
of them. There is a portrait of Roger Kemble with white hair
by Sir Thomas Lawrence. In it he is shown as striking and
aristocratic, and his features are repeated in his progeny.
Roger was born in 1721 in Hereford and was a Catholic.

Roger Kemble married Sarah Ward, daughter of John Ward,
a well known strolling manager, in 1753 in Cirencester, England. Sarah was born in Clonmell, Ireland, while her parents
were acting there, seventeen years before and was a protestant.
Her father had asked her not to marry an actor, and when he
was overruled, said, "Sarah, you have not disobeyed me. I
told you never to marry an actor, and you have married a
man who neither is nor ever can be an actor." There is a
portrait of Sarah Ward Kemble by Lawrence. Henry James
referred to it, calling it the portrait "of the old lioness."

Thomas Campbell, a Kemble biographer, says of Roger and
Sarah Kemble, "They were both of them tall and comely per-
sonages. The mother had a somewhat austere stateliness of
mien, but it seems to have been from her that the family inherited their genius and force of character. The father had
all the suavity of the old school of gentlemen." And James
Boaden says, "I have been all my life particularly observant
of the manners of men at table. I have never yet seen greater
ease nor higher polish than were exhibited by Mr. Kemble.
Mrs. Kemble had very uncommon vivacity and point in her
conversation. As I sat next to her at dinner, I had full opportunity to remark and enjoy the soundness of her judgment and
the peculiar energy of her expressions. I should fancy, among
her own sex, that she must have been deemed like Dr. Johnson,
a tremendous converser."

Campbell says again of the Roger Kembles, "Persons who
cannot for a moment disjoin their idea of human dignity from
that of station, will perhaps be surprised that I should speak

of the dignified manner of a pair who lived by the humble vocation which I have mentioned (strolling players). It is nevertheless true that the presence and demeanor of this couple might have graced a court. Mr. and Mrs. Kemble were of this description. Besides, in spite of all our prejudices against the players' vocation, irreproachable personal character will always find its leaven in the general esteem."

The Roger Kembles had no settled home. They strolled with their cart, their children, their belongings, and their stage properties from town to town giving theatrical performances in public squares and fair grounds by day, and in taverns, unused barns, and inns at night. It was their sole means of support. They paused only long enough in villages for their eight daughters and four sons to be born and were often in need. Fanny's father, Charles, as a boy was once so hungry that he stole turnips from a field and ate them raw. The Roger Kembles did not want their children to be actors, but of the eight who lived to maturity, all were at one time on the stage. Those who did not make a name for themselves gave up acting.

Their oldest child was Mrs. Siddons, the next oldest, John Philip; Charles was eighteen years younger. Sarah, after much family protest, was finally allowed at eighteen to marry William Siddons, an actor in her father's company. Sarah and William Siddons left the Kemble troup and found engagements in the provinces. John Philip, who was intended for the priesthood, and Charles, years later than his brother, were both sent to the English Catholic College at Douay, France. They learned to declaim Latin verse and studied Greek and became proficient French scholars. On John Philip's return he announced that he would be an actor, and he often played in the provinces with Mrs. Siddons. When Charles finished college, he too went on the stage. As a child he had taken children's parts in his parents' troupe like all the Kembles, and he had later also acted children's roles with his brother and sister when they were recognized stars. By 1802 the Kembles were established at Covent Garden and were the reigning theatrical family of England.

One hundred years before Roger Kemble, Oliver Cromwell had closed all theatres in England and ordered actors arrested and whipped. They were to be treated as rogues. Traditionally, boys played women's parts. The Puritans considered the theatre sinful. Superstitions then sprang up concerning actors, and mysterious disappearances and thefts were attributed to them. They became suspected outcasts and fled the cities. And so it was owing to Cromwell that the theatre known and favored in Shakespeare's time did not descend uninterrupted to the following generations. The bad name and disdain engendered towards players during his rule lasted many decades. Though Charles II, twenty years after Cromwell, had granted Royal Patents to two London theatres, giving them the exclusive rights to produce dramas, nevertheless the children of Roger Kemble had to carve their way into social acceptance, and owing to their talents, were favorites of the aristocracy. One more obstacle had stood between the profession of acting and respectability for many years. Women began playing women's parts for the first time in the reign of Charles II, but the public was aware of the many flaunted liaisons between actresses and royalty. The first women on the English stage vied with each other for the protection of rich, titled men, and actresses were considered women of easy virtue. For almost two hundred years after the Restoration only the Royal Patent theatres had the right to give plays in London. The Theatre Royal Drury Lane and the Theatre Royal Covent Garden, in both of which the Kembles achieved their greatest fame, were the Patent theatres. They were repertory theatres and in rivalry with each other.

The Theatre Royal Covent Garden, in whose history the Kembles played a leading part, came under the control of John Philip on his purchase of a sixth share of it in 1802. He and Mrs. Siddons had reached the peak of their success in Drury Lane, then under the management of Richard Brinsley Sheridan. Sheridan often did not pay them, did not pay the stage hands or scene painters, and would be followed out of the stage door by crowds of men who worked for him begging aloud for their wages lest they starve. And so it seemed an act of Providence and a glorious opportunity for the Kembles to be free of Sheridan and Drury Lane when a friend of John Philip's advanced him twenty-three thousand pounds, enabling him to become part owner of Covent Garden, and he was asked to be stage manager at two hundred pounds a year. He invited Mrs. Siddons and Charles to work for him. If all went well, Kemble would earn twenty-five thousand pounds a year. It was the first step in the Kembles' owner-management of Covent Garden and seemed to be a stride toward assured prosperity. But it was in fact the beginning of an involvement that led, after John gave his share to his brother, Charles, in 1821, to mounting debts, six suits in Chancery, and to the eventual loss of the Theatre, postponed for a few years by the heroic efforts of young Fanny.

The Covent Garden Theatre in which Fanny acted was the second theatre of that name to stand on the northwest corner of Covent Garden Market, then as now an open square in the heart of London's west end. The original theatre had been built in 1732, and only six years after John Philip bought his share, it burned down. The new theatre was built on the same site and completed after the fire in the same year, 1808. He continued as owner-manager, and as well as plays he produced operas and concerts as was the custom of the Patent Theatres.

The neighborhood of Covent Garden was famous for its great variety of lusty amusements. Bachelors and rakes, men fleeing domestic monotony, titled and rich, humble and ragged, found nightly pleasures there. It was a region of brothels, at that time called bagnios. There were coffee houses, gaming houses, taverns, clubs where men ate beef steaks and drank ale and talked till dawn. There were cock fights and bull baiting—a man's world. In this age and in the reign of George III the Kembles first acted in London. When the Prince Regent assumed authority he presented an example of bigamy, being married simultaneously to Mrs. Fitzherbert and Queen Caroline. And as Sovereign he continued to set the pace in drinking, gorging, and gaming, but was as well a patron of the arts.

Untouched by the amoral times, the Kembles worked hard and seriously. John Philip strove to give performances of

Shakespeare more faithful to the text than in current use, while all the Kembles also played the accepted repertory. They acted plays by Oliver Goldsmith, Farquahar, Vanbrugh, Congreve, and Sheridan as well as the now forgotten popular, bombastic and harrowing melodramas without merit. Mrs. Siddons played whatever gave her scope to reduce her public to tears, hysterics, swoonings, and convulsions, and men wept as hard as women. Many people were overcome by her and had to be carried out. But her name rests on her Shakespearian roles. Dr. Johnson said of her, "Neither praise nor money depraved her." Her young niece, Fanny Kemble, twenty years later played many of the same parts, as they were current theatrical fare, though she was too immature for most of them and could not reduce her audience to pulp the way her aunt had.

The Kembles depended for their livelihood on continuously pleasing the mercurial, vociferous, and vituperative audiences of the late eighteenth and early nineteenth century London. By 1829 when Fanny came on the stage, the public was somewhat toned down and more sentimental. But even in her day men sat in the pit, often on backless benches, with their hats on. The top gallery of Covent Garden was screened by lattice work, and the stage could barely be seen from it. The gallery was a place of assignation and unseemly conduct.

In the days when the Kembles acted in Drury Lane, and when they first established themselves at Covent Garden, a new play seldom held the stage more than a few nights at a time, but the old successes were repeated as many as fifty times during the season. There were no afternoon performances. The curtain went up at six, and performances lasted until midnight six days a week, from September to June. The evening began with a one act play, followed by a four or five act drama with the great actors who were the main attraction; then came a farce, ballet, pantomime or extravaganza. Those arriving after nine o'clock paid half price. It was the custom to bring hot food into the theatre bought in the neighboring streets, and meat pies, baked potatoes, ale in mugs were consumed during the evening. Audiences were rowdy and scurrilous. Thomas Burke says in "English Night Life," "actors and actresses had not only to work well for their masters but to work hard." The audience shouted disapproval of the actors and pelted them with fruit, but actors were accustomed to abuse and humbly strove to please. Great actors such as Edmund Kean would come back onto the stage amid hoots and catcalls, carrying a sign begging pardon for a poor performance and for being drunk.

The Kembles' day was still the day of mangled Shakespeare. Romeo and Juliet was given with an implied happy ending, and so was Hamlet. John Philip, though taking infinite pains and talking to Dr. Johnson about the meaning and interpretation of the great Shakespearian speeches, altered the text of Henry VIII when he played Cardinal Wolsey to the Queen Katherine of Mrs. Siddons and used horses on the stage in Henry V. Charles Kemble for the first time dressed the production of Romeo and Juliet in which Fanny made her debut in Italian fourteenth century costumes, but Fanny wore a white satin ball dress of her own day.

The Kembles' mammoth debt on Covent Garden was partly due to misfortune. When the original theatre burned down, there were debts still outstanding on the money loaned for its construction. In order to build a new theatre without delay, not only were shares sold in it, but titled friends of John Philip advanced thousands of pounds on which interest had to be paid, and neither the first nor the second debt was amortized. So that when Charles accepted casually his brother's gift of his share in the Theatre, there was no prospect but only a nebulous hope that somehow these debts could be kept running indefinitely and the Theatre could hold its place in public favor against Drury Lane.

Lit by thousands of candles and with many open grates to heat the Green Rooms, it was the fate of London theatres to perish in flames. Nothing remained of Covent Garden Theatre after it burned in 1808. The fire began after midnight when the Theatre was dark, and the twenty lives lost were those of firemen and spectators. In the fire Mrs. Siddons lost all her jewelry and her collection of lace, including a veil which had belonged to Marie Antoinette. Costumes, acting versions of plays, scenery, and stage properties dating from the first season were lost. After the fire John Philip showed the fortitude of the Kembles which marked the entire life of his niece, Fanny. In one year and on the same site a new Theatre Royal Covent Garden was built. Pomp and ceremony marked its opening. It was the biggest, handsomest, most opulent theatre in London.

The second Theatre Royal Covent Garden held 2,800 people and proved to be too big for any play in which an actor's face should be seen clearly in order to follow subtle nuances of expression. Fanny Kemble's voice could be heard distinctly in it, but she says that French farces with French troupes always proved a failure in the Theatre on account of its size. It was a splendid opera house, and the only success that Charles Kemble had with it until his young daughter filled the house was with operas.

From contemporary sources, Henry Saxe Wyndham in "The Annals of Covent Garden Theatre" gave this description of the second Theatre: "It was copied from the Temple of Minerva at Athens, was 200 feet in width . . . four fluted columns supported the portico. The grand entrance hall under the portico . . . fronting onto Bow Street was about 40 feet square, with stone staircases and red porphyry pillars and white veined marble walls."

The stage, Boaden says, "was the most perfect with which I am acquainted." Wyndham continues, "On the left of the stage were passages to the three Green Rooms, the principal one of which was handsomely furnished with crimson seats and curtains."

Charles Kemble was so burdened with ancient debts on the Theatre when he became manager that even if he had succeeded by adroit showmanship in filling it season after season, eventually its creditors would have demanded settlement. Theatre owners of that era, history proves, were never solvent. Charles was not a brilliant manager, though as an actor he was so firmly established that he gave successful performances of Shakespeare in English in Paris. As a producer he blundered often and had no flair for pleasing the public with new presentations. Not only was Drury Lane outstripping him, but other theatres, though not permitted by Royal Patent to give plays, were flourishing. There were operas, oratorios, concerts, circuses, extravaganzas, pantomimes and ballets vying nightly for patronage. A crisis was reached for the Kembles in 1829 when the creditors, owing to half full houses, ordered the sale of the Theatre. Providence briefly favored Charles when his daughter, Fanny, assumed the staggering burden and became the wheelhorse of the Theatre. Once again crowds flocked to Covent Garden, and the family who for generations had labored solely for the stage, had yet another member in high public esteem.

CHAPTER II

Childhood, Girlhood, and Debut

Henry James who became a close friend and admirer of Fanny Kemble in her later years wrote of her, "Her various books, springing in every case but two or three straight from the real, from experience; personal and natural, humorous and eloquent, interesting as her character and her life were interesting, have all her irrepressible spirit, or if the word be admissible, her spiritedness . . . the geniality . . . of her temperament makes everything she wrote what is called good reading. She wrote exactly as she talked, observing, asserting, complaining, confiding, contradicting, crying out and bounding off, always effectually communicating. Last not least, she uttered with her pen as well as with her lips the most agreeable uncontemporary, self-respecting English, as idiomatic as possible and just as little common." And so James did not consider her writing typical of the nineteenth century, but after a hundred years it reveals for us the gentle formalities, niceties and conventions in manners and in speech of her day.

Thus her writing has various usages and expressions now outmoded. It also glows with many hues, the essence of her fluid pen, which rapid as quicksilver became the instrument of her heart. Her felicitous use of her immense erudite vocabulary gives shape to her thoughts, allowing her imagination to roam in lyric heights, and her shocked senses to give tongue in forceful and exact words. She was able to write of herself from earliest childhood, leaving the stamp of her feminine awareness of her relationship to her family, close friends and surroundings, in her letters and journals as well as displaying the masculine timbre of her intellect. It was not as an actress, nor primarily as a woman, but for her intellect that she was valued by famous men. They sought her company as Henry James did for the stimulation of their minds.

Fanny Kemble did not publish "Records of a Girlhood" until she was middle aged. This volume is in part recollections, and in part it is letters dating from her seventeenth to her twenty-second year, thus making a narrative of charm, drama, and near catastrophe. The letters were to her dearest friend, Miss Harriet St. Leger, who returned them to Fanny three decades later. She wove them into the story of her early years. The letters show the worries and excitement of her daily life in the midst of the impending ruin about to engulf her family. The recollections begin before the letters, are interlarded with the letters, and keep the sequence of events moving forward, telling what the letters do not cover. Fanny has mellowed by the time she writes of the past, and the sharp edge of immediacy has become often the philosophic cadence of her intellect, in contrast to the vibrant emotions and assertions in the letters.

All dates and facts relating to when she played what part in Covent Garden in passages written in retrospect by Fanny Kemble are subject to doubt. It is of no great importance how many times she played which role or exactly the year or the month in which she first played it. Substantially all her statements are true, and this slight variation of dates when compared with the authentic records of Covent Garden is of small importance.

Fanny begins her "Records of a Girlhood" by writing of her mother's earliest years. Fanny says that so much has been written about her father that she will say nothing about his youth.

My mother was the daughter of Captain Decamp, an officer in one of the armies that revolutionary France sent to invade republican Switzerland. He married the daughter of a farmer from the neighborhood of Berne. From my grandmother's home you could see the great Jungfrau range of the Alps, and I sometimes wonder whether it is her blood in my veins that so loves and longs for those supremely beautiful mountains.

Not long after his marriage my grandfather went to Vienna,

where, on the anniversary of the birth of the great Empress-King, my mother was born, in 1774, and named after her, Maria Theresa. In Vienna, Captain Decamp made the acquaintance of a young English nobleman, Lord Monson (afterwards the Earl of Essex), who, with an enthusiasm more friendly than wise, eagerly urged the accomplished Frenchman to come and settle in London. In an evil hour my grandfather adopted this advice and came to England. It was the time when the emigration of the French nobility had filled London with objects of sympathy, and society with sympathizers with their misfortunes. Among the means resorted to for assisting the many interesting victims of the Revolution were representations, given under the direction of Le Texier, of juvenile dramas by young French children. These performances became one of the fashionable frenzies of the day.

Among the little actors of Le Texier's troupe my mother attracted the greatest share of public attention by her beauty and grace, and the truth and spirit of her performance. The little French fairy was eagerly seized upon by admiring fine ladies and gentlemen, and snatched up into their society, where she was fondled and petted and played with; passing whole days in Mrs. Fitzherbert's drawing room (commoner wife of George IV), and many a half hour on the knees of her royal and disloyal husband, the Prince Regent, one of whose favorite jokes was to place my mother under a huge glass bell, made to cover some large group of precious Dresden china.

Meantime, while the homes of the great and gay were her constant resort, the child's home was becoming sadder, and her existence and that of her parents more precarious and penurious day by day. From my grandfather's first arrival in London, his chest had suffered from the climate; the instrument he taught was the flute, and it was not long before decided disease of the lungs rendered that industry impossible. He endeavored to supply its place by giving French and drawing lessons, and so struggled on under the dark London sky, and in the damp, foggy, smoky atmosphere, while the poor foreign wife bore and nursed four children.

It is impossible to imagine anything sadder than the condition of such a family, with its dark fortune closing round and over it, and its one little human jewel, sent forth from its dingy case to sparkle and glitter, and become of hard necessity the single source of light in the growing gloom of its daily existence.

How far my mother was hurt by the combination of circumstances that influenced her childhood I know not. As I remember her, she was a frank, fearless, generous, and unworldly woman, and had probably found in the subsequent independent exercise of her abilities the shield for these virtues.

Mrs. Charles Kemble wrote, and they were successfully published and acted, several light comedies, and it was as a comedian that she made a success of acting as a grown woman.

After six years spent in bitter struggle with disease and difficulties of every kind, my grandfather, still a young man, died of consumption, leaving a widow and five little children, of whom the eldest, my mother, not yet in her teens, became from that time the breadwinner and sole support.

After her marriage to my father, Charles Kemble, July 2, 1806, my mother remained but a few years on the stage.

I am persuaded that whatever qualities of mind or character I inherit from my father's family, I am more strongly stamped with those which I derive from my mother. To the fine senses of a savage rather than a civilized nature, she joined an acute instinct of correct criticism in all matters of art, and a general quickness and accuracy of perception, and brilliant vividness of expression, that made her conversation delightful. Had she possessed half the advantages of education which she and my father labored to bestow upon us, she would I think have been one of the most remarkable persons of her time.

She had a fine and powerful voice and a rarely accurate musical ear; she moved so gracefully that I have known persons who went to certain provincial promenades frequented by her only to see her walk; she was a capital horsewoman; her figure was beautiful, and her face very handsome and strikingly expressive.

I was born on the 27th of November, 1809, in Newman Street, Oxford Road, the third child of my parents, whose eldest, Philip, named after my uncle, died in infancy. The second, John Mitchell, lived to distinguish himself as a scholar, devoting his life to the study of his own language and the history of his country in their earliest period, and to the kindred subject of Northern Archaeology.

She was christened Frances Anne; there were also two younger children in the family, Adelaide and Henry.

Of Newman Street I have nothing to say. Our next house, after Newman Street, was at a place called Westbourne Green, now absorbed into an endless avenue of "palatial" residences. At this period of my life, I have been informed, I began, after the manner of most clever children, to be exceedingly troublesome and unmanageable, my principal crime being a general audacious contempt for all authority, which, coupled with a sweet-tempered, cheerful indifference to all punishment made it extremely difficult to know how to obtain of me the minimum quantity of obedience indispensable in the relations of a tailless monkey of four years and its elders. I never cried, and I never sulked, I never resented, lamented, or repented either my ill-doings or their consequences, but accepted them alike with a philosophical buoyancy of spirit which was the despair of my poor bewildered trainers.

Fanny's behavior during her very first few years is characteristic of many children who later grow into well known people. She shows the vitality and independence, which, combined with her talent, enabled her to achieve three successful careers.

About this time it was determined that I should be sent to school in France. My father was extremely anxious to give me every advantage that he could, and Boulogne, where there was a girl's school of some reputation, was chosen as not too far from home to send a mite seven years old, to acquire the French language and begin her education. And so to Boulogne I went, to a school in the oddly named "Rue tant perd tant paie," in the old town, kept by a rather sallow and grim, but still vivacious old Madame Faudier, and received her penal bread and water with the comment "Bon pour la digestion!" and the retributive stripes this drew upon me, "Bon pour la circulation!" I was a sore torment, no doubt, to poor Madame Faudier, who, on being once informed by some alarmed passers in the street that one of her "demoiselles" was perambulating the house roof, is reported to have exclaimed in a paroxysm of rage and terror, "Ah, ce ne peut etre que cette diable de Kemble!" and sure enough it was I. Having committed I know not what crime, I had been thrust for chastisement into a lonely garret, where, having nothing earthly to do but look about me, I discovered (like a prince in the Arabian Nights) a ladder leading to a trap-door and presently was out on a sort of stone coping, which ran around the steep roof of the high, old-fashioned house, surveying with serene satisfaction the extensive prospect landward and seaward, unconscious that I was at the same time an object of terror to the beholders in the street below. I was snatched from the perilous delight of this bad eminence, I was (again, I think, rather like the Arabian prince) forthwith plunged into the cellar; where I curled myself up on the upper step, close to the heavy door that had been locked upon me, partly for the comfort of the crack of light that squeezed itself through it, and partly, I suppose, from some vague idea that there was no bottom to the steps, derived from my own terror rather than from any precise historical knowledge of oubliettes and donjons, with the execrable treachery of stairs suddenly ending in mid-darkness over an abyss. I suppose I suffered a martyrdom of fear. Less justifiable than banishment to lonely garrets or dark incarceration in cellars was another device, adopted to impress me with the evil of my ways, and one which seems to me so foolish in its cruelty, that the only amazement is, how anybody entrusted with the care of children could dream of any good result from such a method of impressing a little girl not eight years old. There was to be an execution in the town of some wretched malefactor, who was condemned to be guillotined, and I was told that I should be taken to see this supreme act of legal retribution, in order that I might know to what end evil courses conducted people. Whether it was ever intended that I should witness the ghastly spectacle of this execution, or whether it was expressly contrived that I should come too late, I know not; it is to be hoped that my doing so was not accidental, but mercifully intentional. Certain it is, that when I was taken to the Grande Place the slaughter was over; but I saw the guillotine, and certain gutters running red with what I was told (whether truly or not) was blood, and a sad-looking man, busied about the terrible machine, who, it was said, was the executioner's son, all which lugubrious objects, no doubt, had their due effect upon my poor childish imagination and nervous system, with a benefit to my moral nature which I should think highly problematical.

The Kembles were not deliberately subjecting their seven-year-old daughter to barbarous treatment when they sent her to Boulogne to school. In that day English children were customarily handed over at an early age to schools and tutors with complete faith on the part of the parents that they were doing what was best. Neither Charles Kemble nor Maria Theresa Decamp had attended school when they were seven, and it was a step up for their daughter to be sent to a French boarding school. Being locked into the attic and then into the cellar were merely usual punishments meted out to little girls, when boys would have been flogged. The nightmarish experience of being taken to see the guillotine would have been the undoing of many English children, the guillotine not being used in England, but there was an inner core of tenacious fortitude in Fanny that now stood by her and enabled her to maintain emotional equilibrium and not be haunted into lasting bad dreams. The school in Boulogne could have been nothing but harmful to Fanny, but she did not lose her health or high spirits there.

I left Boulogne when I was almost nine years old, and returned home where I remained upwards of two years before being again sent to school. During this time we lived chiefly at a place called Craven Hill, Bayswater, where we occupied at different periods three different houses. A row of very fine elm trees was separated only by the carriage road from the houses, whose front windows looked through their branches upon a large, quiet, green meadow. Certainly this was better than the smoke and din of London. To my father, however, the distance was a heavy increase of his almost nightly labor at the theatre. Omnibuses were no part of London existence then; a hackney coach (there were no cabs, either four-wheelers or hansoms) was a luxury to be thought of only occasionally, and for part of the way; and so he generally wound up his hard evening's work with a five mile walk from Covent Garden to Craven Hill.

Fanny says nothing about the dangers to pedestrians on a long midnight walk alone in London. Charles was taking a risk each time he walked to Craven Hill. There were frequent attacks by highwaymen, and the unarmed were often beaten and robbed. Covent Garden up to 1826 rented pistols and blunderbusses to actors who lived at a distance, charging two shillings a month for these firearms. It was typical of Charles that he should let his family live in the country so that his wife and children could be happy and that he should face this fatigue and danger. He considered the health and happiness of his wife and children first during his whole marriage and showed himself a devoted husband and father.

I imagine that my education must have been making but little progress during the last year of my residence at Craven Hill. I had no masters, and my Aunt Dall could ill supply the want of other teachers; moreover, I was extremely troublesome and unmanageable, and had become a tragically desperate young person, as my determination to poison my sister, in revenge for some punishment which I conceived had been unjustly inflicted upon me.

At the end of the summer I departed for Paris with my mother and Mrs. Charles Matthews. We travelled in the "malle poste," and I remember but one incident connected with our journey. Some great nobleman in Paris was about to give a grand banquet, and the *conducteur* of our vehicle had been prevailed upon to bring up the fish for the occasion in large hampers on our carriage, which was then the most rapid public conveyance on the road between the coast and the capital. The heat was intense, and the smell of our "luggage" intolerable. My mother complained and remonstrated in vain; the name of the important personage who was to entertain his guests with this delectable fish was considered an all-sufficient reply. At length the contents of the baskets began literally to ooze out of them and stream down the sides of the carriage; my mother threatenced an appeal to the authorities at the Bureau de Poste, and finally we got rid of our pestiferous load.

I was now placed in a school in the Rue d'Angouleme, Champs Elysees; a handsome house, formerly somebody's private hotel, with porte cochers, cour d'honneur, a small garden beyond, and large, lofty groundfloor apartments opening with glass doors upon them.

At the school there was a constant use of the Bible among us. I cannot call the reading and committing to memory of the Scriptures, as we performed those duties, by the serious name of study. But the Bible was learnt by heart in certain portions and recited before breakfast every morning, and read aloud before bedtime every evening by us. To me my intimate knowledge of the Bible has always seemed the greatest benefit I derived from my school training.

Of the secular portion of the education we received, the French lady who was Mrs. Rowden's partner directed the principal part. Our lessons of geography, grammar, history, arithmetic, and mythology (of which latter subject I suspect we had a much more thorough knowledge than is at all usual with young English girls) were conducted by her.

These studies were all pursued in French, already familiar to me as the vehicle of my elementary acquitments at Boulogne; and this soon became the language in which I habitually wrote, spoke, and thought, to the almost entire neglect of my native tongue, of which I never thoroughly studied the grammar till I was between fifteen and sixteen, when, on my presenting, in a glow of vanity, some verses of mine to my father, he said with his blandest smile, after reading them, "Very well, very well indeed! My dear, don't you think, before you write poetry, you had better learn grammar?" a suggestion which sent me crestfallen to a diligent study of Lindley Murray. But grammar is a perfectly uncongenial matter to me, which my mind absolutely refuses to assimilate. I have learned Latin, English, French, Italian, and German grammar, and do not know a single rule of the construction of any language whatever. Moreover, to the present day, my familiar use of French produced uncertainty in my mind as to the spelling of all words that take a double consonant in French and only one in English.

Moreover, in my own case, both in Italian and German, though I understand for the most part what I read and what is said in these languages, I have had but little exercise in speaking them and have been amused to find myself, while travelling, taken for an Italian as well as for a German, simply by dint of the facility with which I imitated the accent of the people I was among, while intrepidly confounding my moods, tenses, genders, and cases in the determination to speak and make myself understood in the language of whatever country I was passing through.

I remained in Paris till I was between fifteen and sixteen years old, and then it was determined that I should return home.

The three uninterrupted years in Paris proved to be the most serene of Fanny's life. She was away from the worry and turmoil of her home, the Kembles moving repeatedly from house to house in or near London, the excitement connected with the hoped-for success of new plays which as a whole did not succeed, and the frequent hysteria of her mother. It was a very monotonous life in the French school, and she obviously applied herself diligently to the studies which, though limited, furnished her mind with a thorough knowledge of the Bible and French classical literature. The pedantic teaching of the piano and the hours of practice gave her an admirable facility and fluency on the keyboard. She does not speak of being homesick, and these three years were certainly a sound educational foundation and gave her intellectual resources which served her well in her strenuous and harassed future. Her schooling was far superior to the average English girl's and quite remarkable for the daughter of actors.

My father came to fetch me, and the only adventure I met with on the way back was losing my bonnet, blown from my head into the sea on board the packet, which obliged me to purchase one as soon as I reached London; and having no discreeter guide of my proceedings, I so far imposed upon my father's masculine ignorance in such matters as to make him buy for me a full-sized Leghorn flat, under the circumference of which enormous sombrero I seated myself by him on the outside of the Weybridge coach, and amazed the gaping population of each successive village we passed through with the vast dimensions of the thatch I had put on my head.

Weybridge was not then reached by train in half an hour from London; it was two or three hours' coach distance: a rural, rather deserted looking, and most picturesque village.

We had left London in the afternoon, and did not reach Weybridge until after dark. I had been tormented the whole way down by a nervous fear that I should not know my mother's face again; an absence of three years, of course, could not justify such an apprehension, but it had completely taken possession of my imagination and was causing me much distress, when, as the coach stopped in the dark village inn, I heard the words, "Is there anyone here for Mrs. Kemble?" uttered in a voice which I knew so well, that I sprang, hat and all, into my mother's arms, and effectually got rid of my fear that I should not know her.

Her rural yearnings had now carried her beyond her suburban refuge at Craven Hill, and she was infinitely happy in her small cottage habitation on the outskirts of Weybridge and the edge of its picturesque common.

It was then that Mrs. Kemble daily indulged in her favorite outdoor occupation of fishing which became a major interest for her. Doubtless it took her mind off the family's burden with the Theatre and soothed her edgy nerves. She walked daily to the nearby streams and fished for hours on end.

Perhaps it was hardly fair to expect my father to relish extremely a residence where he was as nearly as possible too high and too wide, too long and too large, for every room in the house. He used to come down on Saturday and stay till Monday morning, but the rest of the week he spent at what was then our home in London, No. 5 Soho Square; it was a handsome, comfortable, roomy house, and has now, I think, been converted into a hospital.

I have said that I followed no systematic studies after I left school; but from that time began for me an epoch of indiscriminate, omnivorous reading, which lasted until I went upon the stage, when all my own occupations were necessarily given up for the exercise of my profession. Besides reading every book that came within my reach, I now commenced the still more objectionable practice of scribbling verses without stint or stay; some I suppose, in very bad Italian, and some, I am sure, in most indifferent English; but the necessity was on me, and perhaps an eruption of such rubbish was a safer process than keeping it in the mental system might have proved; and in the meantime this intellectual effervescence added immensely to the pleasure of my country life, and my long, rambling walks in that wild, beautiful neighborhood.

Our happy Weybridge summers, which succeeded each other for three years, had but one incident of any importance for me—my catching the small pox, which I had very severely. A slight eruption from which my sister suffered was at first pronounced by our village Aesculapius to be chicken pox, but presently assumed the more serious aspect of varioloid. My sister, like the rest of us, had been carefully vaccinated; but the fact was then by no means so generally understood as it is now, that the power of the vaccine dies out of the system by degrees, and requires renewing to insure safety. My mother, having lost her faith in vaccination, thought that a natural attack of varioloid was the best preservative from small pox, and my sister having had her seasoning so mildly and without any bad result but a small scar on her long nose, I was sent for from London, where I was, with the hope that I should take the same light form of the malady from her; but the difference of our age and constitution was not taken into consideration, and I caught the disease indeed, but as nearly as possible died of it, and have remained disfigured by it all my life.

I was but little over sixteen, and had returned from school a very pretty-looking girl, with fine eyes, teeth, and hair, a clear, vivid complexion, and rather good features. The small pox did not affect my three advantages first named, but besides marking my face very perceptibly, it rendered my complexion thick and muddy and my features heavy and coarse, leaving me so moderate a share of good looks as quite to warrant my mother's satisfaction in saying when I went on the stage, "Well, my dear, they can't say we have brought you out to exhibit your beauty." Plain I certainly was, but I by no means always looked so; and so great was the variation in my appearance at different times, that my comical old friend, Mrs. Fitzhugh, once exclaimed, "Fanny Kemble, you are the ugliest and the handsomest woman in London!" And I am sure if a collection were made of the numerous portraits that have been taken of me, nobody would ever guess any two of them to be likenesses of the same person.

Fanny, writing 53 years later in retrospect, touches impersonally on the catastrophe of the loss of her beautiful complexion and regular features from small pox. It was the first heavy blow of her life and Fanny did not bow to fate, but took in her stride this major calamity. She says nothing of the horror she felt on first looking into the mirror when the illness was over. The Kembles were famous for their beauty, and even her mother is referred to by contemporary biographers as beautiful. The family was not planning to have her act, as they had resolved to keep their children off the stage. But even though Fanny was not counting on her beauty for her livelihood, her good looks which she had taken for granted were marred.

> Among the principal interests of my London life at this time was the production at our theatre of Weber's opera, "Der Freischütz." Few operas I believe have had a wider or more prolonged popularity; none certainly within my recollection ever had anything approaching it.

> We went to hear it until we literally knew it by heart, and such was my enthusiasm for it that I contrived to get up a romantic passion for the great composer.

"Der Freischütz" was filling Covent Garden night after night in the season of 1824–25 and was simultaneously being given at two other theatres. Charles Kemble was desperately hoping to produce another opera that would find equal favor with the public. Most of the plays he had produced since accepting his share of Covent Garden from his brother John had not filled the Theatre, and his indebtedness was increasing. In August, 1825, he went to Bad Ems, Germany, to ask Carl Maria von Weber to write an opera for Covent Garden and concluded the contract by paying him one thousand pounds. A libretto by the English novelist James Robinson Planche based on the fairy tale of "Oberon" by Wieland was commissioned at the same time, and so the opera "Oberon" came into being. Charles took with him to Germany Sir George Smart, Conductor of the London Philharmonic Society Concerts, and of opera at Covent Garden during Charles' proprietorship. Sir George was in Germany to see Beethoven and ask him about the tempi of his symphonies. Weber came to London to conduct "Der Freischütz," and rehearse "Oberon" and conduct its first performance.

Weber took up his abode at the house of Sir George Smart, our excellent old friend . . . a capital musician and very worthy man. Weber continued to reside in Sir George's house the whole of his stay in London, and died there soon after the production of his "Oberon."

"Oberon" was not the success of "Der Freischütz," and the Kembles' worries continued to mount.

Sir George Smart was the first person who presented Mendelssohn to me. I had been acting Juliet one night, and at the end of the play was raised from the stage by my kind old friend, who had been in the orchestra during the performance with the great composer, then a young man of nineteen, on his first visit to England. He brought letters of introduction to my father and made his first acquaintance with me in my graveclothes.

Upon my uncle John's death his widow had returned to England and fixed her residence at a charming place called Heath Farm, in Hertfordshire. Mrs. Kemble invited my mother to come and see her soon after she settled in Hertfordshire, and I accompanied her thither. Cashiobury Park thus became familiar ground to me and remains endeared to my recollection for its own beauty, for the delightful days I passed rambling about it, and for the beginning of that love bestowed upon my whole life by Harriet St. Leger.

Harriet St. Leger now spoken of for the first time by Fanny Kemble in her "Records of a Girlhood," was the Irish spinster who became almost on sight the dearest, the most intimate, life-long friend of Fanny Kemble's. She lived at Ardgillan Castle, Ireland. Fanny says of her,

And so I here first knew the dearest friend I have ever known. The device of her family is "Haut et Bon": it was her description. She was about thirty years old when I first met her at Heath Farm; tall and thin, her figure wanted roundness and grace, but it was straight as a dart, and the vigorous, elastic, active movements of her limbs, and firm, fleet, springing step of her beautifully made feet and ankles, gave to her whole person and deportment a character like that of the fabled Atalanta.

Miss St. Leger was the person to whom Fanny wrote, as they so seldom saw each other, always once a week, often twice a week, and sometimes twice a day for forty years. Miss St. Leger returned all of Fanny's letters to her amounting to thousands. When Fanny as an old woman settled for a time in America, she edited these letters into the story of her life.

Miss St. Leger led a secluded, monotonous life in Ireland, broken by several dreary trips to European watering places in search of health, accompanied by a friend, Miss Alice Wilson, and in the end Miss St. Leger became blind. She had nothing to offer Fanny but ultraconservative advice, and asked endless questions about religious dogma. Fanny describes Miss St. Leger as always wearing heavy clumsy boots made for her by a maker of men's boots, and garments that were designed to clothe her somberly, of no fashion or cut, but made of the finest wool or sheerest lawn, and as immaculate and particular about her person. Occasionally Miss St. Leger came to London and stayed with the Kembles for a short time, and infrequently and at long intervals Fanny spent a few days at Ardgillan Castle. Often there was half a world between them, but in temperament and life experience, they were a universe apart. They seldom saw each other, and their correspondence reached staggering proportions. Fanny kept Miss St. Leger's letters to read again for strength and comfort until her nomadic life made it impossible.

What can be thought of such a relation between two so utterly different women? Though letter writing was part of every day for many literate people in the nineteenth century, and there are innumerable volumes of published letters of well known men and women, there are no letters from a famous woman to an unknown woman covering forty years. Why was Fanny drawn to Miss St. Leger who was twelve years older and shared none of Fanny's delight in living? Miss St. Leger was austere and outwardly serene, while Fanny gave way to her emotions. Miss St. Leger was in complete contrast to the women of the Kemble family, nor was she like the women in London society whom the Kembles knew. Fanny's letters must have been a feast to her: her one contact with vivid throbbing life. The questions asked and advice given by Miss St. Leger can be seen in Fanny's answers. Miss St. Leger always asked some abstract question such as "What do you think of Calvinism?" Sometimes Fanny wrote her that she had no time to answer her questions, but often she did answer.

Fanny apparently had to have someone to write to without reservation and displays an astonishing candor and self-evaluation even at the age of eighteen. Fanny had to have someone who would accept eagerly and seriously her telling of her daily battles with her emotions, and the huge perplexing burdens of her existence. She felt that Miss St. Leger gave her sage counsel, and she became not only a safety valve but at times a much hoped for, and needed, ballast to Fanny so often seething in the tempests of life.

> About this time (1827) I began to be aware of the ominous distresses and disturbances connected with the affairs of the theatre (Covent Garden), that were to continue and increase until the miserable subject became literally the sauce to our daily bread; embittering my father's life with incessant care and harassing vexation; and of the haunting apprehension of that ruin which threatened us for years, and which his most strenuous efforts only delayed, without averting it.
>
> The proprietors were engaged in a lawsuit with each other and finally one of them threw the whole concern into chancery; and for years that dreary chancery suit seemed to envelop us in an atmosphere of palpitating suspense or stagnant uncertainty, and to enter as an inevitable element into every hope, fear, expectation, resolution, event, or action of our lives.
>
> How unutterably heart-sick I became of the very sound of its name, and how well I remember the expression on my father's careworn face one day as he turned back from the door out of which he was going to his daily drudgery at the theatre, to say to my aunt who had reproached him with the loss of a button from his rather shabby coat, "Ah, Dall, my dear, you see it is my chancery suit."

Still in 1827:

My father is in Paris, where he was to arrive yesterday and where tomorrow he will act in the first regularly and decently organized English theatre that the French ever saw.

After three years at Weybridge Fanny says to Miss St. Leger: "We are going to remove to Westminster on account of Henry's schooling as soon as we can part with this house."

They had had to take Henry, Fanny's younger brother, out of boarding school and place him in a day school because they could not afford boarding school but were determined that he should finish his education. In the same letter to Miss St. Leger she says:

I have been writing a great deal of poetry—at least I mean it for such, and I hope it is not all very bad, as my father has expressed himself surprised and pleased at some things I read him lately. I wish I could send you some of my perpetrations, but they are for the most part so fearfully long that it is impossible.

I am writing a journal, and its pages, like many pleasant hours of conversation, are a whimsical medley of the sad, the sober, the gay, the good, the bad, and the ridiculous; not at all the sort of serious, solemn journal you would write.

This is the first time that Fanny speaks of keeping a journal. It must be in the earliest and never-referred-to-again diary that the accounts of the major happenings in her early life, such as her opening in Juliet, were recorded and used by her when she edited her "Recollections" for publication.

My life at home at this time became difficult and troublesome, and unsatisfactory to myself and others; my mind and character were in a chaotic state of fermentation that required the wisest, firmest, and gentlest guidance. I was vehement and excitable, violently impulsive, and with a wild, ill-regulated imagination.

Fanny spent most of 1828 in Edinburgh with Mrs. Henry Siddons, the widow of her aunt's son. Mrs. Henry Siddons and her husband had been managers of a theatre in Edinburgh. Fanny became extremely fond of her cousin and speaks with admiration of the steadying influence Mrs. Siddons was to her. Fanny roamed the countryside for hours by herself by day, but in the evening she became part of the intellectual

circle which gathered almost nightly in her cousin's house
and had ample opportunity to express her feelings and convictions, matching her brains against those of older people.
Two of the men who frequented her cousin's house were
George Combe and his brother, Dr. Andrew Combe. Both
were well known at that time and published books which
caused many controversies. George Combe was a well known
phrenologist, practising what he believed was a science,
proving that the shape of human skulls established the characteristics of each individual. He and his brother from this early
date became life-long friends of Fanny, and she wrote George
Combe many letters asking his advice and telling him things
about herself which she told no one else. The letters were
never published and have recently been found. But in her
"Records of a Girlhood," she merely speaks frequently of
him during this year in Scotland. She says of herself that she
gained emotional equilibrium and became more religious without undergoing any extreme religious experiences. She writes
in her "Record" of the Kembles' religious observances at home.

> In my childhood in my father's house we had no special religious
> training; our habits were those of average English Protestants of
> decent respectability. My mother read the Bible to us in the morn-
> ing before breakfast; Mrs. Trimmer's and Mrs. Barbauld's Scripture
> histories and paraphrases were taught to us; we learnt our cate-
> chism and collects, and went to church on Sunday, duly and de-
> corously, as a matter of course. Grace was always said before and
> after meals by the youngest member of the family present; and I
> remember a quaint, old fashioned benediction which when my
> father happened to be at home at our bedtime we used to kneel
> down by his chair to receive, and with which he used to dismiss us
> for the night: "God bless you! Make you good, happy, healthy, and
> wise." These, with our own daily morning and evening prayers,
> were our devotional habits and pious practices.

Fanny returned from this happy year in Scotland to her
family at St. James St., Buckingham Gate, Westminster and
found her family as usual beset by financial difficulties.
Charles had been arrested on the street for the Theatre's debts
although he owed no private debts. She wrote to Harriet,
making the first mention of her first play, "Francis I."

I am extremely busy, dearest Harriet, and extremely elated about my play; I know I mentioned it before to you, but you may have reckoned it as one of the soap bubbles which I am so fond of blowing, admiring, and forgetting; however, when I tell you that I have finished three acts of it, and that the proprietors of Covent Garden have offered me, if it succeeds, two hundred pounds, you will agree that I have some reason to be proud as well as pleased.

Moreover, my father has offered me either to let me sell my play to a bookseller, or to buy it for the theatre at fifty pounds.

I feel almost ashamed of saying anything about myself, after the two or three scoldings you have sent me of late. Perhaps while my blue devils found vent in ridiculous verses, they did not much matter; but their having prompted me lately to throw between seven and eight hundred pages (about a year's work) into the fire, seems to me now rather deplorable.

In January, 1828 Fanny wrote to Harriet:

They are in sad want of a woman at both the theatres (Covent Garden and Drury Lane), I've half a mind to give Covent Garden one. Don't be surprised. I have something to say to you on this subject, but have not room for it in this letter.

In March, 1828 again to Harriet:

My father is now in Edinburgh. He has been absent from London about a week. I had a conversation with him about the stage some time before he went, in which he allowed that should our miserably uncertain circumstances finally settle unfavorably, the theatre might be an honorable and advantageous resource for me; but that at present he should be sorry to see me adopt that career. As he is the best and kindest father and friend to us all, such a decision on his part was conclusive, as you will easily believe; and I have forborne all further allusion to the subject, although on some accounts I regret being obliged to do so.

Charles, even though his situation was worsening, was still determined to keep his daughter off the stage, and a month later Fanny writes:

Dearest Harriet, in my last letter want of time and room prevented my enlarging on my hint about the stage, but as far as my own determination goes at present, I think it is the course that I shall most likely pursue. You know that the independence of mind and body seems to me the greatest desideratum of life. I am not

patient or restrained or submissive to authority, and my head and
heart are engrossed with the idea of exercising and developing the
literary talent which I think I possess. This is meat, drink, and sleep
to me; my world, in which I live and have my happiness; and moreover, I hope, my means of fame (the prize for which I pray).
. . . I do not think I am fit to marry, to make an obedient wife
or affectionate mother. My imagination is paramount with me and
would disqualify me, I think, for the everyday, matter of fact cares
and duties of the mistress of a household and head of a family. I
think I should be unhappy and the cause of unhappiness to others
if I were to marry. Now, if I do not marry, what is to become of
me in the event of anything happening to my father? His property
is almost all gone. I doubt if we shall ever receive one pound from
it. Is it likely that, supposing I were willing to undergo the drudgery
of writing for my bread, I could live by my wits and the produce
ᴏᶠ my brain; or is such an existence desirable?

Fanny shows remarkable insight and self-evaluation at nineteen.

Perhaps I might attain to the literary dignity of being the lioness
of a season, asked to dinner parties "because I am so clever"; perhaps my writing faculty might become a useful auxiliary to some
other less precarious dependence; but to write to eat—to live, in
short—that seems to me to earn hard money after a very hard
fashion. The stage is a profession that people who have a talent for
it make lucrative, and which honorable conduct may make respectable; one which would place me at once beyond the fear of
want and that is closely allied in its nature to my beloved literary
pursuits.

My father said the other day, "There is a fine fortune to be made
by any young woman of even decent talent on the stage now." A
fine fortune is a fine thing. To be sure, there remains a rather material question to settle, that of even "decent talent." In some respects no girl intending herself for this profession can have had
better opportunities of acquiring just notions on the subject of
acting. I have constantly heard refined and thoughtful criticism on
our greatest dramatic works, and in every various way of rendering
them effective on the stage. I have been lately frequenting to the
theatre, and seen and heard observingly, and exercised my own
judgment and critical faculty to the best of my ability, according
to these same canons of taste by which it has been formed. Nature

has certainly not been favorable to me as might have been wished, if I am to embrace a calling where personal beauty if not indispensable is so great an advantage. But if the informing spirit be mine, it shall go hard if with a face and voice obedient to my emotions as mine are, I do not in some measure make up for the want of good looks. My father is now proprietor and manager of the theatre, and those certainly are favorable circumstances for my entering on a career which is one of great labor and some exposure, at the best, to a woman, and where a young girl cannot be too prudent herself, nor her protectors too careful of her. I hope I have not taken up this notion hastily, and I have no fear of looking only on the bright side of the picture, for ours is a house where that is very seldom seen.

Fanny is oblivious of one cardinal fact; she has had no training, has served no apprenticeship in small parts, and has never stood before the footlights.

P.S. My father's income is barely eight hundred a year. John's (her older brother) expenses since he has been at college have been nearly three. Five hundred a year for such a family as ours is very close and careful work, dear Harriet, and if my going on the stage would nearly double that income, lessen my dear father's anxieties for us all, and the quantity of work which he latterly had often felt too much for him, and remove the many privations which my dear mother cheerfully endures, as well as the weight of her uncertainty about our future provision, would not this be a "consummation devoutly to be wished?"

She continues in her "Record":

The constantly darkening prospects of that unlucky theatre threw a gloom over us all; sometimes my father used to speak of selling his share in it for anything he could get for it (and Heaven knows it was not likely to be much!) and going to live abroad; or sending my mother with us to live cheaply in the south of France. My own former fancy about going on the stage and passionate desire for a lonely, independent life in which it had originated, had died away with the sort of moral and mental effervescence which had subsided during my year's residence in Edinburgh.

It was in the autumn of 1829, my father being absent on a professional tour in Ireland, that my mother, coming in from walking one day, threw herself into a chair and burst into tears. She had been evidently much depressed for some time past, and I was alarmed at her distress, of which I begged her to tell me the cause. "Oh, it has come at last," she answered; "our property is to be sold. I have seen that fine building all covered with placards and bills of sale; the theatre must be closed, and I know not how many hundred poor people will be turned adrift without employment." I believed the theatre employed regularly seven hundred persons in all its different departments, without reckoning the great number of what were called supernumeraries, who were hired by the night at Christmas, Easter, and on all occasions of any specially showy spectacle. Seized with a sort of terror like the Lady of Shallott, that "The curse had come upon me," I comforted my mother with expressions of pity and affection, and as soon as I left her, wrote a most urgent entreaty to my father that he would allow me to act for myself, and seek employment as a governess, so as to relieve him at once at least of the burden of my maintenance. I brought this letter to my mother and begged her permission to send it, to which she consented; but I afterward learned she wrote by the same post to my father requesting him not to give a positive answer to my letter until his return to town. The next day she asked me whether I seriously thought I had any real talent for the stage. My school day triumphs in Racine's "Andromaque" were far enough behind me, and I could only answer, with as much perplexity as good faith, that I had not the slightest idea whether I had or not. She begged me to learn some part and say it to her that she might form some opinion of my power, and I chose Shakespeare's Portia, then as now my ideal of a perfect woman—the wise, witty woman, loving with all her soul and submitting with all her heart to a man whom everybody but herself (who was the best judge) would have judged her inferior; the laughter-loving, light-hearted, true-hearted, deep-hearted woman, full of keen perception, of active efficiency, of wisdom prompted by love, of tenderest unselfishness, of generous magnanimity; noble, simple, humble, pure; true, dutiful, religious, and full of fun; delightful above all others, the woman of women. Having learned it by heart, I recited Portia to my mother, whose only comment was, "There is hardly passion enough in this part to test any tragic power. I wish you would study Juliet for me." Study to me then, as unfortunately long afterward, simply meant to learn by heart, which I did again, and repeated my lesson to my mother, who again heard me without any observation whatever. Meantime my father returned to town and my letter remained unanswered, and I was wondering in my mind what reply I should receive to my urgent entreaty, when one morning my mother told me she wished me to recite Juliet to my father; and so in the evening I stood up before them both and with indescribable trepidation repeated my first lesson in tragedy.

They neither of them said anything beyond "Very well—very nice, my dear," with many kisses and caresses, from which I escaped to sit down on the stairs halfway between the drawing room and my bedroom and got rid of the repressed nervous fear I had struggled with while reciting in floods of tears. A few days after this my father told me he wished to take me to the theatre with him to try whether my voice was of sufficient strength to fill the building; so thither I went. That strange looking place, the stage with its racks of pasteboard and canvas—streets, forest, banqueting halls, and dungeons—drawn apart on either side, was empty and silent; not a soul was stirring in the indistinct recesses of its mysterious depths, which seemed to stretch indefinitely behind me. In front, the great amphitheatre, equally empty and silent, wrapped in its gray holland covers, would have been absolutely dark but for a long sharp, thin shaft of light that darted here and there from some height and distance far above me and alighted in a sudden vivid spot of brightness on the stage. Set down in the midst of twilight space, as it were, with only my father's voice coming to me from where he stood hardly distinguishable in the gloom, in those poetical utterances of pathetic passion I was seized with the spirit of the thing; my voice resounded through the great vault above and before me, and completely carried away by the inspiration of the wonderful play, I acted Juliet as I do not believe I ever acted it again, for I had no visible Romeo, and no audience to thwart my imagination; at least I had no consciousness of any, though in truth I had one. In the back of one of the private boxes, commanding the stage but perfectly invisible to me, sat an old and warmly attached friend of my father's, Major D........, a man of the world, of London society, a passionate lover of the stage, an amateur actor of no mean merit, the best judge in many respects that my father could have selected, of my capacity for my profession and my chance of success in it. Not till after the event had justified my kind old friend's prophecy did I know that he had witnessed that morning's performance, and joining my father at the end of it had said, "Bring her out at once; it will be a great success." And so three weeks from that time I was brought out, and it was a "great success." Three weeks was not much time for preparation of any sort for such an experiment, but I had no more to become acquainted with my fellow actors and actresses, not one of whom I had ever spoken with or seen—off the stage—before; to learn all the technical business as it was called, of the stage; how to carry myself toward the audience, which was not—but was to be—before me; how to concert my movements with the movements of those I was acting with, so as not to impede or intercept their efforts, while giving the greatest effect of which I was capable to my own.

Fanny's parents in desperation decided to have her attempt the part best suited to her, and gamble on her hoped-for inherited talent. They were beyond reasonable consideration for her, stubbornly heedless of the great risk, of forcing on her this desperate measure. They must have discussed with each other at length the wisdom of this momentous step. How could Fanny succeed with no training?

I do not wonder when I remember this brief apprenticeship to my profession that Mr. Macready once said that I did not know the elements of it. Three weeks of morning rehearsals of the play at the theatre, and evening consultations at home as to colors and forms of costume; what I should wear, how my hair should be dressed, etc. etc.,—in all which I remained absolutely passive in the hands of others, taking no part and not much interest in the matter,—ended in my mother's putting aside all suggestions of innovation, like the adoption of the real, picturesque costume of mediaeval Verona (which was, of course, Juliet's proper dress), and determining in favor of the traditional stage costume for the part, which was simply a dress of plain white satin with a long train, with short sleeves and a low body; my hair was dressed in the fashion in which I usually wore it; a girdle of fine paste brilliants, and a small comb of the same, which held up my hair, were the only theatrical parts of the dress, which was perfectly simple and as absolutely unlike anything Juliet ever wore as possible.

My mother, though undoubtedly very anxious that I should look well, was of course far more desirous that I should act well, and judged that whatever rendered my dress most entirely subservient to my acting, and least an object of preoccupation and strange embarrassment to myself, was, under the circumstances of my total inexperience and brief period of preparation, the thing to be chosen, and I am sure that in the main she judged wisely. The mere appendage of a train—three yards of white satin—following me wherever I went, was to me a new and would have been a difficult experience to most girls. As it was, I never knew after the first scene of the play what became of my train and was greatly amused when Lady Dacre told me the next morning that as soon as my troubles began I had snatched it up and carried it on my arm, which I did quite unconsciously, because I found something in the way of Juliet's feet.

The lack of proper rehearsals is shown here by Fanny without her realizing it. If she had been perfect in the part, as she should have been, she would have learned to walk without having her train interfere, or had she planned to pick it up, she should have known when to do it.

My frame of mind under the preparations that were going forward for my debut appears to me now curious enough. Though I had found out that I could act and had acted with a sort of frenzy of passion and entire self-forgetfulness the first time I ever uttered the wonderful conception I had undertaken to represent, my going on the stage was absolutely an act of duty and conformity to the will of my parents, strengthened by my own conviction that I was bound to help them by every means in my power. The theatrical profession was, however, utterly distasteful to me, though acting itself, that is to say, dramatic personation, was not; and every detail of my future vocation, from the preparation behind the scenes to the representations before the curtain was more or less repugnant to me. Nor did custom ever render this aversion less; and liking my work so little, and being so devoid of enthusiasm, respect, or love for it, it is wonderful to me that I ever achieved any success in it at all. The dramatic element inherent in my organization must have been very powerful to have enabled me without either study of or love for my profession to do anything worth anything in it.

But this is the reason why, with an unusual gift and many unusual advantages for it, I did really so little; why my performances were always uneven in themselves and perfectly unequal with each other, never complete as a whole, however striking in occasional parts, and never at the same level two nights together; depending for their effect upon the state of my nerves and spirits, instead of being the result of deliberate thought and consideration,—study, in short, carefully and conscientiously applied to my work; the permanent element which preserves the artist, however inevitably he must feel the influence of moods of mind and body, from ever being at their mercy.

I brought but one half the necessary material to the exercise of my profession, that which nature gave me; and never added the cultivation and labor requisite to produce any fine performance in the right sense of the word; and coming of a family of real artists have never felt that I deserved that honorable name.

The wonderful candor and detachment of this evaluation of her Juliet is also typical of all her criticisms of herself in every part she later played. She saw herself as clearly as if she were a rival actress. She did not let her feelings come between her and what she knew was not perfect, and her judgment was not clouded by egotism. In a letter to Harriet from St. James Street, September 24, 1829, she voices her excitement and anxiety about her coming debut:

My dear Harriet, I am going on the stage! The nearest period talked of for my debut is the first of October, at the opening of the Theatre; the furthest, November; but I almost think I should prefer the nearest, for it is a very serious trial to look forward to, and I wish it were over. Juliet is to be my opening part, but not to my father's Romeo; there would be many objections to that; he will do Mercutio for me. I do not enter more fully upon this, because I know how few things can be of interest to you in your present state of feeling, but I wished you not to find the first notice of my entrance on the stage of life in a newspaper. God bless you, dearest Harriet, and grant you better hopes.

At about the same time she wrote in her Journal:

My father not acting Romeo with me deprived me of the most poetical and graceful lover of his day; but the public, who had long been familiar with his rendering of the part of Romeo, gained as much as I lost by his taking that of Mercutio, which has never since been so admirably represented, and I dare affirm will never be given more perfectly. The graceful ease and airy sparkling brilliance of his delivery of the witty fancies of that merry gentleman, the gallant defiance of his bearing toward the enemies of his house, and his heroically pathetic and humorous death scene, were beyond description charming. He was one of the best Romeos, and incomparably the best Mercutio, that ever trod the English stage.

The part of Romeo was given to Mr. Abbot, an old fashioned

favorite with the public, a very amiable and worthy man, old enough to have been my father, whose performance, not certainly of the highest order, was nevertheless not below in offensive mediocrity. But the public who were bent upon doing more than justice to me, were less than just to him; and the abuse showered upon his Romeo, especially by more enthusiastic admirers of the male sex, might, I should think, have embittered his stage relations with me to the point of making me an object of detestation to him all through our theatrical lives.

The report of the approaching appearance on the stage had excited a good deal of interest among the acquaintances and friends of my family, and occasioned a renewal of cordial relations which had formerly existed but ceased for some time between Sir Thomas Lawrence and my father and mother.

Sir Thomas Lawrence, then sixty-one years old and President of the Royal Academy, had painted the crowned heads of Europe and England, and was a sought-after ornament in fashionable London.

Lawrence's enthusiastic admiration for my uncle John and my aunt Mrs. Siddons, testified by the numerous striking portraits in which he has recorded their personal beauty and dramatic picturesqueness, led to a most intimate and close friendship between the great painter and the eminent actors and subsequently to very painful circumstances which estranged him for years from all our family, and forbade all renewal of the relations between himself and Mrs. Siddons which had been so cruelly interrupted.

Sir Thomas Lawrence had behaved in a flagrant and inexcusable way to Mrs. Siddon's young daughters, Sarah and Maria. He had asked Mrs. Siddons for permission to court Sarah, the elder, and became engaged to her, and then told Mrs. Siddons he was in love with Maria. Then he broke the engagement to Sarah and became engaged to Maria. Both girls had tuberculosis, and Maria died shortly, after exacting a promise from Sarah that she would never marry Lawrence. Sarah died a few months after her sister. In unpublished fragments of Fanny's Journal before Fanny met Lawrence she said of him, "he, whose wanton and heartless duplicity planted the death that conquered them both in their bosoms."

It was years after these events that Lawrence, meeting my father accidentally in the street one day, stopped him and spoke with great feeling of his sympathy for us all in my approaching trial (debut on the stage) and begged permission to come and see my mother and become acquainted with me, which he accordingly did; and from that time till his death which occurred but a few months later, he was unwearied in acts of friendly and affectionate kindness to me. He came repeatedly to consult with my mother about the disputed point of my dress and gave his sanction to her decision upon it.

When in town Lawrence never omitted one of my performances, always occupying the stage box and invariably sending me the next morning a letter full of the most detailed and delicate criticism, which, combined with expressions of enthusiastic admiration with which this discriminating and careful review of my performance invariably terminated, was as strong a dose of the finest flattery as could well have been offered to a girl of my age on the very first step of her artistic career. I used to read over the last of these remarkable criticisms, invariably, before going to the theatre, in order to profit by every suggestion of alteration or hint of improvement they contained; and I was in the act of reperusing the last I ever received from him when my father came in and said, "Lawrence is dead." (January 7, 1830)

I had been sitting to him for some time previously for a pencil sketch which he gave my mother; it was his last work and certainly the most beautiful of his drawings. He had appointed a day for beginning a full-length, life-size portrait of me as Juliet, and we had seen him only a week before his death. The shock of this event was terrible to me, although I have sometimes since thought it was fortunate for me rather than otherwise. I think it not at all unlikely that had our intercourse continued and had I sat to him for the projected portrait of Juliet, in spite of the forty years' difference in our ages and my knowledge of his disastrous relations with my cousins, I should have become in love with him myself, and been the fourth member of our family whose life he would have disturbed and embittered.

All being in due preparation for my coming out, my rehearsals were the only interruption to my usual habits of occupation, which I pursued very steadily in spite of my impending trial. On the day of my first appearance I had no rehearsal for fear of over-fatigue, and spent my morning as usual in practicing the piano, walking in the enclosure of St. James' Park opposite our house, and reading in "Blunt's Scripture Characters" (a book in which I was then deeply interested) the chapters relating to St. Peter and Jacob. I do not know whether the nervous tension which I must have been enduring strengthened the impression made upon me by what I read, but I remember being quite absorbed by it, which I think was curious, because certainly such subjects of meditation were hardly allied to the painful undertaking so immediately pressing upon me. But I believe I felt imperatively the necessity of moderating my own strong nervous emotion and excitement by the fulfillment of my accustomed duties and pursuits, and above all by withdrawing my mind into higher and serener regions of thought as a respite and relief from the pressure of my alternate apprehensions of failure and hope of success.

Fanny actually was able to give her attention to St. Peter and Jacob the day of her first appearance. This is an example of the strong grip she had on herself which seldom failed her. She says years later that it was only through systematic habits, customs, and routine that she could maintain an even keel through times of severe stress.

My mother, who had left the stage for upward of twenty years, determined to return to it on the night of my first appearance, that I might have the comfort and support of her being with me in my trial. We drove to the Theatre very early, indeed while the late autumn sunlight yet lingered in the sky; it shone into the carriage upon me, and as I screened my eyes from it, my mother said, "Heaven smiles on you, my child." My poor mother went into her dressing room to get herself ready and did not return to me for fear of increasing my agitation by her own. My dear Aunt Dall and my maid and the theatre dresser performed my toilet for me, and at length I was placed in a chair, with my satin train carefully laid over the back of it, and there I sat, ready for execution, with the palms of my hands pressed convulsively together, and the tears I in vain endeavored to repress welling up into my eyes and brimming slowly over, down my rouged cheeks—upon which my aunt with a smile of pity renewed the color as often as these heavy drops made unsightly streaks in it. Once and again my father came to the door, and I heard his anxious "How is she?" to which my aunt answered, sending him away with words of comforting cheer. At last, "Miss Kemble called for the stage, ma'am!" accompanied with

a brisk tap at the door, started me upright on my feet, and I was
led round to the side scene opposite to the one from which I saw
my mother advance on the stage; and while the uproar of her reception filled me with terror, dear old Mrs. Davenport, my nurse, and
dear Mr. Keely, her Peter, and half the dramatis personae of the
play (but not my father who had retreated, quite unable to endure
the scene) stood round me as I lay, all but insensible, in my aunt's
arms. "Courage, courage, dear child! poor thing, poor thing!" reiterated Mrs. Davenport. "Never mind 'em, Miss Kemble!" urged
Keely, in that irresistibly comical, nervous, lachrymose voice of
his, which I have never since heard without a thrill of anything but
comical association; "Never mind 'em! Don't think of 'em, any
more than if they were so many rows of cabbages!" "Nurse!" called
my mother, and on waddled Mrs. Davenport, and turning back
called in her turn, "Juliet!" My aunt gave me an impulse forward,
and I ran straight across the stage, stunned with the tremendous
shout that greeted me, my eyes covered with mist and the green
baize flooring of the stage feeling as if it rose up against my feet;
but I got to my mother and stood like a terrified creature at bay,
confronting the huge theatre full of gazing human beings. I do not
think a word I uttered during this scene could have been audible;
in the next, the ballroom, I began to forget myself; in the following
one, the balcony scene, I had done so, and for aught I knew I was
Juliet; the passion I was uttering, sending hot waves of blushes all
over my neck and shoulders, while the poetry sounded like music
to me as I spoke it, with no consciousness of anything before me,
utterly transported into the imaginary existence of the play. After
this I did not return into myself till all was over, and amid a tu-
multuous storm of applause, congratulation, tears, embraces, and a
general joyous explosion of unutterable relief at the fortunate ter-
mination of my attempt, we went home. And so my life was determined, and I devoted myself to an avocation which I never
liked or honored, and about the very nature of which I have never
been able to come to any decided opinion. A business which is
incessant excitement and my fictitious emotion seems to me unworthy
of a man; a business which is public exhibition, unworthy of a
woman. I never presented myself before an audience without a
shrinking feeling of reluctance, or withdrew from their presence
without thinking the excitement I had undergone unhealthy, and
the personal exhibition odious.

Nevertheless I sat down to supper that night with my poor, rejoicing parents well content, God knows! with the issue of my trial; and still better pleased with a lovely little Geneva watch, the first I had ever possessed, all encrusted with gold work and jewels, which my father laid by my plate, and I immediately christened Romeo, and went, a blissful girl, to sleep with it under my pillow.

Fanny went instantly to sleep after her great success, and her father still treating her like a little girl gave her a mere trinket as a reward. There was no present that Charles Kemble could have given his daughter which could possibly express the magnitude of her achievement or his gratitude, but even so a watch seems pitifully inadequate. The Charles Kembles surely did not fall to sleep at once that night after supper with their children. They must have been congratulating each other and too excited, thanking heaven for giving them a daughter capable of such a triumph.

CHAPTER III

Success in England

The skies had lifted for the Charles Kembles. Fanny, after the first night as Juliet, became the leading lady of Covent Garden and the sensation of London. Her success for three years in London and the Provinces made it possible for Charles Kemble to continue as Actor-Manager, and 13,000 pounds of debt on the Theatre were paid back as a result of full houses. The Reviewer in the London Times for October 6, 1829 wrote:

> The general apprehension that the public might be deprived, for a time at least, of so considerable a source of amusement as this Theatre has always afforded, and which the difficulties that beset it seemed to encourage, were removed by its opening last night. We are sincerely glad to be able to say, too, that it opened with such *eclat,* as gives glorious promise that those apprehensions will be wholly put an end to. The tragedy of Romeo and Juliet was selected for the commencement, and in addition to the attractions which were held out by an extremely judicious and powerful cast, was that of the first appearance of Mr. C. Kemble's daughter, Miss Fanny Kemble, as the heroine. The public discussions whch have lately taken place respecting the theatre, have given a painful notoriety to the untoward circumstances in which Mr. Kemble has been placed; and it is most probable that some feelings of sympathy had been excited among the audience in favour of the young lady, whose first essay in the profession she has chosen was made for the express purpose of assisting to stem the dangers which assailed her father. Although this consideration might have brought some persons to the theatre last evening, the young candidate displayed talents of so high an order, that the audience quitted it convinced that her claims to the public encouragement are unquestionable, and that her success would have been certain even if she had not appeared under the circumstances which have excited a strong personal interest in her

behalf. Miss Kemble is very young, probably about 18, tall, of graceful and well proportioned figure; her features resemble her mother's,
but not so much as to be strikingly like her. They are very agreeable,
and her dark eyebrows and eyelashes which are extremely handsome, give them a power of expression admirably adapted for the
stage. Her voice is flexible and of considerable volume, and her
utterance so perfectly distinct that her lower tones are always audible and effective. On her first entrance she seemed to feel very sen-
sibly the embarrassment of the new and overwhelming task she
had undertaken. She ran to her mother's arms with a sort of in-
stinctive impulse and almost immediately recovered her composure.
From that time, although there was occasionally something like
timidity in her manner, there was not the slightest portion of awk-
wardness, or even of that want of self-possession which might have
been well pardoned in so young an actress. Upon the whole we do
not remember to have ever seen a more triumphant debut. That
Miss Kemble has been well and carefully instructed, as of course
she would be, is clear; but it is no less clear that she possesses qualifications which instruction could not create, although it can bring
them to perfection.

The enthusiasm that marked Fanny's initial appearance on
any stage and which proved a financial success was not shared
by the diarist, Charles Greville. He and his brother Henry
were friends of the Kemble family, and in later years they
both saw a great deal of Fanny. Charles was alone in his
opinion, as her reception had been overwhelming, but sentiment played no part in Charles Greville's judgment, and complete detachment and dry facts are always reported by him
in his voluminous diary published since his death. Charles
Greville wrote on November 9, 1829:

> I saw Miss Fanny Kemble for the first time on Friday, and I was
> disappointed. She is short, ill made, with large hands and feet, an
> expressive countenance though not handsome, fine eyes, teeth, and
> hair, not devoid of grace and with great energy and spirit, her voice
> good, though she has a little of the drawl of her family. She wants
> the pathos and tenderness of Miss O'Neill, and she excites no emo-
> tion; but she is very young, clever, and may become a very good,
> perhaps a fine, actress. Mrs. Siddons was not so good at her age.
> She fills the house every night.

Fanny's first letter of interest to George Combe, whom she had seen frequently during the year she had spent in Edinburgh with her cousin Mrs. Henry Siddons, was written on September 7, 1830 and concerns her convictions on the way the part of Juliet should be played. It was written one year after she first acted the role, but her life was so crowded and she was working so hard that she did not have time to explain in a letter her interpretation of Juliet.

You give me leave in your last kind letter to me to continue our Shakespearean discussions, for despite your quotation from Mrs. Harry [Siddons] I still think Juliet's love purely that of instinct—I saw Mrs. Henry Siddons act Juliet when I was staying with her in Edinburgh; and I was then struck with the beauty but at the same time the incorrectness of her conception of the part—I then had *not* thought of the thing at all as a matter of art, but every line of Shakespeare's Juliet was familiar to my mind, and in the pure, intellectual, and comparatively *cold* creation of Mrs. Harry I did not recognize the passionate young Italian girl—Now there are two ways in which Juliet may be represented—As Shakespeare wrote her, that is, with all the passion which exists in those passages which our education and state of society have rendered it necessary to omit—the second is the modification of the passion so as to convey no more of it than is expressed in what Juliet has to say as the play now stands, this I have endeavored to render mine—but I cannot think we are justified in totally altering an author's conception. If Juliet as Shakespeare wrote her be unfit to be presented to an audience of the nineteenth century, let her be banished to the library—but if she still holds her place on the stage, let her retain at least her individuality and come before us like the vision of the warm South—Juliet's love is like the red of a damask rose, full, rich, and glowing over every part of the flower.

This letter states how Fanny believed the part of Juliet should be acted; when Sir Thomas Lawrence re-entered the Kemble family circle, he wrote five letters to Fanny pointing out to her how she could improve her playing of the part. These letters have recently been found, and prove that he had a great and flattering interest in Fanny's performance of Juliet. As a young man he had considered going on the stage. His knowledge of the part of Juliet and his astute criticism and advice must have been of the utmost value to Fanny. The concentration and sensitiveness with which he watched and listened to her show that he was an artist with an understanding of an art that was not his own. His finite observations and his reasons for changing the inflections and emphasis of lines and single words could only be understood by an actress and prove that he knew the part of Juliet by heart.

He could not keep away from the Kembles' house, repeatedly called and asked Fanny to play and sing for him, and had begun a full length oil portrait of her as Juliet when he died. This short episode at the very beginning of Fanny's life as an actress was certainly stimulating to her, and the praise which his wish for her improvement implied was one of her greatest successes. His instructions to her are clear, but the formality of his letters and oblique phrasing at first make it hard to see that he is taking a romantic interest in her.

The best way of presenting these letters of Lawrence to Fanny is to leave out irrelevant details about comings and goings and only include the salient facts of his approbation and criticism of her. In speaking of her performance he says:

You have already effected an almost impossibility. Against the *Genius* of your family—against the probable influence of affection and the unconscious habits of imitation, you have fix'd an impression of the originality of your conceptions and power, that gives increasing stability to your success. The public toast to your Genius and go each night in expectation either of new or improved beauties. What if before Juliet parts from us for a long season you give them another novelty (if your judgment do not reject it) in the mode of rendering these lines? "these trembling limbs—*pale lips,* and *swimming* EYES—DEATH'S *in thy face!!!!"*

I believe that the manner in which you speak this is perfectly original. In itself a fine conception—with variety of tone and action to recommend it. It is the despairing conclusion of the dreadful symptoms she has seen. *But,* it is JULIET who utters it, and it has a sort of compassionate despair in it that is not LOVE! "Poor fellow thou art then dying" is a meaner language, the sort of sentiment that the uplifted hands and deepened tone of voice convey. Is there not something in the piercing TERROR of the thought though despair be the essence of it, more allied to the respect and homage of her love? He is her world! his loss, her annihilation!

The person who can seem to pity can survive. The mind that as it were *proclaims* the doom of the lov'd object is at that moment its superior, and not the victim of its fate. What the maddening thought flashes like heaven's lightning on her (and at what a moment!) the utterance of it (were it possible) should be a shriek! For what was even the shade of Tybalt to her startled fancy but the forerunner of the ill that is then the dreadful fact.

"Give me my Romeo, Night! and when he dies, take him and cut him out in little stars" etc. You *tell* Night to make stars of him. What, if in the mode of speaking this you were to say, "Do but make *stars* of him and he will give such splendor to the heavens" etc. Can I draw it? "Give me my Romeo, Night—and when he dies—take him and cut him out in *little stars!* and he will make the face of *heaven so fine* that *all the world will be in love with night* and pay no homage to the garish sun." I acknowledge the entire success of this passage with the audience, and there is the wise old saying "let well alone"—and not even Mrs. Kemble would resign the delight of hearing you applauded—but we are talking of truth and Juliet.

I have thus, dear Madam, ventur'd to bestow a more than royal tediousness upon you, yet it comes from one of the humblest and most faithful of your subjects, me, and the other slaves of the Lamp. I can not tell you how long a time I have been out of its service.

On October 16, 1829 he wrote her:

You make me shrink from the recollection of my own temerity, when you tell me of the condescending attention with which it has been received. You may remember that some time since when I last saw you play the character of Juliet, you were a little annoy'd in the closing scene by your hair coming into your eyes and concealing your countenance. As it was noticed by every other person in the house, I thought myself justified in suggesting the wig as security against its again occurring. I hope, however, tonight not only to see your hair "in undisturbed possession of your head" but your head in its rightful dominion over it. I beg to say how sincerely gratified I am by Mrs. Kemble's acquiescence, with your consent, in my professional request.

Fanny had accepted to sit for the pencil drawing which she says was her favorite picture of herself. In another letter Lawrence says:

How exactly you touched the note (on Wed. night) in "some word there was" etc. . . . It was with the same truth that you gave the line on the Monday "that *one word* BANISHED hath slain TEN THOUSAND *Tybalts.*"

Should Winchester of Eton dictate the pronounciation of "Amen?" The one I acknowledge has more solemnity if the vowel be not *too* open. I have a treasure of information for you! How rejoic'd you will be to know that not merely in the musty many editions "as it is acted" but absolutely in the present Prompter's Book itself, it is "cursed" and not "ACCURSED Friar." I know you have been longing to use it (whose prudery was it?) You feel that this vexatious syllable makes the whole passage "hang fire" and prevents its going off as it should and as your genius would make it. Can you give a note higher and of more *piercing* agony to *"Patience!!, Talk't* thou of PATIENCE *to a Wretch like me!!!"* Tis now the recollection of above five and thirty years that rushes to me the whole *Theatre* ringing with these notes!

In still another letter he says;

A little—*a wee*—bit too much of varied inflection in the following passage "and therefore both the wind-swift Cupid wing" etc. *Doves draw Love* for *"Doves* draw Love." All is but one stream of impetuous thought.

In every future work of mine that may at all address itself to the imagination—the heart—or the reasoning faculty, you shall be the monitor to whom I shall refer it, if you choose to bestow the time. But I write as if my career was still before me—as if life were not fading from me, and I had been recalled to past impressions only by a genius that will have [word undecipherable] the youth of its course when, I am ever present to it, I shall for many years have existed only in my works, and be restored by them to her remembrance.

P.S. If it should happen to be perfectly convenient to you I propose to begin your picture in oil in the first week of the next month. In this, we have nothing but fogs and darkness. I saw the engraving from the drawing last night. It will very soon be finished, and I think very successfully.

On October 28, 1829 he wrote:

I hope our first appointment stands good for tomorrow and will be not too fatiguing to you, that you will likewise sit to me on Friday. My present disappointment will thus delay the progress of the drawing but a day.

On November 3, he wrote to Mrs. Kemble:

My dear Madam,
  The sitting of today will probably be chiefly for the person. I am
perfectly satisfied with the general dress in which Miss F. Kemble
comes to me, but I could wish an alteration in the muslin collar,
which would be better if less smooth and stiff, and possibly of a
lighter material. This bother, however, may not be necessary, for
I well know the transmuting skill of the laundress; the sleeves of my
bishops often vying with rigid orthodoxy of their wigs.
  If any two or three light handkerchief shawls should be lying near
you, don't say "you need not bring those"—one of them may be
useful.
  I shall hope for the honor of seeing you with Miss Kemble at
twelve o'clock.

Fanny was the sensation of London. She was so hard worked
that she let two months go by before writing to Harriet St.
Leger about her debut:

> James St., Buckingham Gate
> December 14, 1829

My trial is over, and thank heaven, most fortunately. Our most
sanguine wishes could hardly have gone beyond the result, and at the
same time that I hail my success as a source of great happiness to
my dear father and mother. You say it is a very fascinating occupation; perhaps it is, though it does not appear to me so, and I think it
carries with it drawbacks enough to operate as an antidote to the
vanity and love of admiration which it can hardly fail to foster.

This piously phrased and truly Victorian letter is typical of
Fanny up to that date. She is the dutiful, humble daughter
of her era, thinking of her mother and father before herself.
  She is here writing to Miss St. Leger what Miss St. Leger
would approve of and not what she suffered on her opening
night. Fanny continues in the same letter:

We have all cause for heartfelt thankfulness when we think what
a light has dawned upon our prospects lately so dismal and overcast.
My own motto in all this must be as far as possible, "Beget a temperance in all things." I trust I shall be enabled to rule myself by it,
and in the firm hope that my endeavor to do what is right will be

favored and assisted, I have committed myself, nothing doubting, to the stormy sea of life.

"Beget a temperance in all things," is exactly what Fanny could not accomplish through her life except when she bowdlerized the account of her debut for Miss St. Leger. Mostly in her letters she withheld nothing, but the unctuous ring may have convinced Miss St. Leger that Fanny rode through her first appearance on the stage in this frame of mind.

The journal resumes:

When I saw the shop windows full of Lawrence's sketch of me and knew myself the subject of almost daily newspaper notices, when plates and saucers were brought to me with small figures of me as Juliet and Belvidera on them, and finally when gentlemen showed me lovely buff-colored neck handkerchiefs which they had bought and which had, as I thought, pretty lilac-colored flowers all over them, which proved on nearer inspection to be minute copies of Lawrence's head of me, I not unnaturally in the fullness of my inexperience believed in my own success.

I have since known more of the manufacture of public enthusiasm and public triumphs, and remembering to how many people it was a matter of vital importance that the public interest should be kept alive in me, and Covent Garden filled every night I played, I have become more skeptical upon the subject.

It is certain, however, that I played Juliet upward of a hundred and twenty times running, with all the irregularity and unevenness of immature inequality of which I have spoken as characteristics which were never corrected in my performances. My mother, who never missed one of them, would sometimes come down from her box and folding me in her arms say only the very satisfactory words, "Beautiful, my dear!" Quite as often if not oftener, the verdict was, "My dear, your performance was not fit to be seen! I don't know how you ever contrived to do the part decently; it must have been by some knack or trick which you appear to have entirely lost the secret of; you had better give the whole thing up at once than go on doing it so disgracefully ill." This was awful and made my heart sink down into my shoes, whatever might have been the fervor of applause with which the audience had greeted my performance.

Fanny had had to learn the part so quickly that it was absurd of her mother to expect her to give an even, let alone a fine, performance every night. Merely telling her what scenes she had played badly without insisting that she go over those scenes again and again until she had achieved perfection was useless. Mrs. Kemble had learned to act from long experience, but being aware that she had thrust Fanny on the stage and that so far all was going well, she evidently did not wish to impose any more drudgery on Fanny. Taking the long range view, it would have been much better for them all if Fanny had applied herself daily to acquire the fundamentals of her craft.

My life now became settled in its new shape. I acted regularly three times a week; I had no rehearsals, since "Romeo and Juliet" went on during the whole season, and some mornings were still my own. I always dined in the middle of the day (and invariably on the mutton-chop, so that I might have been a Harrow boy for diet). I was taken by my aunt early to the theatre, and there in my dress-ingroom sat through the entire play when I was not on the stage, with some piece of tapestry or needlework with which during the intervals of my tragic sorrows I busied my fingers; my thoughts being occupied with the events of my next scene and the various effects it demanded. When I was called for stage my aunt came with me, carrying my train that it might not sweep the dirty floor behind the scenes, and after spreading it out and adjusting the folds carefully as I went on, she remained at the side scene till I came off again, then gathered it on her arm, and folding a shawl around me, escorted me back to my dressing room and tapestry; and so my theatrical evenings were passed. My parents would not allow me to go into the green room where they thought my attention would be distracted from my business, and where I might occasionally meet with undesirable associates. My salary was fixed at thirty guineas a week, and the Saturday after I came out I presented myself for the first and last time at the treasury of the theatre to receive it, and carried it, clinking, with great triumph to my mother, the first money I ever earned.

It would be difficult to imagine anything more radical than the change which three weeks had made in the aspects of my whole life. From an insignificant schoolgirl I had suddenly become an object of general public interest. I was a little lion in society, and the town talk of the day. Approbation, admiration, adulation, were showered upon me; every condition of my life had been altered as by the wand of a fairy. Instead of the twenty pounds a year which my poor father squeezed out of his hard-earned income for my allowance, out of which I bought (alas with how much difficulty, seeing how many other things I would buy!) my gloves and shoes, I now had an assured income, as long as my health and faculties were unimpaired, of at least a thousand a year; and the thirty guineas a week at Covent Garden, and much larger remuneration during provincial tours, forever forbade the sense of destitution productive of the ecstasy with which only a short time before I came out I had found wedged into the bottom of my money drawer in my desk a sovereign that I had overlooked and so had sorrowfully concluded myself penniless till next allowance. Instead of trudging long distances afoot through the muddy London streets when the hire of a hackney coach was matter of serious consideration, I had a comfortable and elegant carriage; I was allowed at my own request to take riding lessons and before long had a charming horse of my own and was able to afford the delight of giving my father one, the use of which I hoped would help to invigorate and refresh him. The faded, threadbare, turned, and dyed frocks which were my habitual wear were exchanged for fashionably made dresses of fresh colors and fine textures in which I appeared to myself transfigured. Our door was besieged with visitors, our evenings bespoken by innumerable invitations; social civilities and courtesies poured in upon us from every side in an incessant stream; I was sought and petted and caressed by persons of conventional and real distinction, and every night that I did not act, I might if my parents had thought it prudent to let me do so, have passed in all the gaiety of the fashionable world and the great London season. So much cordiality, sympathy, interest, and apparent genuine goodwill seemed to accompany all these flattering demonstrations that it was impossible for me not to be touched and gratified—perhaps too unduly elated. If I was spoiled and my head turned, I can only say I think it would have needed a strong head not to be so; but God knows how pitiful a preparation all this tinsel, sudden success, and popularity formed for the duties and trials of my afterlife.

For some time after my first coming out I lost my sleep almost entirely, and used to lie wide awake the greater part of the night. With more use of my new profession this nervous wakefulness wore off; but I was subject to very frequent and severe pains in the side which any strong emotion almost invariably brought on, and which were relieved by nothing but exercise on horseback. The refreshment

of this panacea for bodily and mental ailments was always such to
me that often, returning from balls where I had danced until daylight, I used to feel that if I could have an hour's gallop in the fresh
morning air, I should be revived beyond all sleep that I could then
get.

One day when I had gone to the riding school more for exercise
than a lesson and was taking a solitary canter in the tan for my own
amusement, the little door under the gallery opened and Captain
Fozzard, the riding teacher, appeared, introducing a middle-aged
woman and a young girl who remained standing there while he advanced toward me and presently began to put me through all my
most crucial exercises, apparently for their edification. I was always
delighted to go through these particular feats which amused me
excessively and in which I took great pride. So I sat through them
all till upon a sign from the elder lady, Fozzard with extreme defer-
ence opened the door and escorted them forth, and then returning to
dismount me informed me that I had given a very satisfactory sample
of his teaching to the Duchess of Kent and the Princess Victoria, the
latter of whom was to be placed under his tuition forthwith. This
was the first time I ever saw the woman who holds the most exalted
position in the world, the Queen of England.

During the early days of her triumph, she wrote an undated
letter to Harriet from James St., Buckingham Gate:

I hope you will excuse the delay and believe me when I assure you
that not only the effort you made in going to the theatre, but your
seeing me at all, are appreciated by me as very strong marks of your
affection for me.

Now let me say something to you about Lady C. . . . L. . . .'s
criticism of my performance. As to my Aunt Siddons—look at her,
Harriet; look at her fine person, her beautiful face; listen to her
magnificent voice; and supposing that I were as highly endowed
with poetical dramatic imagination as she was (which I certainly am
not), is it likely that there can ever be a shadow of comparison between her and myself, even when years may have corrected all that
is at present crude and imperfect in my efforts?

Wait; have patience; by and by I hope I shall do better. It is very
true that to be the greatest actress of my day is not the aim on
which my happiness depends. But having embraced this career I
think I ought not to rest satisfied with any degree of excellence
short of what my utmost endeavor will enable me to attain in it.

As Fanny says that she plays Juliet upwards of one hundred times during her first season, it must be assumed that when she speaks in her journal of her second part it must be 1830–31.

The second part assigned to me by the theatre authorities was Belvidera, in Otway's "Venice Preserved." I had never read the play until I learned my part, nor seen it until I acted it. It is, I believe, one of the longest female parts on the stage, but I had still my schoolgirl capacity for committing quickly to memory and learned it in three hours. Acting it was a very different matter. I was no longer sustained by the genius of Shakespeare, no longer stimulated by the sublime passion and exquisite poetry. Juliet was a reality to me. Belvidera seemed to me a sort of lay figure in a tragic attitude, a mere "female in general." There was nothing in the part itself that affected my feelings or excited my imagination, and the miserable situations into which the poor creature was thrown throughout the piece revolted me. In this piece too I came at once into the unfavorable light of full comparison with my aunt's performance of the part, which was one of her famous ones. A friend of hers and mine, my dear and excellent William Harness, said that seeing me was exactly like looking at Mrs. Siddons through the diminishing end of an opera glass. I disliked the play and the character of Belvidera, and I am sure I must have played it very indifferently.

The next piece in which I appeared was Murphy's "Grecian Daughter," (I played Euphrasia), a feeble and inflated composition, as inferior in point of dramatic and poetical merit to Otway's "Venice Preserved" as that is to any of Shakespeare's masterpieces. It has situations of considerable effect, however, and the sort of parental and conjugal interest that infallibly strikes sympathetic chords in the pater familias bosom of an English audience. The choice of the piece had in it, in my opinion, an ingredient of bad taste, which, objectionable as it seemed to me, had undoubtedly entered into the calculation of the management as likely to increase the effect and success of the play; I mean the constant reference to Euphrasia's filial devotion, and her heroic and pious efforts in behalf of her old father—incidents in the piece which were seized upon and applied to my father and myself by the public, and which may have perhaps added to the feeling of the audience, as they certainly increased my dislike for the play. Here, too, I again encountered the formidable impression which Mrs. Siddons had produced in the part, of which, in spite of the turbid coldness and stilted emphasis of the style, she had made a perfect embodiment of heroic grandeur and classical grace.

Again to Harriet:

James St., Buckingham Gate
January 17, 1830

We are all tolerably well; I am quite so, and rejoice daily in that strength of consititution which, among other of my qualifications, entitles me to the appellation of the "Shetland pony."
P.S. This is my summer tour—Bath, Edinburgh, Dublin, Liverpool, Manchester, and Birmingham.

To Harriet:

James St., Buckingham Gate
March 9, 1830

I have been so busy all this day, signing benefit tickets, that I hardly feel as if I could write anything but "25th March, F.A.K."
I was sorry that the newspapers should give you the first account of my Mrs. Beverly, but my time is so taken up with "an infinite deal of nothing" that I have not had an hour to call my own till this evening, and this evening is my only unengaged one for nearly three weeks to come.
I do not think I ever spent a more miserable day than the one in which I acted Mrs. Beverly for the first time. Stage nervousness, my father and mother both tell me, increases instead of diminishing with practice; and certainly, as far as my own limited experience goes, I find it so. The first hazard, I should say, was not half so fearful as the last; and though on the first night that I ever stood upon the stage I thought I never could be more frightened in my life, I find that with each new part my fear has augmented in proportion as previous success would have rendered it more damaging to fail. However, all went well with me till the last act, when my father's acting and my own previous state of nervousness combined to make my part of the tragedy anything but feigning; I sobbed so violently that I could hardly articulate my words, and at the last fell upon the dead body of Beverly with a hysterical cry that had all the merit of pure nature, if none other, to recommend it. Fortunately the curtain fell then, and I was carried to my dressing room to finish my fit in private.

Fanny was to act Portia in *The Merchant of Venice* on the 25th of March. She continues in her letter to Miss St. Leger:

> I shall be much frightened, I know, but I delight in the part; indeed, Portia is my favoritest of all Shakespeare's women. She is so generous, affectionate, wise, so arch and full of fun, and a true lady that I think if I could but convey her to my audience as her creator has conveyed her to me, I could not fail to please them.
>
> I go out a great deal, and that I like very much whenever there is dancing, but nothing else. My own home spoils me for society; perhaps I ought not to say it, but after the sort of conversation I am used to the usual jargon of society seems poor stuff; but you know when I am dancing I am "O'er all the ills of life victorious." John [her oldest brother] has taken his degree and Adelaide [a younger sister] is quite well and almost more woman than I am; my father desires his love to you, to which I add mine; Henry [her youngest brother] has left us for Paris.

Charles and Fanny began their provincial tour in Edinburgh, by tradition considered a hard city for actors, owing to the proverbial cold Scottish audiences. In London theatre-goers still stood up and cheered when a favorite first came on stage and interrupted all famous scenes with thunderous applause. Actors dreaded Edinburgh. Fanny and her father had played a few performances, and the newspaper criticisms of Fanny were lukewarm. Although they had good houses, Fanny was chilled by the lack of applause. It was the first time she had played outside of London. She writes in her journal:

> Of the proverbial frigidity of the Edinburgh audience I had been forewarned, and of its probably disheartening effect upon myself. Mrs. Harry Siddons had often told me of the intolerable sense of depression with which it affected Mrs. Siddons, who, she said, after some of her grandest outbursts of passion, to which not a single expression of applause or sympathy had responded, exhausted and breathless with the effort she had made, would pant out in despair, under her breath, "stupid people, stupid people!"
>
> Among the delightful occurrences of last week I must record our breakfasting with Walter Scott. I was wonderfully happy. To whom, since Shakespeare, does the reading world owe so many hours of perfect, peaceful pleasure, of blessed forgetfulness of all things miserable and mean in its daily life? The party was a small but in-

teresting one: Sir Walter and his daughter Anne, his old friend Sir Adam Ferguson and Lady Ferguson, and Miss Ferrier, the authoress of "Marriage" and "Inheritance." Sir Walter was most delightful, and I even forgot all awful sense of his celebrity in his kind, cordial, and almost affectionate manner toward me. He is exceedingly like all the engravings, pictures, and busts of him with which one is familiar, and it seems strange that so varied and noble an intellect should be expressed in the features of a shrewd, kindly, but not otherwise striking countenance.

Scott's opinion of my acting, which would of course have been very valuable to me, let it have been what it would, was written to his friend and editor (eheu!), Ballantyne, who was also the editor of one of the principal Edinburgh papers in which unfavorable criticisms of my performances had appeared, and in opposition to which Sir Walter told him he was too hard upon me, and that for his part he had seen nothing so good since Mrs. Siddons. This encouraging verdict was courteously forwarded to me by Mr. Ballantyne himself who said he was sure I would like to possess it. The first time I ever saw Sir Walter Scott, my father and myself were riding slowly down Princes Street, upon which Scott was walking; he stopped my father's horse which was near the pavement and desired to be introduced to me. Then followed a string of cordial invitations which previous engagements and our work at the theatre forbade our accepting, all but the pressing one with which he wound up, that we would at least come and breakfast with him. The first words he addressed to me as I entered the room were, "You appear to be a very good horsewoman, which is a great merit in the eyes of an old Border-man."

From Edinburgh Charles and Fanny went by public mail coach to Glasgow to act, and on June 28 Fanny wrote to Miss Cox, a friend from the year that she spent in Edinburgh with her cousin, Mrs. Harry Siddons.

As soon as we arrived here [in Glasglow] the mail was surrounded, which I in my modesty attributed to the anxiety of the worthy citizens of Glasgow to hear news of the King [King George IV, then fatally ill], but herein I was deceived, for it was *my* Majesty and not *His* which excited their curiosity, and we drove from the inn to our present quarters with an escort of about two hundred shabby looking individuals, ragged urchins, pale faced mechanics etc. to my infinite amusement and at the same time confusion.

Fanny describes to Miss St. Leger her ride with the engineer, Stephenson, on the first railroad. His invitation to the Charles Kembles and Fanny shows how prominent they were, and also that Fanny as an individual must have pleased him. The ride that she describes was one of the very first, a trial run before the official opening and was even a greater compliment than being included in the large group of prominent people at the opening.

I will give you an account of my yesterday's excursion. A party of sixteen persons was ushered into a large courtyard where under cover stood several carriages of a peculiar construction, one of which was prepared for our reception. It was a long-bodied vehicle with seats placed across it, back to back. The one we were in had six of these benches and was a sort of uncovered char a banc. The wheels were placed upon two iron bands which formed the road and to which they are fitted, being so constructed as to slide along without any danger of hitching or becoming displaced, on the same principle as a thing sliding on a concave groove. The carriage was set in motion by a mere push, and having received this impetus, rolled with us down an inclined plane into a tunnel, which forms the entrance to the railroad. This tunnel is four hundred yards long (I believe) and will be lighted by gas. At the end of it we emerged from darkness, and the ground becoming level, we stopped. We were introduced to the little engine which was to drag us along the rails. She (for they make these curious little fire horses all mares) consisted of a boiler, a stove, a small platform, a bench, and behind the bench a barrel containing enough water to prevent her being thirsty for fifteen miles, the whole machine not bigger than a common fire engine. She goes upon two wheels which are her feet and are moved by bright steel legs called pistons; these are propelled by steam, and in proportion as more steam is applied to the upper extremities (the hip joints I suppose) of these pistons, the faster they move the wheels; and when it is desirable to diminish the speed, the steam, which unless suffered to escape, would burst the boiler, evaporates through a safety valve into the air. The reins, bit, and bridle of this wonderful beast is a small steel handle which applies or withdraws the steam from its legs or pistons, so that a child might manage it. The coals which are its oats were under the bench, and there was a small glass tube affixed to the boiler with water in it, which indicates by its fullness or emptiness when the creature wants water, which is immediately conveyed to it from its reservoirs. There is a chimney to the stove, but as they burn coke there is none of the dreadful black smoke which accompanies the progress of a steam vessel. This snorting little animal which I felt rather inclined to pat, was then harnessed to our carriage, and Mr. Stephenson having taken me on the bench of the engine with him, we started at about ten miles an hour. The steam horse being ill adapted for going up and down hill, the road was kept at a certain level and appeared sometimes to sink below the surface of the earth and sometimes to rise above it. Almost at starting it was cut through the solid rock which formed a wall on either side of it about sixty feet high. You can't imagine how strange it seemed to be journeying on thus, without any visible cause of progress other than the magical machine with its flying white breath and rhythmical, unvarying pace between these rocky walls which are already clothed with moss and ferns and grasses, and when I reflected that these great masses of stone had been cut asunder to allow our passage thus far below the surface of the earth, I felt as if no fairy tale was ever half so wonderful as what I saw. Bridges were thrown from side to side across the top of these cliffs, and the people looking down upon us from them seemed like pigmies standing in the sky. I must be more concise though, or I shall want room. We were to go only fifteen miles, that distance being sufficient to show the speed of the engine and to take us on to the most beautiful and wonderful object on the road. After proceeding through this rocky defile we presently found ourselves raised upon embankments ten or twelve feet high. We then came to a swamp of considerable extent on which no human foot could tread without sinking, and yet it bore the road which bore us. This had been the great stumbling block in the minds of the Committee of the House of Commons, but Mr. Stephenson has succeeded in overcoming it. A foundation of hurdles, or as he called it, basket work, was thrown over the morass, and the interstices were filled with moss and other elastic matter. Upon this the clay and soil were laid down, and the road does float, for we passed over it at the rate of five and twenty miles an hour and saw the stagnant swamp water trembling on the surface of the soil on either side of us. I hope you understand me. The embankment had gradually been rising higher, and in one place where the soil was not to form banks, Stephenson had constructed artificial ones of woodwork, over which the mounds of earth were heaped, for he said that though the woodwork would rot, before it did so the banks of earth which covered it would have been sufficiently consolidated to support the road.

We had now come fifteen miles and stopped where the road traversed a wide and deep valley. Stephenson made me alight and led me down to the bottom of this ravine, over which, in order to keep his road level, he has thrown a magnificent viaduct of nine arches, the middle one of which is seventy feet high. He explained to me the whole construction of the steam engine, and said he could soon make a famous engineer of me, which considering the wonderful things he has achieved, I dare not say is impossible. His way of explaining himself is peculiar but very striking, and I understood without difficulty all that he said to me. We then rejoined the rest of the party, and the engine having received its supply of water, the carriage was placed behind it, for it cannot turn, and was set off at its utmost speed, thirty-five miles an hour, swifter than a bird flies (for they tried the experiment with a snipe). You cannot conceive what that sensation of cutting the air was; the motion is as smooth as possible, too. I could have either read or written, and as it was I stood up, and with my bonnet off "drank the air before me." The wind which was strong, or perhaps the force of our own thrusting against it, absolutely weighed my eyelids down. When I closed my eyes this sensation was quite delightful and strange beyond description; yet strange as it was, I had a perfect sense of security and not the slightest fear. At one time to exhibit the power of the engine, having met another steam carriage which was unsupplied with water, Mr. Stephenson caused it to be fastened in front of ours, moreover a wagon laden with timber was also chained to us, and thus propelling the idle steam engine and dragging the loaded wagon which was beside it, and our own carriage full of people behind, this brave little she-dragon of ours flew on. Farther on she met three carts which, being fastened in front of her, she pushed on before her without the slightest delay or difficulty. When I add that this pretty little creature can run with equal facility either backward or forward, I believe I have given you an account of all her capacities.

Now for a word or two about the master of all these marvels with whom I am horribly in love. He is a man of from fifty to fifty-five years of age. His face is fine, though careworn, and bears an expression of deep thoughtfulness. His mode of explaining his ideas is peculiar and very original, striking, and forcible, and although his accent indicates strongly his north country birth, his language has not the slightest touch of vulgarity or coarseness. He has certainly turned my head.

Four years have sufficed to bring this great undertaking to an end.

The railroad will be opened upon the sixteenth of next month. The Duke of Wellington is coming down to be present on the occasion, and I suppose what with the thousands of spectators and the novelty of the spectacle, there will never have been a scene of more striking interest. The directors have kindly offered us three places for the opening which is a great favor for people are bidding almost anything for a place I understand, but I fear we shall be obliged to decline them, as my father is most anxious to take Henry over to Heidelberg before our season of work in London begins which will take place on the first of October.

London will be particularly gay this winter, and the king and queen it is said are fond of dramatic entertainments, so that I hope we shall get on well. You will be glad to hear that our houses here have been very fine and that tonight, Friday, which was my benefit, the theatre was crowded in every corner. We do not play here anymore, but on Monday we open at Manchester.

Fanny and her mother did after all ride on the open railroad car on the official opening date in the carriage back of the Duke of Wellington. A huge crowd gathered to see the railroad, and the Duke, but he was hissed at Manchester by the workers in the textile mills who feared the encroachment of machinery in their industry.

Her next letter to Harriet was written from Dublin in August, 1830:

My reception on Monday was quite overpowering, and I was escorted back to the hotel after the play by a bodyguard of about two hundred men, shouting and hurrahing like mad; strange to say they were people of perfectly respectable appearance. My father was not with us, and they opened the carriage door and let down the steps when we got home and helped us out, clapping and showering the most fervent expressions of goodwill upon me and Aunt Dall, whom they took for my mother. One young man exclaimed pathetically, "Oh, I hope ye're not too much fatigued, Miss Kemble, by your exertions!" They formed a line on each side of me, and several of them dropped on their knees to look under my bonnet as I ran laughing, with my head down, from the carriage to the house. I was greatly confused and a little frightened, as well as amused and gratified, by their cordial demonstration.

The humors of a Dublin audience, much as I had heard of them before going to Ireland, surprised and diverted me very much. The second night of our acting there, as we were leaving the theatre by the private entrance, we found the carriage surrounded by a crowd eagerly waiting for our coming out. As soon as my father appeared there was a shout of "Three cheers for Misther Charles!" then came Dall, and "Three cheers for Misthriss Charles!" then I, and "Three cheers for Miss Fanny!" "Bedad, she looks well by gaslight!" exclaimed one of my admirers. "Och, and bedad, she looks well by daylight too!" retorted another, though what his opportunity for forming that flattering opinion of the genuineness of my good looks had been I cannot imagine. When I was acting Lady Townley, in the scene where her husband complains of her late hours and she insolently retorts, "I won't come home till four tomorrow morning," and received the startling reply with which Lord Townley leaves her, "Then, madam, you shall never come home again," I was apt to stand for a moment aghast at this threat, and one night during this pause of breathless dismay, one of my gallery auditors, thinking I suppose that I was wanting in proper spirit not to make some rejoinder, exclaimed, "Now then, Fanny!" which very nearly upset the gravity produced by my father's impressive exit, both in me and in the audience.

The Kembles had a most successful tour of the provinces during Fanny's first summer on the stage, 1830, and returned to London knowing that the King and Queen had requested a command performance of "The Provoked Husband," in which Fanny played Lady Townley. This Hanoverian monarch did not ask for Shakespeare.

In the course of the winter there was an episode in which Charles felt his honor was at stake. Fanny gives her version of the beating her gentle, mannerly father gave the journalist, Richard Westmacott, editor of a newspaper called *The Living Age*. Westmacott had acted small parts, but there is no record of his having played in the Covent Garden Company. He became a hack writer, and then the editor of the *Age* and took particular pleasure in writing disagreeable things about the Kemble family, and particularly about Fanny during her first season. Westmacott was also a professional blackmailer, and his newspaper dealt in "exposure" of scandals in prominent families. On October 17, 1830 when Fanny was starting her second season at Covent

Garden Westmacott published a verse which he claimed had been
sung by Fanny's first cousin, the son of Horace Twiss, brother-in-
law to Charles who had been very briefly an actor but was not a
success. Besides the abusiveness he had showered on Fanny in his
paper which was hard for Charles to bear, Charles must have
been particularly stung by the last line of the verse, as it had
become obvious to the London public that it was Fanny who
had retrieved Charles Kemble's fortune.

> My feelings I cannot dissemble,
> A shame to turn off such a man!
> For I am the nephew of Kemble,
> The father of "my daughter, Fan."

A few days later Charles went without Fanny to see "The
Duenna" at Covent Garden. Westmacott was in his box.
Charles armed himself with a theatrical club and waited for
Westmacott. Charles struck him and reportedly knocked him
senseless. This might have led to a suit against Charles by
Westmacott, but the reputable London newspapers, *The Times,
The Post,* and *The Literary Gazette,* sided with Charles, and
nothing more came of this incident.

To Harriet:

Great Russell Street, October 24, 1830
I wonder whether you have heard that my father has been
thrashing the editor of the Age newspaper, who it seems took offence
at my father's not appearing on sufficiently familiar terms with him
somewhere or other when they met, in revenge of which "coldness"
(as he styles it) he has not ceased for the last six months abusing us
every week in his paper. From what I hear I was the especial mark
of his malice. Of course I need not tell you that knowing the character of this publication I should never have looked at it, and the
circumstance of my name appearing in its columns would hardly
have been an inducement to me to do so. I knew nothing, therefore,
of my own injuries but heard general expressions of indignation
against Mr. Westmacott and saw that my father was extremely
exasperated upon the subject. The other night they were all going
to the play and pressed me very much to go too, but I had something I wished to write and remained at home. On their return my
father appeared to me much excited, and I was informed that having

unluckily come across Mr. Westmacott, his wrath had got the better of his self-command, and he had bestowed a severe beating upon that individual. I could not help looking very grave at this, for though I should have been very well satisfied if it could have rained a good thrashing upon Mr. Westmacott from the sky, yet as I do not approve of returning injuries by injuries, I could not rejoice that my father had done so. I suppose he saw that I had no great satisfaction in the event, for he said, "The law affords no redress against such attacks as this paper makes on people, and I thought it time to take justice in my own hands when my daughter is insulted." He then repeated some of the language made use of with reference to me, and I could not help blushing with indignation to my finger's ends. Perhaps under the circumstances, it is not surprising that my father has done what he has, but I think I should have admired him more if he had not. Mr. Westmacott means to bring an action against him, and I am afraid he will have to pay dearly for his momentary indulgence of temper.

To Harriet:

Great Russell Street, March 8, 1831

Tuesday evening I played Belvidera. I was quite nervous at acting it again after so long a period. After the play my father and I went to Lady Dacre's and had a pleasant party enough. Lord Melbourne desired to be introduced to me, and I think if he likes, he shall be the decrepit old nobleman you were so afraid of me marrying. I was charmed with his face, voice, and manner. We dine with him next Wednesday week, and I will write to you word if the impression deepens.

On Wednesday, the 23rd she continues:

I promised to tell you something of our late dinner at Lord Melbourne's but have left myself neither space nor time. It was very pleasant, and I fell out of my love for our host (who, moreover, is absorbed by Mrs. Norton) and into another love with Lord ...., Lord T.............'s son, who is one of the most beautiful creatures of the male sex I ever saw. Unluckily he does not fulfill the necessary conditions of your theory and is neither as old nor as decrepit as you have settled the nobleman I am to marry is to be, so he won't do.

On March 25, 1831 in a letter to George Combe Fanny shows the contemplative, philosophical side of her nature in sharp contrast to her gruelling daily life on the stage and in London society. She tells him that she has been reading the essays and sermons of William Ellery Channing, the American Unitarian Abolitionist Clergyman. It is extraordinary to learn that Fanny's intellectual leanings had no boundaries; that she could address her attention almost simultaneously to learning a role, writing a play, and finding nourishment for her mind in something so completely unrelated to anything in her existence as the writings of Channing. It is this wide scope of her intellect that later brought her friendships with the great men of her era. She writes to Combe:

> I have been reading some of Channing's works—I admire him more than any writer of the present day.

In this paragraph Fanny speaks for the first time of Emily Fitzhugh who became a life-long, trusted friend:

> We dine with the Fitzhughs on Tuesday week, I like Emily much though she will talk of human souls as "vile." I gave her Channing to read.

Of great importance is what Fanny says in her journal about her visit to Newgate Prison. It is the first time she shows her humanitarian interests which became a major factor in the life she was to lead on her husband's plantation and changed her whole existence. She was always upholding the down-trodden, and years later says that little girls in Brussels should not sacrifice their lives to make lace, as lace should be made by machinery. From her early years her heart was touched by pity for others:

> I had the great honor of accompanying Mrs. Fry on one of her visits to Newgate, but from various causes received rather a painful impression instead of the different one I had anticipated. Her divine labor of love had become famous, and fine ladies of fashion pressed eagerly to accompany her or to be present at the Newgate exhortations. The unfortunate women she addressed were ranged opposite their less excusable sister sinners of the better class, and I hardly dared to look at them so entirely did I feel out of my place by the side of Mrs. Fry and so sick for their degraded attitude and position. If I had been alone with them and their noble teacher, I would assuredly have gone and sat down among them. On the day I was there

there was a poor creature sat in the midst of the congregation attired differently from all the others who was pointed out to me as being under sentence of transportation for whatever crime she committed. Altogether I felt broken-hearted for them and ashamed for us.

Fanny in August, 1831 wrote to George Combe:

I have been *living*—I mean that my existence has been a string of incessant duties, pleasures, of various occupations and perplexing interests—*quiet* I never know, and this species of life creates occasionally in me so strong a sense of mental exhaustion that I almost fancy at two and twenty I feel the weary longing for silence and solitude and rest that should belong to those who have gone further on their pilgrimage than I have yet.

It is not surprising that Fanny is exhausted. While she was acting every night and going out in society, she was also working on her play, "Francis I," which she had started when she was seventeen. Upon finishing it, she at once began work on her second, "The Star of Seville."

Saturday, January 14th, 1832

After dinner I came up to my room and set to work like a little galley slave, and by tea time I had finished my play. Oh, joy forever! MY TASK IS DONE! I came down rather tipsy and proclaimed my achievement.

My father says perhaps they will bring out "The Star of Seville" which notion sometimes brings back my old girlish desire for "fame." Every now and then I feel quite proud at the idea of acting in a play of my own at two and twenty, and then I look again at my "good works," this precious play, and it seems to be no better than "filthy rags." Is it as good a second piece of work ought to be? I cannot tell. I think so differently of it at different times that I cannot trust my own judgment.

Thursday, January 26th, 1832

Murray was most kind and goodnatured and liberal about all the arrangements of publishing "Francis I" and "The Star of Seville." He will take them both, and defer the publication of the first as long as the managers of Covent Garden wish him to do so. (As there was some talk just then of bringing out "The Star of Seville" at the Theatre, it was thought better not to forestall its effect by the publication of "Francis I.")

Fanny bought with the four hundred pounds paid for her first play the commission in the British Army for her younger brother, Henry. She says Henry, after he left college, was idling about the house doing nothing and was a very beautiful boy. He wanted to be an officer in the Navy, but his mother could not bear the thought of his going to sea, and he to please her went into the army. Commissions had to be paid for, and the Kembles had no money to buy him his commission until Fanny used the money from her play. This great act of generosity was typical of her whole life, and though she earned money for her support during most of her active years, she always acted and read for the benefit of other people whenever she felt it right to do so.

Saturday, February 4th
As it is now determined that "Francis I" is to be brought out, I received official notice that it was to be read in the Green Room today.

"Francis I" was given in Covent Garden with Fanny playing an older woman, but the play was not a success and was only given a few times. It was played in the provinces with Fanny as the younger woman and was a success in Edinburgh. But the only reasons it played in Covent Garden for those few nights were affection and courtesy to Fanny; it did nothing towards solving the theatre's financial problems, and Charles was summoned to the Court of Chancery as the theatre neared bankruptcy.

I rode with Henry, and after I got home told my father that his horse was quite well and would be fit for use on Saturday. He replied sadly that his horse must be sold, for that from the first, though he had not liked to vex me by saying so, it was an expense he could not conscientiously afford. I had expected this for certainly when from day to day a man may be obliged to declare himself insolvent, keeping a horse does seem rather absurd. He then went on to speak about the ruin that is falling upon us, and dismal enough it is to stand under the crumbling fabric we have spent body, substance, and all but soul, to prop and to see that it must inevitably fall and crush us presently. Yet from my earliest childhood I remember this has been hanging over us. I have heard it foretold, and there is no reason why it should now take any of us by surprise, or stick us with sudden dismay. Thank God our means of existence lie within ourselves. While health and strength are vouchsafed to us there is no need to despond. It is very hard and sad to become so far on in life, or rather so far into age, as my father is without any hope of support for himself and my mother but toil, and that of the severest kind, but God is merciful.

Months before Charles Kemble had discussed the advisability of going to America in the hope that the money they would certainly earn there could be used toward the Covent Garden debt. Fanny writes in her Journal for July 7th, 1831:

> At dinner as we were talking about America and I was expressing my disinclination ever to go thither, my father said: "If my cause (Our Chancery suit) goes ill before the Lords, I think the best thing I can do will be to take ship from Liverpool and sail to the United States." I choked a little at this, but presently found voice to say, "Ebben son pronta," but he replied, "no, that he should go alone." That you never should, my own dear father!—But I do hate the very thought of America.

It is true when Fanny says that they are being ruined as part owners of Covent Garden and its debts, which dated from 1732, even before John Philip Kemble had bought his share with borrowed money. But as actor-manager of the Theatre Charles was in a position of great importance in London. In the continuing rivalry with Drury Lane, stemming from the founding of both theatres, the Kembles were catering to and molding British theatrical taste, producing what they hoped would be popular successes, keeping abreast of the entertainment world, introducing opera such as Weber's "Oberon" into England, and Mendelssohn's music to accompany "Midsummer Night's Dream." Had they only been individual actors, they would not have been entangled financially, but they would not have been such an important part of British theatrical history.

> My father and I need scarcely remain without engagements, either in London or the provinces. If our salaries are smaller, so must our expenses be. The house must go, the carriage must go, the horses must go, and yet we may be sufficiently comfortable and very happy—unless, indeed, we have to go to America, and that will be

dreadful. What can, in spite of his interest, make him [Charles] so loath to leave that ponderous ruin? Even today, after summing up all the sorrow and care and toil and waste of life and fortune which that concern has cost his brother, himself, and all of us, he exclaimed, "Oh if I had but 10,000£ I could set it all right again even now!" My mother and I actually stared at this infatuation. If I had twenty, or a hundred thousand pounds, not one farthing would I give to the redeeming of that fatal millstone which cannot be raised, but will infallibly drag everything tied to it down to the level of its own destruction.

The crisis for the Kembles and the Covent Garden Theatre was worsening. The other shareholders in the Theatre told Charles that some steps must be taken to pay the Theatre debts, and there was no hope of the Kembles being able to pay off any of them.

Saturday, March 10, 1832

My father continued to walk up and down for nearly half an hour without uttering a syllable, and at last flung himself into a chair and leaned his head and arms on the table. I was horribly frightened and turned as cold as stone, and for some minutes could not muster up courage enough to speak to him. At last I got up and went to him, and on my touching his arm, he started up and exclaimed, "Good God, what will become of us all?" I tried to comfort him and spoke for a long time, but much I fear as a blindman speaks of colors. What I dread most of all is that my father's health will break down.

During this anxious time, Fanny has a very significant conversation with her aunt, Adelaide Decamp, her mother's sister. As a young girl, Aunt Dall, as she was called by the Kemble children, was penniless and was sent to live with one of Charles Kemble's married sisters in the country where she became engaged to the son of the local squire of good family. When the squire was told of the engagement, he read a proclamation from the steps of the town hall stating that his son was illegitimate, and if he married Adelaide Decamp, he would be cut off without a shilling. The young man then fled to the colonies, and Miss Decamp made her home for the rest of her life in the Charles Kemble household. Fanny says of her in her journal:

Without any home but my father's house, without any means of subsistence but the small pittance which he was able to give her in most grateful acknowledgement of her unremitting care of us, without any joys or hopes but those of others, without pleasure in the present or expectation in the future, apparently without memory of the past, she spent her whole life in the service of my parents and their children and lived and moved and had her being in a serene, unclouded, unvarying atmosphere of cheerful, self-forgetful content that was heroic in its absolute unconsciousness.

July 22, 1831

Long and edifying talk with dear Dall upon my prospects in marrying. "While you remain single," says she, "and choose to work, your fortune is an independent and ample one. As soon as you marry, there's no such thing. Your position in society," says she, "is both a pleasanter and more distinguished one than your birth or real station entitles you to, but that also is the result of your professional exertions and might, and probably would, alter for the worse if you left the stage, for after all, it is mere frivolous fashionable popularity." I ought to have got up and made her a courtesy for that. So that it seems I have fortune and fame (such as it is)—positive, real advantages which I cannot give with myself, and which I cease to own when I give myself away, which certainly makes my marrying anyone or anyone marrying me rather a solemn consideration. For I lose everything, and my marrying gains nothing in a worldly point of view—says she—and it's incontrovertible and not so pleasant. So I took up Dante and read about devils boiled in pitch which refreshed my imagination and cheered my spirits very much.

During Fanny's first two years on the stage she played the young heroines in Shakespeare's plays and the young heroines in the popular melodramas that she disliked so much. In the winter of 1831–32, however, Charles had to give in to the Board of Directors of Covent Garden, composed of the other shareholders, who could dictate to him what roles Fanny would play, and she was asked to play Queen Katherine in *Henry VIII* and Lady Macbeth. They were the two most famous roles of Mrs. Siddons, and Fanny was too young and inexperienced for either of them. But in hopes of having full houses, and as she had been seen many times in her young roles, she was obliged to act them. She says in a letter to Harriet St. Leger:

October 3, 1831

I need not tell you what my feeling about acting Queen Katherine is, but I cannot help thinking the management short sighted. I think their real interest as far as I am concerned, which they overlook for some immediate tangible advantage, is not to destroy my popularity by putting me into parts which I must play ill, and not to take from my future career characters which require physical as well as mental maturity, and which would be my natural resources when I no longer become Juliet and her youthful sisters of the drama.

I am sorry to say my father is pronounced worse today. He has a bad sideache, and they are applying mustard poultices to overcome it. There is a real and terrible anxiety, dear Harriet. The Theatre, too, is going on very ill, and he is unable to give it any assistance, and for the same reason I can do nothing for it, for all my plays require him except Isabella and Fazio, and these are worn threadbare. It is all very gloomy, but, however, time doth not stand still and will some day come to the end of the journey with us.

Negotiations are pending between the partners which it is hoped may eventually terminate in some arrangement with the creditors about the property.

I think it would be a wise thing if I were to go to America and work till I have made 10,000£, then return to England and go the round of the provinces and act for a few nights leave-taking in London. Providence would then perhaps find less difficulty in adjusting my plans for the future. That is what I think would be well for me to do, supposing all things remain as they are, and God preserves my health and strength. It will not do to verify all Poitier's lugubrious congratulation to his children in the vaudeville on their marriage:

> Ji! Ji! mariez-vous
> Mettez-vous dans la misere!
> Ji! Ji! mariez-vous
> Mettez-vous la corde au cou.

Fanny has despondently quoted the French doggerel about marriage which is exactly what happened to her three years later.

Friday, January 27th, 1832

A long discussion after breakfast about the necessity of one's husband being clever. Ma foi, je n'en vois pas la nécessité. People don't want to be entertaining each other all day long. Very clever men don't grow on every bush, and middling clever men don't amount to anything. I think I should like to have married Sir Humphry Davy. A well assorted marriage, as the French say, seems to me like a well arranged duet for four hands. The treble, the woman, has all the brilliant and melodious part, but the whole government of the piece, the harmony, is with the bass which really leads and sustains the whole composition and keeps it steady, and without which the treble for the most part runs to tune merely and wants depth, dignity, and real musical importance.

In Fanny's marriage there was no question of this harmony. Her husband was a loud, quenching bass with a sustaining pedal blurring and drowning out the treble.

In June, 1832, the Kembles finally decided to go to America for two years, hoping to bring back enough money to pay off some debts and continue in Covent Garden which was leased to Pierre Laporte who was going to give nothing but operas. In June and July the Kembles toured in the provinces before sailing from Liverpool for America. Aunt Dall was travelling with them, and Mrs. Kemble said good-bye to them in Liverpool before they sailed. Harriet St. Leger was also with them for a short time.

Aunt Dall had the steadiness and sound health which were lacking in Fanny's mother, so it was natural that she should go to America to look after Fanny as her mother could not have made such a journey. Also, the Kembles' oldest son, John Mitchell, was studying in Germany and occasionally came home, Henry's regiment had not yet been sent out of England, and Adelaide was still a schoolgirl.

July 4th, 1832, Edinburgh

How sad it will be in that strange land beyond the sea among those strange people, to whom we are nothing but strangers! But this is a foolish weakness. It must be, and what a world of strength lies in those two little words! . . . At the theatre the house was very good, and I played well.

July 7, 1832

Miserable day of parting, of tearing away and wrenching asunder! At eleven we were obliged to go to rehearsal, and when we returned found my mother busy with her packing. When she was gone I sat down beside my father with a book in my hand, not reading, but listening to his stifled sobbing, and every now and then, in spite of my determination not to do it, looking up to see how far the ship had moved. (Our windows looked over the Forth.)

Mrs. Kemble was taking a steamer back to London on the River Forth.

CHAPTER IV

The Kembles go to America:
Conquest of the New World

After an unhappy parting with her mother and Harriet St. Leger, Fanny and her father took a tremendous, bold step. On Wednesday, August 1, 1832, they sailed to America from Liverpool on the three-masted packet boat, the "Pacific," one of the largest, fastest packet boats of her day. Her topsails were square rigged, and although she often took forty days from Liverpool to New York, she sometimes made the east-bound crossing in seventeen days. There were individual cabins for the first-class passengers, expensively furnished, and the food was equal to that of a good hotel. But Fanny says there were only three other women besides herself in the first class. Five to eight hundred steerage passengers could be crammed on board, bringing their own food. It took the Kembles thirty-one days to reach New York.

Fanny and her father were leaving their home and country to try their fortune in the United States. They were not the first English actors to go to America. Edmund Kean had had a successful engagement in New York, and Fanny's aunt, Elizabeth Kemble, acting under the name of Mrs. Whitelock, had preceded them and returned safely to London to retire. She is described as being much like Mrs. Siddons in appearance, but coarser and less talented. She had acted in Philadelphia at the Walnut St. Theatre in 1814 before President Washington and a stage box full of Indians. Charles and Fanny were far better known than she, and it was their hope not merely to support themselves, but with their earnings to resume the proprietorship of Covent Garden.

The journey was a fateful one for Fanny as she met Pierce Butler in Philadelphia and married him and left the stage. But during the crossing she met William Hodgkinson, the son of a tenant of the Duke of Norfolk. He made a success of his life in America and was a friend to Fanny all her life. She also met a Mr. Staley of Philadelphia and saw much of him during all her Philadelphia visits, and he apparently was one of her suitors.

The Kembles waited several days in Liverpool for the "Pacific," as adverse winds prevented her from entering the harbor. As soon as Fanny and Aunt Dall had settled themselves in their cabin, Fanny began the Journal in which she described all she saw and did during her American tour. The Journal not only caused serious trouble with her husband when she published it a year after her marriage, but also hurt the feelings of many of the people who had befriended her. Fanny felt competent and assured in making tart and often vitriolic statements about people, manners, and customs as she first saw them in America, and as a whole, comparing them unfavorably to England.

She resented going to America and was convinced that she would not like it. Though she doesn't say so, she evidently was keeping her American Journal with a view to publishing it and so carefully writing down things she thought would be interesting later. She had the bad example of Mrs. Trollope and Captain Hamilton who had lectured in America, pointing out to their audiences their shortcomings when compared with accepted English social customs, and who had caused such rancor and universal ill feeling in the United States that English travellers who were known to be writing about America were in great disfavor. Both Mrs. Trollope and Captain Hamilton had published their American experiences, but neither one of them had the flair for expression or the gift of observation that Fanny had. The press was mostly against her in speaking of her Journal, as touchiness about any criticism of American customs was the vogue of the day.

None of the Journal is written in retrospect the way much of her "Records of a Girlhood" is, which was so highly praised by Henry James. She shows an astonishing maturity, an almost unnatural interest in all phases of American life, including politics and slavery, and writes philosophical paragraphs showing her to be thoughtful and introspective, but displaying an intellect with wide horizons. It is startling to read many of her opinions which are often a hundred years ahead of the aspirations and convictions of women of her day. Her total independence of mind is shown repeatedly as well as her high standard of artistic judgment. She is not in the least a twenty-two-year-old successful actress, thinking of nothing but herself and interested in nothing but her next performance. Her mind embraces every aspect of the new world in which she is travelling.

Although she published her Journal in 1835, leaving all names blank, now for the first time those names are known. They were filled in by Fanny years later in the copy she gave to Mr. Charles B. Sedgwick of Syracuse, New York, not to be confused with Charles Sedgwick of Boston, whose family were the staunchest friends in America of Fanny Kemble. So now the Journal is brought to life by names of the well known people and the names of ordinary people who became her admirers and friends and prove her to have been an instant favorite everywhere. Pierce Butler's courtship can be traced in it.

Wednesday, August 1, 1832

Another break in my Journal, and here I am on board the "Pacific" bound for America, having left home and all the world behind—Well!

After dinner the ladies adjourned to their own cabin, and the gentlemen began to debate about regulating the meal hours. They adopted the debating society tone, called my poor father to the chair, and presently I heard, oh horror (what I had not thought to hear again for six weeks) the clapping of hands. They sent him in to consult us about the dinner hour, and we having decided four o'clock, the debate continued with considerable merriment. Oh my home, my land, England, glorious England! from which this bragging big baby was born, how my heart yearns towards your earth!

On my back all day. Mercy, how it ached too! The ship reeled about like a drunken thing. I lay down and began reading Byron's life.

Fanny spent the voyage of thirty days studying the Bible, studying German, reading Dante in Italian, writing in her Journal, and when the weather was possible, walking on the decks.

I sat downstairs in my cabin all day, the very spirit of doggerel possessed me, and I poured forth rhymes as rapidly as possible, and they were as bad as possible—wrote Journal. In looking over my papers fell in with the "Star of Seville"—some of it is very good. I'll write an English tragedy next. Dined at table—our heroes have drunk wine and are amicable. After dinner went on deck, and took a short walk. Saw the sun set.

Fanny describes her voyage in a letter to George Combe written on September 29 after landing in New York.

My dear Sir, Our fellow passengers were as far as vocation goes all much of a kind—travelling agents for mercantile houses— dealers in cottons and hardware, but in spite of this sameness of pursuit, I found enough to amuse my observing faculties in the pe-culiarities of each individual as called into action by the various befallings of a long sea voyage. We had English Scotch Irish and Americans on board, and the national characteristics were strik-ingly manifested by their respective samples. One thing, however, they all agreed in which was being most kind and attentive to me, so that indeed, much of the wretchedness and discomfort attending upon a month's residence within such narrow limits was done away with. My father who is not a good sailor bore the rough weather but badly. Poor Aunt Dall was on her back the whole time. As for your humble servant, she was working reading writing walking singing dancing eating drinking sleeping and being sick between each won-derful activity and zeal. I believe the whole crew thought I was possessed with a dancing devil and fairly wished me at the bottom of the sea, for I quadrilled and reeled their souls out of their bodies to say nothing of their soles off their shoes.

Fanny recounts the last day of her voyage in the Journal, September 5, 1832:

Breakfasted at table for the first time since I've been on board the ship; I did hope, the last. After breakfast put my things to rights, tidied our cabin for prayers and began looking out the lessons. While doing so the joyful sound "Land, land!" was heard aloft. I rushed on deck and between the blue waveless sea and the bright un-clouded sky lay the wished-for line of the darker element. 'Twas Long Island. Hail, strange land! My heart greets you coldly and sadly! Oh how I thought of Columbus, as with eyes strained and on tiptoes our water-weary passengers stood after a summer's sail of thirty days welcoming their mother earth. The day was heavenly though intensely hot; the sky utterly cloudless, and by that same token, I do not love a cloudless sky. They tell me that it is their American weather almost until Christmas. That's nice for those who like frying.

I had desired the mate to call me by sunrise, and accordingly in the midst of a very sound and satisfactory sleep, Mr. Curtis shook me roughly by the arm, informing me that the sun was just about to rise. Towards midday we had to thank heaven for an incident. A brig had been standing aft against the horizon for some hours past, and we presently descried a boat rowing towards us from her. The distance was some five miles, the sun broiling. We telescoped and stood on tiptoe, they rowed stoutly, and in due time boarded us. She was an English brig from Bristol, had been out eleven weeks distressed by contrary winds and was in want of provisions. Our dear captain supplied them with everything they wanted, and our poor steerage passengers sent their mite to the distressed crew in the shape of a sack of potatoes.

After this the whole day was one of continual excitement, near-ing the various points of land, greeting vessels passing us, and watching those bound on the same course. At about four o'clock a schooner came alongside with a news collector. He was half de-voured with queries. News of the cholera, reports of the tariff and bank questions were loudly demanded. Poor people, how anxiously they looked for replies to the first. As the evening darkened, the horizon became studded with sails. At about eight o'clock we dis-covered the Highlands of Neversink, the entrance to New York Harbour, and presently the twin lights of Sandy Hook glimmered against the sky. We were all in high spirits, a fresh breeze had sprung up, we were making rapidly to land, the lovely ship with all sails set curtseying along the smooth water. The captain alone seemed anxious and was eagerly looking out for the pilot. Cheering resounded on all sides, rockets were fired from the ship's stern, we were all dancing, when suddenly a cry was echoed round of "A pilot" and close under the ship's side a light graceful little schooner

shot like an arrow. She lay to but proved only a news boat. While
however all were gathered round the collector, the pilot boat came
alongside and the pilot on board. The captain gave up the cares
and glories of command, and we danced an interminable country
dance. Came up and dawdled on deck, saw them cast anchor,
away went the chain, down dropped the heavy stay, the fair ship
swung round, and there lay New York before us with its clustered
lights shining like a distant constellation against the dark outline
of land. Remained on deck till very late, was going to bed when the
gentlemen entreated us to join their party once more. We did so,
sang all the old songs, laughed at all the old jokes, drank our own
and each other's health, wealth, and prosperity, and came to bed
at two o'clock. Our cradle rocks no longer, we have reached our
destination, thank God! I did so with all my soul.

Tuesday, September 4
New York, America

It is true by my faith, there it is written, here I sit, I am myself
and no other, this is New York and nowhere else—Oh, "singular
strange!" Our passengers were all stirring and about at peep of day,
and I got up myself at half past six. We breakfasted and packed
ourselves into our shawls and bonnets, and at half past nine the
steamboat came alongside to take us to shore. It was different from
any English steam boat I ever saw, having three decks and being
consequently a vessel of very considerable size. We got on board
her all in the misery and rain, and as we drifted in, our passengers
collected to the side of the boat and gave "the dear old lady" three
cheers. Mr. Hodgkinson and Mr. Staley went to secure apartments
for us at the American Hotel, and after bidding goodby to the sea,
we packed ourselves into a hackney coach and progressed. The
houses are almost all painted glaring white or red. The other favorite colors appear to be pale straw color and gray. They have all
green venetian shutters which give an idea of coolness, and almost
every house has a tree or trees in its vicinity which looks pretty
and garden-like. We reached our inn, the gentlemen were waiting
for us and led us to our drawing room. I had been choking for the
last three hours and could endure no more but sobbed like a wretch
aloud. There was a piano in the room to which I flew with the ap-
petite of one who has lived on the music of the speaking trumpet
for a month. That, and some iced lemonade and cake presently restored my spirits. I went on playing and singing till I was exhausted
and then sat down and wrote Journal.

Our drawing room being large and pleasant, the table was laid in it. Our dinner was a favorable specimen of eating as practiced in this new world; everything good, only in too great a profusion, the wine drinkable, and the fruit beautiful to look at, in point of flavor it was infinitely inferior to English hothouse fruit or even fine espalier fruit raised in a good aspect. Everything was wrapped in ice, which is a most luxurious necessity in this hot climate, but the things were put on the table in a slovenly, outlandish fashion—fish, soup, and meat at once, and pudding, tarts, and cheese at another once; no finger glasses, and a patched table cloth. In short, a want of that style and neatness which is found in every hotel in England. The waiters too reminded us of the half savage highland lads that used to torment us under that denomination in Glasgow—only that they were wild Irish instead of wild Scotch. The streets were brilliantly lighted, the shops through the trees, and people parading between them reminded me very much of the Boulevards. We left the gentlemen and went downstairs, where I played and sang for three hours. On opening the door I found a junta of men sitting on the hall floor round it and smoking. Came up for coffee, most of the gentlemen were rather elated. We sang and danced and talked and seemed exceedingly loath to say goodbye.

Wednesday, September 5th, 1832

I have been in a sulky fit half the day, because people will keep walking in and out of our room without leave or license, which is coming a great deal too soon to Hope's idea of Heaven. I am delighted to see my friends, but I like to tell them so and not that they should take it for granted. When I made my appearance in my dressing gown (my clothes not being come, and the day too hot for a silk pelisse) great was my amazement to find our whole ship's company assembled at the table. After breakfast they dispersed, and I sat writing Journal and playing and singing.

Fanny had written to George Combe on September 29:

The aristocracy here is one of wealth which I hold to be nearly as contemptible as that nobility of mere birth, my reverence for which amused you so much—the man who has made his fortune by trade looks down with infinite disdain upon the man who is building his upon the same foundation. Wholesale turns up his nose at Retail. I have heard such expressions as "the lower orders finding their level—exclusive—select"—all the jargon in fact of our high English circle. Their omnibuses are carriages of rank, all being "My Lady this, that, or 'tother." They are as tenacious of a Judgeship or a Militia military title as ever German Baron was of his countless quarterings. In short the very essence of aristocratic feeling prevails here, and 'tis my own belief that this country will soon lose the form as it certainly has the spirit of a Republic.

Fanny writes in her Journal of September 6, "My father is ten years younger since he came here already." She continues on September 9:

I do nothing but look out of window all the blessed day long. I did not think in my old age to acquire so Jezebel a trick, but the park (as they entitle the green opposite our windows) is so very pretty and the streets so gay, with their throngs of smartly dressed women, and so amusing with their abundant proportion of black and white caricatures, that I find my window the most entertaining station in the world. My father dined out. Dall and I dined tete-a-tete. Poor Dall has not been well today. She is dreadfully bitten by the mosquitoes which, I thank their discrimination, have a thorough contempt for me and have not come near me. Then only things that bother me are little black ants which I find in my wash-hand basin and running about in all directions.

The fish of these waters may be excellent in the water, but owing to the want of care and niceness with which they are kept after being caught, they are very seldom worth eating when brought to table. They have no turbot or soles, a great national misfortune. Their best fish are rock fish, bass, shad, and sheep's head. Cod and salmon I have eaten, but from the above cause they were never comparable to the same fish at the English table. The lobsters, crabs, and oysters are all gigantic, frightful to behold, and not particularly well flavored. Their size makes them tough and coarse.

The climate of this country is the scape-goat upon which all the ill looks and ill health of the ladies is laid. But while they are brought up as effeminately as they are, take as little exercise, live in rooms like ovens during the winter, and marry as early as they do, it will appear evident that many causes combine with an extremely variable climate to sallow their complexions and destroy their constitutions.

A change seems to have taken place in Fanny's disposition after landing in America. In London she always appeared good-mannered and amenable, but in the United States she was perpetually commenting brusquely on every occurrence in daily life that differed from English customs and manners. Not only was she furious with having to act the play "Fazio" with an old actor, Mr. Keppel, whom she knew to be incompetent, but she took umbrage at the deportment of the shopkeepers who obviously were doing their best to please her. She later explains a conversation she had with the proprietor of a shoe store who told her that owing to the shortage of labor it was impossible to employ clerks who were either civil to customers or interested in their work as there were more places open to them than could possibly be filled. She soon learned that neither the dressmaker, milliner, nor shoemaker would take any pains to fit her or try to be prompt. She did not pause to reflect that London tradespeople had for generations been striving to please their patrons, or their patrons would do their shopping elsewhere. When this Journal of Fanny's was first published passages such as the following about her trying to buy some cloth in a store led to virulent attacks by the American press, and it was only praised by a few magazines. The Journal had a splendid sale, and as contemporary Americana it is now of the greatest value and used often as a reference book. Fanny brought a fresh mind and an Englishwoman's point of view to her Journal.

Monday, September 17th

Rose at eight. At twelve went to rehearsal (Park Theatre). The weather is intolerable. I am in a state of perpetual fusion. The theatre is the coolest place I have yet been in; I mean at rehearsal when the front is empty and the doors open and the stage so dark that we are obliged to rehearse by candlelight. That washout man who failed in London when he acted Romeo with me is to be my Fazio. Let us hope he will know some of his words tomorrow night, for he is at present most innocent of any such knowledge. After rehearsal walked into a shop to buy some gauze. The shopman called me by my name, entered into conversation with us, and one of them, after showing me a variety of things which I did not want, said that they were most anxious to show me every attention and render my stay in this country agreeable. A Christian, I suppose, would have met those benevolent advances with an infinitude of thankfulness and an outpouring of grateful pleasure, but for my own part, though I had the grace to smile and say thank you, I longed to add, "but be so good as to measure your ribands and hold your tongue." I have no idea of holding parley with clerks behind a counter, still less of their doing so with me. So much for my first impression of the courtesy of this land of liberty. I should have been much better pleased if they had called me "Ma'am" which they did not.

The Kembles were not actors arriving in New York with no hope of meeting prominent members of New York society. Charles had been given a letter of introduction from Mr. Vaughan, the British Minister to the United States, to Mr. Philip Hone, a former Mayor of New York City, and a prominent business man and philanthropist. Mr. Hone wrote in his diary:

September 15, 1832

Miss Kemble, like all young persons who have become celebrated, has many and strong admirers. But many dislike her on first acquaintance. Her manners are somewhat singular. Allowance should be made for the peculiarity of her situation, just arrived among strangers, with a consciousness that she is viewed as one of the lions of the day, and as such the object more of curiosity than of affection. Her behavior would be attributed naturally to timidity, were it not that at times she appears to be perfectly self-possessed. She talks well, but will only talk when, and to whom, she chooses. She sat at my side at dinner, and I certainly had no reason to complain of her, for I lost my dinner in listening to her and in endeavoring to make myself agreeable. She has certainly an air of indifference and nonchalance not at all calculated to make her a favorite with the beaux. Indeed, Henry Hone and I think that she prefers married men. Her fault appears to be an ungracious manner of receiving the advances of those who desire to pay her attention. This may proceed from the novelty of her situation and may soon be removed. But now is her time to make friends if she wants them. She sang and played for us in the evening. Her voice is not sweet, but has great force and pathos. I am confirmed in my opinion that she has astonishing requisites for the stage. Her features separately are not good, but combined they make a face of great and powerful expression. I am of the opinion that she does not like her profession. It is not her favorite theme of conversation; necessity, rather than choice, has led her to adopt it.

Journal, Tuesday, September 18th

Rose at eight. At eleven went to rehearsal. Mr. Keppel is just as nervous and as imperfect as ever. What on earth will he, or shall I, do tonight! Came home, got things out for the theatre and sat like any stroller stitching for dear life at my dress. Mr. H. [Fanny did not fill in this name] and his nephew called. The latter asked me if I was at all apprehensive. No, by my troth, I am not, and that not because I feel sure of success, for I think it very probable the Yankees may like to show their critical judgment and independence by damning me, but because, thank God, I do not care whether they do or not. The whole thing is too loathsome to me for either failure or success to affect me in the least, and therefore I feel neither nervous nor anxious about it.

They acted the farce of "Popping the Question" first in order, I suppose to get the people in their places before the play began. Poor Mr. Keppel was gasping for breath. He moved my compassion infinitely. I consoled and comforted him all I could, gave him some of my lemonade to swallow for he was choking with fright, sat myself down with my back to the audience, and up went the curtain. Owing to the position in which I was sitting, and my plain dress, most unheroine-like in its make and color, the people did not know me and would not have known me for some time if that stupid man had done as I kept bidding him, gone on. But instead of doing so, he stood stock still, looked at me and then at the audience, whereupon the latter caught an inkling of the truth and gave me such a reception as I get in Covent Garden Theatre every time I act a new part. The house was very full. All the Hones were there and Colonel Sibell. Mr. Keppel was frightened to death, and in the very second speech was quite out. It was in vain that I prompted him; he was too nervous to take the word and made a complete mess of it. This happened more than once in the first scene, and at the end of the first act as I left the stage I said to Dall, "It's all up with me, I can't do anything now," for having to prompt my Fazio, frightened by his fright, annoyed by his forgetting his crossings and positions, utterly unable to work myself into anything like excitement, I thought the whole thing must necessarily go to pieces. However, once rid of my encumbrance, which I am at the end of the second act, I began to move a little more freely, gathered up my strength, and set to work comfortably by myself. Whereupon the people applauded, I warmed (warmed, quoth? the air was steam) and got through very satisfactorily, at least so it seems. My dresses were very beautiful, but oh, the mosquitoes had made dreadful havoc with my arms which were covered with hills as large and red as Vesuvius in an eruption.

. . . To bed, to sleep—to sleep—perchance to be bitten!

Aye, there's the scratch . . . And in that sleep of ours what bugs may come must give us pause.

Came to bed at half past twelve, weary and half melted away. The ants swarm on the floors, on the tables, in the beds, about one's clothes. The plagues of Egypt were a joke to them. Horrible! It makes one's life absolutely burdensome to have creatures creeping about one and all over one night and day in this fashion, to say nothing of those cantankerous stinging things, the mosquitoes.

Philip Hone entered in his diary after returning from "Fazio" on Tuesday, September 18:

Miss Fanny Kemble made her first appearance this evening in the character of Bianca, in Millman's tragedy, "Fazio." It is a fine part, well calculated for a display of the strongest passions of the female heart,—love, hate, and jealousy. I have never witnessed an audience so moved, astonished, and delighted. Her display of the strong feelings which belong to the part was great beyond description, and the expression of her wonderful face would have been a rich treat if her tongue had uttered no sound. The fifth act was such an exhibition of female powers as we have never before witnessed, and the curtain fell amidst the deafening shouts and plaudits of an astonished audience. On the whole I am quite satisfied that we have never seen her equal on the American stage.

The reviewer of the *New York Mirror* wrote on Wednesday, September 19 of Fanny's first appearance in America as follows:

The curtain rose and discovered two characters, the one a man, the other a young female, slight but gracefully formed, seated at a table, drawing, with her back partly towards the audience, so as to preclude any immediate recognition. Her companion had proceeded some time in his opening speech before she turned and discovered a sweet new face, glowing with soul and feeling, and the large, dark eyes of Miss Fanny Kemble, half lifted to the audience who returned their glances with long, hearty, and reiterated thunders of applause. The deafening peals at length died away into a hushed and pervading silence, and the low tones of a silvery voice rose in the silence, tremulously sweet, and at once seducing every heart. We were surprised, delighted. She was different from our anticipations and much beyond them. As the play proceeded, the audience were frequently thrown off their guard by some sudden and peculiarly felicitous display. Of these, some were received with an universal low murmur of approbation, others with loud applause. Several of the most exquisite but quiet features of touching tenderness such as resembled the flashes of the elder Kean were apparently overlooked. The curtain fell to loud and prolonged plaudits, and we may safely assert that a more brilliant effect has rarely if ever been produced on the American stage.

Fanny for the first time is made aware of the social position of colored people in the United States, a subject on which she could not possibly have had any thought before she came to America:

> Journal, Thursday, 20th.
> By the bye, Essex, the colored steward for the sailship "Pacific," called this morning to fetch away the captain's claret jug. He asked my father for an order [a free ticket to the theatre], adding with some hesitation, "It must be for the gallery if you please, sir, for people of color are not allowed to go to the pit or any other part of the house." I believe I turned black myself I was so indignant. Here's aristocracy with a vengeance! Went to the theatre. The house was very full and dreadfully hot. My father acted Romeo beautifully. I looked very nice, and the people applauded my gown abundantly.

Charles Kemble was not well received in New York. They found his acting too slow, lacking virility, and did not like the long pauses that he made between sentences and often between words. He played Hamlet without Fanny for his opening in New York, and the following night she acted in "Fazio" with the hopeless Mr. Keppel. The Kembles then dismissed Keppel who had been engaged to play Romeo to Fanny's Juliet because Fanny told her father that she would not act with Keppel, and so Charles Kemble played Romeo on her first appearance as Juliet in New York. It was at once apparent that it was Fanny and not her father who was the attraction, and this remained true for the whole American

tour. Charles Kemble could not fill a house without her, and
she sometimes acted every night in the week, which no actress
in those days did in London.

Came to bed in tremendous dudgeon. The few critiques that I have
seen upon our acting have been upon the whole laudatory. One was
sent to me from a paper called "The Mirror" which pleased me very
much. It was written with great taste and feeling and was evidently
not the produce of a common press hack. There appeared to me in
all the others the true provincial dread of praising too much, a sort
of jealousy of critical freedom, which together with the established
nil admirari of the press seems to keep them in a constant dread
of being thought enthusiastic. They need not be afraid. Enthusiasm
may belong to such analysis as Schlegel's or Channing's, but has
nothing in common with the paragraphs of a newspaper, the inditers
of which, in my poor opinion seldom go beyond the very threshhold
of criticism, i.e. the discovery of faults.

I am infinitely amused at the extreme curiosity which appears to
me to be the besetting sin of the people here. A gentleman whom
you know very slightly will sit down by your table during a morning
visit, turn over every article upon it, look at the cards of the various
people who have called upon you, ask half a dozen questions about
each of them, as many about your own private concerns, and all this
as though it were a matter of course that you should answer him,
which I feel greatly inclined occasionally not to do.

Went into a shop to order a pair of shoes. The shopkeepers in this
place with whom I have hitherto to deal are either condescendingly
familiar or insolently indifferent in their manner. Your washer-
woman sits down before you while you are standing speaking to her,
and a shop boy bringing things for your inspection, not only sits
down, but keeps his hat on in your drawing room. All this is bad.
It has its origin in a vulgar misapprehension which confounds ill
breeding with independence and leads people to fancy that they
elevate themselves above their condition by discharging its duties
and obligations discourteously.

Her American Journal is full of surprises. She continually
displays her deep interest in matters of national importance
to Americans only, and in no way pertaining to her daily life
of acting. The worry and fatigue of performing before audiences in a new country, on whose favors and judgments her
future and that of her family depended, did not absorb or

dull her intellect. She had already shown herself a keen observer of all that was new to her. But the compassion she instantly felt for the slaves as fellow human beings mark her now as a woman with immense comprehension of suffering. To hear of cruelty was enough; she was stirred. Indifference was not part of her nature, and her conscience, so quickly aroused, bade her heart speak out in protest. Though this is the first mention of slavery, it was followed in a few months by others and observations on the American political scene.

Ogden Hoffman called and sat with us during dinner, telling us stories of the flogging of slaves as he himself had witnessed it in the South that forced the color into my face, the tears into my eyes, and strained every muscle in my body with positive rage and indignation. He made me perfectly sick with it.

I was horrified at Dr. Charles Mifflin's account of the state of the negroes in the South. To teach a slave to read or write is to incur a penalty of fine or imprisonment. They form the larger proportion of the population by far, and so great is the dread of insurrection on the part of the white inhabitants that they are kept in the most brutish ignorance and too often treated with the most brutal barbarity in order to insure their subjection. Oh! what a breaking asunder of old manacles there will be some of these fine days, what a fearful rising of the black flood, what a sweeping away as by a torrent of oppressions and tyrannies, what a fierce and horrible retaliation and revenge for wrong so long endured—so wickedly inflicted.

It seems Carolina is in a state of convulsions. Reports have arrived that the Nullifiers and Unionists have had a fight in Charleston and that lives have been lost. "Bide a wee" as the Scotchman says. We talk a good deal on the other side of the water of matters that are far enough off, but as for America, the problem is not yet solved, and this very crisis is threatening to slacken the bonds of brotherhood between the states and shake the Union to its centre. The interests of the northern states are totally different from, and in some respects opposite to those of the southern ones.

Mr. Keppel who had been dismissed by Charles Kemble was given one more try, which proved to be his last. He begged to be reinstated in the company, and letters had been written to the newspapers protesting his dismissal.

Monday, 24th

Rose at eight, went and took a bath. After breakfast went to rehearsal. "Venice Preserved" with Mr. Keppel who did not appear to
me to know the words even, and seemed perfectly bewildered at
being asked to do the common business of the piece. "Mercy on me!
what will he do tonight?" thought I. I determined not to go upon the
stage again with that gentleman for a hero. At the end of the play
the clever New Yorkians actually called for Mr. Keppel! and this
most worthless clapping of hands, most worthlessly bestowed upon
such a worthless object, is what by the nature of my craft I am bound
to care for. I spit at it from the bottom of my soul! We came home
tired and thoroughly disgusted and found no supper. The cooks,
who do not live in the house but come and do their work, and depart home whenever it suits their convenience, had not thought it
proper to stay to prepare any supper for us, so we had to wait for
the readiest things that could be procured out of doors for us—this
was pleasant—very! At last appeared a cold, boiled fowl, and some
monstrous oysters that looked for all the world like an antediluvian
race of oysters, "for in those days were giants." Six mouthfuls each.
They were well flavored but their size displeased my eye, and I
swallowed but one, and came to bed.

Fanny continues to describe the discomforts of living in
hotels in America at that time. In the engravings of the
burlesque pamphlet published in 1835, very clever derisive car-
toons illustrating various passages in the Journal, there is one of
Fanny and her father sitting down to supper with a menial carrying over his shoulder an oyster that is so big that he is staggering
under it. It has not been established who drew the pictures of this
pamphlet. The captions under them are quoted from the Journal,
and it proves the popularity of the Journal and that the fame of
Fanny Kemble was so great that anonymous pamphlets such as
this one sold readily.

The universal hour of dining in New York when we first arrived was
three o'clock, after which hour the cooks took their departure, and
nothing was to be obtained fit to eat, either for love or money. This
intolerable nuisance is gradually passing away, but even now, though
we can get our dinner served at six o'clock, it is always dressed at
three, and its excellence may be imagined from that. To say the
truth, I think the system upon which all houses of public entertain-

ment are conducted in this country, is a sample of the patience and long-suffering with which dirt, discomfort, and exorbitant charges may be borne by a whole community without resistance or even remonstrance.

Charles Kemble during the first week of his engagement in New York got an anonymous letter saying that friends of two current American actresses would fill the house at the next performance and hiss him off the stage, as the writer disapproved of English actors coming to America and taking away the patronage which should rightly belong to American stars.

Monday, October 1

It is fortunate for the managers of the Park Theatre and very unfortunate for the citizens of New York that the audiences who frequent that place of entertainment are chiefly composed of the strangers who are constantly passing in vast numbers through this city. It is not worth the while of the management to pay a good company when an indifferent one answers their purpose quite as well. The system upon which theatrical speculations are conducted in this country is having one or two "stars" for the principal characters, and nine or ten sticks for all the rest. The consequence is that a play is never decently acted, and at such times as stars are scarce, the houses are very deservedly empty. The terrestrial audiences suffer much by this mode of getting up plays, but the celestial performers, the stars propped upon sticks, infinitely more.

Having been born and brought up with Shakespeare and the Restoration plays, Fanny could not comprehend why a supposedly educated public was offended by Farquhar's play, "The Inconstant." Fanny was mistaken in taking for granted that the theatre goers in the eastern seaboard cities were as literate as the Covent Garden audiences. All her life in America she was constantly struck by the prissy euphemisms in American conversation and the veering away from ordinary words in general use in London society. She says later in America, "I cannot say I put my leg over the pommel of my saddle as American women do not have legs."

Saturday, October 6th

Rose late. When I came in to breakfast, found Col. Sibell sitting in the parlor. He remained a long time, and we had sundry discussions on topics manifold. It seems that the blessed people here were shocked at my having to hear the coarseness of Farquhar's "Inconstant"—humbug!

Were the morality that I constantly hear uttered a little more consistent not only with right reason, but with itself, I think it might be more deserving of attention and respect. But the mock delicacy which exists to so great a degree with regard to theatrical exhibitions, (in the United States) can command neither the one nor the other.

Monday, 8th

Rose (or horror!) at a quarter of five. Long before I was dressed the first voice I heard was that of Col. Sibell come to look after our luggage and see us off. Dressed, and gathered together my things, and at six o'clock just as the night was folding its soft black wings and rising slowly from the earth, we took our departure from that mansion of little ease, the America, and our fellow-lodgers, the ants, and proceeded to the Philadelphia steamboat which started from the bottom of Barclay St. The servants, who as I said before, were just a quarter as many as the house required, had no bedrooms allotted to them, but slept about anywhere, in the public rooms, or on sofas in drawing rooms let to private families. In short, nothing can exceed the want of order, propriety, and comfort in this establishment, except the enormity of the tribute it levies upon pilgrims and wayfarers through the land. And so, as I said, we departed from there nothing loath.

The morning was dull, dreary, and damp, which I regretted very much. The steamboat was very large and commodious, as all these conveyances are. These steamboats have three stories. The upper one is, as it were, a roofing or terrace on the leads of the second, a very desirable station when the weather is neither too foul nor too fair. The second floor or deck has the advantage of the ceiling above, and yet, the sides being completely open, it is airy and allows free sight of the shores on either hand. The deck below, being the one near the water, is a spacious room completely roofed and walled in, where the passengers take their meals and resort if the weather is unfavorable. At the end of this room is a smaller cabin for the use of the ladies, with beds and a sofa, and all the conveniences necessary if they should like to be sick; whither I came and slept till breakfast time. The breakfast was good, and served and eaten with decency enough.

At about half past ten we reached the place where we leave the river to proceed across a part of the State of New Jersey to the

Delaware. The landing was beyond measure wretched. The shore shelved down to the water's edge, and its marshy, clayey soil, rendered doubly soft and squashy by the damp weather with some slippery planks half immersed in mud was the only road to the coaches that stood ready to receive the passengers of the steamboat. They are shaped something like boats, the sides being merely leathern pieces, removable at pleasure, but which, in bad weather, are buttoned down to protect the inmates from the wet. There are three seats in this machine; the middle one having a movable leathern strap, by way of adossier, which runs between the carriage doors and lifts away to permit the egress and ingress of the occupants of the other seats. Into the one facing the horses Dall and I put ourselves. Presently two young ladies occupied the opposite one and a third lady and a gentleman of the same party sat in the middle seat, into which my father's huge bulk was also squeezed. Finally another man belonging to the same party ensconced himself between the two young ladies. Thus the two seats were filled with three persons, and there should have by rights been a third on ours, for this nefarious black hole on wheels is intended to carry nine. For the first few minutes I thought I must have fainted from the intolerable sensation of smothering which I experienced. However, the leathers having been removed, and a little more air obtained, I took heart of grace and resigned myself to my fate. Away walloped the four horses, and away went we after them, bumping, thumping, and tumbling over the wickedest road, I do think, the hard-heartedest road, that ever wheel humbled upon. Bones of me! what a road! Even my father's solid proportions could not keep their level, but were jerked up to the roof and down again every three minutes. Our companions seemed nothing dismayed by these wondrous performances of a coach and four, but laughed and talked incessantly; the young ladies at the very top of their voices and with the national nasal twang. The ladies were all pretty, but how I wish they could have held their tongues for two minutes.

The few cottages and farmhouses which we passed reminded me of similar dwellings in France and Ireland, yet the peasantry here have not the same excuse for disorder and dilapidation. The farms had the same desolate, untidy, untended look; the gates broken, the fences carelessly put up, the farming utensils sluttishly scattered about a littered yard where the pigs seemed to preside by undisputed right; house windows broken and stuffed with paper or cloths, dishevelled women and barefooted, anomalous looking human young things. None of the stirring life and activity which such places present in England and Scotland; above all, none of the enchanting mixture of neatness, order and rustic elegance and comfort which render so picturesque the surroundings of a farm and the various belongings of agricultural labor in my own dear country.

At the end of fourteen miles we turned into a swampy field the whole fourteen coachfuls of us, and by the help of heaven, bag and baggage were packed into the coaches which stood on the railway ready to receive us. The carriages were not drawn by steam, but by horses, with the mere advantage in speed afforded by the iron ledges, which, to be sure, compared with our previous progress through the ruts, was considerable. Our coachful got into the first carriage of the train, escaping, by way of especial grace, the dust which one's predecessors occasion. This vehicle had but two seats, each of which held four of us. The whole inside was lined with blazing scarlet, which with full complement of passengers on a fine, sunny summer's day, must make as pretty a little miniature hell as may be, I should think. This railroad is an infinite blessing. 'Tis not yet finished, but shortly will be so, and then the whole of that horrible fourteen miles will be performed in comfort and decency in half the time. In about an hour and a half we reached the end of our railroad part of the journey and found another steamboat waiting for us, when we all embarked on the Delaware. Again the enormous width of the river struck me with astonishment and admiration. We passed Bristol and Burlington, stopping at each of them to take up passengers. I sat working, having finished my book, not a little discomfited by the pertinaceous staring of some of my fellow travellers. One improvement they have adopted on board these boats is to forbid smoking, except in the fore part of the vessel. I wish they would suggest that if the gentlemen would refrain from spitting about too, it would be highly agreeable to the female part of the community. The universal practice here of this disgusting trick makes me absolutely sick. Every place is made a perfect piggery of— streets, stairs, steamboats, everywhere—and behind the scenes and on the stage at rehearsal I have been shocked and annoyed beyond expression.

At about four o'clock we reached Philadelphia, having performed the journey between that and New York (a distance of a hundred miles) in less than ten hours, in spite of bogs, ruts, and all other impediments. The manager came to look after us and our goods, and we were presently stowed into a coach which conveyed us to the

Mansion House [3rd St. above Spruce St.], the best reputed inn in Philadelphia. On asking for our bedrooms they showed Dall and myself into a double-bedded room. On my remonstrating against this, the chamber maid replied that they were not accustomed to allow lodgers so much room as a room apiece. However, upon my insisting, they gave me a little nest, just big enough to turn about in but where at least I can be by myself.

Tuesday, 9th

Rose at half past eight. Went and took a bath. On my way thither drove through two melancholy looking squares which reminded me a little of poor old Queen Square in Bristol. [Must have been Independence Square and Washington Square]. The ladies' baths were closed, but as I was not particular, they gave me one in the part of the house usually allotted to the men's use. I was much surprised to find two baths in one room, but it seems to me that the people of this country have an aversion to solitude, whether eating, sleeping, or under any other circumstances.

Took a walk with my father through some of the principal streets. The town is perfect silence and solitude compared with New York. There is a greater air of age about it too, which pleases me. The red houses are not so fiercely red, nor the white facings so glaringly white. In short, it has not so new and flaunting a look, which is a great recommendation to me. The city is regularly built, the streets intersecting each other at right angles.

Politics of all sorts, I confess, are far beyond my limited powers of comprehension. Those of this country as far as I have been able to observe, resolve themselves into two great motives. The aristocratic desire of elevation and separation, and the democratic desire of demolishing and levelling. Whatever may be the immediate cause of excitement or discussion, these are the two master springs to which they are referable. Democrats, or radicals, are for the reelection of General Jackson, but the aristocratic party, which here at all events is the strongest are in favor of Henry Clay.

Wednesday, 10th

Rose at eight. After breakfast trimmed a cap and wrote to dear Harriet. The streets were in an uproar all night; people shouting and bonfires blazing. In short, electioneering fun, which seems to be pretty much the same all the world over. At twelve o'clock sallied forth with Dall to rehearsal. The theatre [Chestnut St. Theatre] is very pretty, not large but well sized, and I should think, favorably constructed for the voice.

Thursday, 11th

Rose rather late. After breakfast wrote Journal. At twelve went to rehearsal. After rehearsal came home, habited, and went to the riding school to try some horses. Merci de moi! what quadrupeds! How they did wallop and shamble about, poor half-broken dumb brutes.

Came home. The enchanting Mr. Head has allowed me a pianoforte, but in bringing it into the room, the stupid slave broke one of the legs off, whereat I was like to faint, for I thought Mr. Head would wish me hanged therefore. Nothing can exceed the civility of the people here, and the House is extremely well kept, quiet and comfortable. Came home in high delight with this Quaker city which is indeed very pretty and pleasant.

Fanny made her first Philadelphia appearance in the Chestnut Street Theatre on Friday, October 12, as Bianca in "Fazio," the same play in which she had opened in New York. She speaks disdainfully of the audience and shows that despite all her protestations to Miss St. Leger in her letters during her first season in London, saying many times that she will not become dependent on the excitement of the theatre, and that she does not find it exciting, she is now stimulated by applause and realizes that her acting is better when she receives acclaim from the audience.

My cough and cold are dreadful. After dinner practised, invented and executed a substitute for the coques de perle in my Bianca dress, and lay down to rest a little before my work. At six went to the theatre. The house was very full, and Dall and my father say that I was extremely ungracious in my acknowledgement of their greeting. I cannot tell; I did not mean to be so. So I made them three curtsies, and what could woman do more. Of course, I can neither feel nor look so glad to see them as I am to see my own dear London people, neither can I be as profound in my obeisance as when my audience is civil enough to rise to me. "There is differences, look you."

My Fazio had a pair of false black whiskers on which distilled a black strip of trickling cement down his cheeks and kept me in agony every time he had to embrace me. My voice was horrible to hear. This audience is the most unapplausive I ever acted to, not excepting my excitable friends north of the Tweed. They were very attentive certainly, but how they did make me work! 'Tis amazing how much an audience loses by this species of hanging back, even where the silence proceeds from unwillingness to interrupt a good performance. Though in reality it is the greatest compliment an actor can receive, yet he is deprived by that very stillness of half his power. Excitement is reciprocal between the performer and the audience; he creates it in them and receives it back again from them, and in that last scene in "Fazio" half the effect that I produce is derived from the applause which I receive, the very noise and tumult of which tends to heighten the nervous energy which the scene itself begets. I know that my aunt Siddons has frequently said the same thing. And besides the above reason for applause, the physical powers of an actor require after any tremendous exertion, the rest and regathering of breath and strength which the interruption of the audience affords him. Moreover, as 'tis the conventional mode of expressing approbation in a theatre, it is chilling and uncomfortable to go toiling on, without knowing whether, as the maid-servants say, "one gives satisfaction or no." They made noise enough, however, at the end of the play. Came home, supped, and to bed, weary to death and with a voice like a cracked bagpipe.

On Friday, October 12, the Kembles opened in Philadelphia, and on Saturday, October 13, Pierce Butler came to call for the first time. It was the turning point in Fanny's life. The marriage proved to be a disaster for both of them, but Fanny merely speaks of Pierce Butler without making any comment, and so the occasion at a glance does not seem a momentous one. She marks by three rows of stars in her Journal the blank she left for his name. However, the whole published Journal is cut up with these rows of stars, even when referring to trivial incidents, and it is impossible to put an interpretation of significance at this particular place in the Journal.

Came down to tea and found a young gentleman sitting with my father; one Mr. .... He was a pretty-spoken, *genteel* youth enough. He drank tea with us and offered to ride with me. He is, it seems, a great fortune. Consequently, I suppose (in spite of his inches) a great man. Now I'll go to bed. My cough's enough to kill a horse.

This is the only reference Fanny makes to Pierce Butler's stature, but she complained of her own smallness, and it can

be assumed that she probably was not as tall as he. Pierce
Butler is referred to by Celia, a negro born on St. Simon
Island, one of his plantations, as "Marse Pierce, little short
one." In an unsigned pencil drawing of Pierce Butler's head
in profile made in London in 1841, he has dark hair curling
over his ears onto his collar and a slightly turned up nose
and determined look. But there are no references to his height
other than these two.

Though Fanny Kemble does not state in her published
Journal why Pierce Butler presented himself to her father
any more than she accounts for the introductions of the
various young men who came to see her, sent her flowers,
and took her riding, years later she explains this. He was
given a letter of introduction to the Kembles by an Englishman, Henry Berkeley, whom Fanny does not mention in her
Journal till November 27, during the Kembles' second visit
in New York. Henry Berkeley obviously looked up the Kembles
and went to see Fanny act because he was travelling in America for pleasure, knew them by reputation, had perhaps seen
them in London, and was the kind of man with cosmopolitan
taste who would naturally be drawn to the Kembles. He was
one of the eighteen children of the Earl of Berkeley, but born
out of wedlock to a butcher's daughter of Gloucester, England,
whom the Earl of Berkeley subsequently married. At this time
he was travelling in the United States with a Mrs. Austin, a
fairly well known English singer, but was not married to her.

After playing "The Gamester" with her father at his benefit, Fanny records in her Journal:

> Mr. Henry Berkeley was behind the scenes, and Ogden Hoffman,
> rapt, in his usual seat. He's a delightful bit of audience.

Ogden Hoffman became extremely attentive to Fanny and is
referred to many times both in New York and Philadelphia.

Fanny wrote in her own hand of Henry Berkeley in the
pages stitched into the Charles Sedgwick copy of the American
Journal years later:

> Henry Berkeley was one of the most profligate and unprincipled
> men I have ever known. He was also one of the most agreeable and

accomplished. He was the most intimate friend of Mr. Pierce Butler who, when first he made his acquaintance, was a mere youth not yet of age. To this Englishman's example and precepts I attribute much of Mr. Butler's subsequent profligacy and want of principle. Henry Berkeley was the person who when we were going to Philadelphia gave my father a letter of introduction to Mr. Butler and so was the means of my first acquaintance with that gentleman. Many years after in England in speaking to my sister of Mr. Butler's ill usage of me, Mr. Berkeley said, "but he is mad. I do not use the word in any but its literal sense. I have known him ever since he was eighteen intimately, and I know he is mad." Mr. Berkeley had studied in England for the bar and for the church, but a fall from his horse while hunting had crippled him, and he gave up all thought of a professional career. He was the finest amateur musician I have ever known and imparted some portion of this fine taste to his disciple, Mr. Butler, among worse things. He has now been for many years member of the House of Commons for the great commercial town of Bristol.

Journal, Monday, October 15

It is delightful to act with my father. One's imagination need toil but little to see in him the very thing he represents, whereas with all other Romeos, although they were much younger men, I have had to do double work with that useful engine, my fancy; first to get rid of the material obstacle staring me in the face, and then to substitute some more congenial representative of that sweetest vision of youth and love. Once only this was not necessary.

The audience here are without exception the most disagreeable I ever played to. Not a single hand did they give the balcony scene or my father's scene with the friar. They are literally immovable. They applauded vehemently at the end of my draught scene and a great deal at the end of the play, but they are nevertheless intolerably dull, and it is all but impossible to act to them.

The house was literally crammed from floor to ceiling. Came home tired and hoarse, though my voice was a good deal better today. Mr. Clark supped with us. My father expected a visit from the haggling Boston manager and chose to have witness to the conference.

Tuesday, 16th

The Boston manager it seems does not approve of our terms, and after bargaining till past two o'clock last night with my father, the latter, wearied out with his illiberal trafficking and coarse vul-

garity of manner, declined the thing altogether, so unless the gentleman thinks better of the matter, we shall not go to Boston this
winter.

The Kembles did come to an agreement with the Boston
manager and had a successful engagement there.

Mr. Staley amused me by telling me that he had heard my be-
haviour canvassed with much censure by some man or other who
met me at Mr. Horne's and who was horrified at my taking up a
book and then a newspaper, and in short, being neither tragical
nor comical at a dinner party. Of course I must seem a very strange
animal to them all, but they seem just as strange to me.

Wednesday, October 17th

The dignified and graceful influence which married women among
us exercise over the tone of manners is utterly unknown here. Married women are either house-drudges and nursery-maids, or if they
appear in society, comparative cyphers, and the retiring, modest,
youthful bearing which among us distinguishes girls of fifteen or
sixteen is equally unknown. Society is entirely led by chits who in
England would be sitting behind a pinafore. The consequence is that
it has neither the elegance, refinement, nor the propriety which belongs to ours, but is a noisy, racketty, vulgar congregation of flirting
boys and girls, alike without style or decorum.

The beautiful villas on the banks of the Schuylkil are all either
utterly deserted and half-ruinous, or let out by the proprietors to
tavern keepers. The reason assigned for this is that during that
season of the year when it would be most desirable to reside there,
the fever and ague take possession of the place and effectually
banish all other occupants.

Fanny is nonplused by the lack of personal attention her
father received in Philadelphia.

It gave me something like a feeling of contempt, not only for the
charities, but for the good taste of the Philadelphians when I found
them careless and indifferent towards one whose name alone is a
passport into every refined and cultivated society in Europe.

Friday, October 26

Mr. and Mrs. Nicholas Biddle and their eldest son, Edward,
called upon us. They are the only inhabitants of this good city who
have done us that honor.

Found an invitation to dinner from the Nicholas Biddles. "One exception makes a rule," say the scholars. By that same token, therefore, the Philadelphians are about the most inhospitable set of people it ever was my good fortune to fall in with. I can only attribute the want of courtesy we met with in Philadelphia to the greater prevalence of that very small spirit of dignity which is always afraid of committing itself.

As far as my yesterday's dinner at the Nicholas Biddle's will allow me to judge, I should say that not only the style of living, but the society is superior to that which I saw in New York. Certainly, both the entertainment itself and the guests were irreproachable; the first in very good taste, the latter appeared to me well informed and very agreeable.

The Unitarian faith was not unknown to Fanny before she came to America, because she speaks of Dr. William Ellery Channing and having read his sermons and essays in a letter to George Combe in 1831. How she came upon the sermons and essays she does not say, and it is startling for an English Episcopalian actress of twenty to be interested in theology. However, she sums up what she thinks the religious needs of the Americans are. Pierce Butler was a Unitarian, and it was through her marriage to him that she worshipped in the First Unitarian Church, Philadelphia, with the Reverend William Furness as pastor. He preached abolition sermons and lost some of his congregation from his outspoken anti-slavery convictions. Fanny's inborn anti-slavery feelings must have been strengthened by her going to the Unitarian Church with Pierce Butler after they were married as well as by talking to Dr. Channing in Boston.

Sunday, October 28

Throughout all the northern states, and particularly those of New England, the Unitarian form of faith prevails very extensively. It appears to me admirably suited to the spiritual necessities of this portion of the Americans. They are a reasoning, not an imaginative race. Moreover, they are a hard-working, not an idle one. It therefore suits their necessities as well as their character to have a religious creed divested at once of mysteries at which the rational mind excepts, and of long and laborious ceremonies which too often engross the time without the attention of the worshipper. Their form of religion is a simple one, a short one, and a cheap one.

After church came home, and began writing to Harriet. Mr. Staley called. He sat for some time mending pens for me, and at half past one Dall, he, and I packed ourselves into a coach and proceeded on to Fair Mount, where we got out and left the coach to wait for us.

The wind was deliciously fresh, and I think as we buffeted along in its face we should have made an admirable subject for Bunbury; I with my bonnet off, my combs out, and all my hair flying about, hooked up to Mr. Staley, who, willow-like, bent over me to facilitate my reaching his arm.

Tuesday, October 30

I think it has not been my good fortune in more than six instances during my residence in this country to find ladies "at home" in the morning. The first reason for this is the total impossibility of having a housekeeper, the American servants steadfastly refusing to obey two mistresses. The being subservient to any appears, indeed, a dreadful hardship to them. Of course, this compels the lady of the house to enter into all those minute daily details which with us devolve upon the superintendent servant, and she is thus condemned, at least for some part of the morning, to the storeroom or the kitchen. In consequence of this, her toilet is seldom completed until about to take her morning promenade, and I have been a good deal surprised, more than once, at being told when I called, that "the ladies were dressing but would be down immediately." This is French, the disorderly slouching about half the morning in a careless undress, being unluckily quite compatible with that exquisite niceness of appearance with which the Parisian ladies edify their streets so much and their homes so little. Another very disagreeable result of this arrangement is that when you are admitted into a home in the morning, the rooms appear as they were never used. There are no books lying about, no work tables covered with evidences of constant use, and if there is a piano, it is generally closed; the whole giving one an uninhabited feel that is extremely uncomfortable. As to a morning lounge in a lady's boudoir or a gentleman's library, the thing's unheard of. To be sure there are no loungers where every man is tied to a counting house from morning till night, and therefore no occasion for those very pleasant sanctums devoted to gossiping; political, literary, and scandalous.

Fanny has this to say about boat travel in America on Saturday, November 10:

To an English person the mere circumstances of being the whole day in a crowd is a nuisance. As to privacy at any time or under any circumstances, 'tis a thing that enters not into the imagination of an American. They do not seem to comprehend that to be from sunrise to sunset one of a hundred and fifty people confined in a steam boat, is in itself a great misery. They live all the days of their lives in throng, eat at ordinaries [public dining rooms] of two or three hundred, sleep five or six in a room, take pleasure in droves, and travel by swarms. The quantity of one's companions in these conveyances [river steamers] is not more objectionable than their quality sometimes. As they are the only vehicles, and the fares charged are extremely low, it follows necessarily that all classes and sorts of people congregate in them, from the ragged Irish immigrant and the boorish back-countryman, to the gentleman of the Senate, the Supreme Court, and the President himself.

After dinner came upstairs, read Grahame, wrote Journal, began my novel under another shape. I can't write prose (query: can I anything else?) I don't know how, but my sentences are the comicallest things in the world. The end forgets the beginning, and the whole is a perfect labyrinth of parenthesis within parenthesis. Perhaps by the bye without other view it would be just as well if I exercised myself a little in writing my own language as the grammar hath it "with elegance and propriety."

Fanny did learn to write well. She outgrew her early labyrinthine sentences which were no more wordy and involved than most nineteenth century writing. She continued to embroider her prose with adjectives, but they were well chosen. At her best she did not allow herself to drift into minor channels when her main theme was of vital interest. In her Georgian Journal her style sometimes becomes staccato: she says that living in Georgia gave her a new view of the South; "an elegant young Carolinian or Georgian gentleman whip in hand, driving a gang of lusty women," and she describes the poor whites as "the most degraded race of human beings claiming an Anglo-Saxon origin that can be found on the face of the earth— filthy, lazy, ignorant, brutal, proud, penniless savages." In her eightieth year she published a novel that Henry James admired, *Far Away and Long Ago*. In it one cannot recognize her earlier manner. In the novel it has become terse, and words are used with economy.

While in Philadelphia a gentleman called on her, whom she does not name, who claimed to be a relation. He told Fanny that he had looked up the Kembles' ancestry and found that they were originally Italian and pirates named Campo Bello, and that the family was the same as the Scottish Campbells. Fanny says, "I have and always have had the greatest love and veneration for old blood. I would rather by far have some barbarous Saxon giant to my ancestor than all the wealth to my dower." She evidently was dismayed by the fact that her grandfather, Rodger Kemble, founder of the Kemble family, had no ancestors that could be verified. She was glad that this so-called kinsman of hers was convinced of the Kembles' ancient lineage.

The bond between Fanny and her father is well illustrated in the following passage. Taking a December midnight walk from the heart of Philadelphia to the Schuykill River was not done by Philadelphians at that time. But the Kembles were English and loved walking and the out-of-doors, and Charles enjoyed the companionship of his daughter who was always happy to go on any form of expedition with him. She enjoyed the walk or she could not have written so lyrically about it. From Third and Spruce Streets, across the Schuylkill River and back is about three miles.

Dined at five. My father out. After dinner sat writing Journal till ten when he returned. The moon was shining soft and full, and he asked me if I would take a walk. I bonneted and booted, and we sallied forth to the Schuylkill. The moon withdrew herself behind a veil of thin white clouds but left a grey, clear light over the earth and through the sky. We reached the Fair Mount bridge at about eleven. The turnpike was fast, and everybody asleep, so we climbed over the gate and very deliberately pursued our way over the strange, dark-looking covered bridge, where the glimmering lamps at distant intervals threw the crossing beams and rafters into momentary brightness that had a strange effect with the surrounding gloom.

The moon, faintly struggling through the clouds now touched the dark pyramids of the cedar trees that rose up into the grey sky, and threw our shadows on the lonely path we were now pursuing, now cast a pale gleam through the rapid clouds that chased one another like dreams across the sky. The air was soft and balmy as the night air of mid August. The world was still, and except for our footfalls as we trudged along, no sound disturbed the universal repose. We did not reach home until after twelve.

On November 4, 1832, the Kembles returned to New York and played a very successful engagement at the Park Theatre for a month. Their first performance of "The Taming of the Shrew" brought five thousand dollars to the box office. They then returned to Philadelphia and once more played at the Chestnut St. Theatre. It was in this second Philadelphia visit that Fanny speaks of going to call on the artist, Thomas Sully, who became a warm friend and who painted thirteen beautiful portraits of her. On this second engagement in Philadelphia, Pierce Butler, whose name is recorded only once in the Journal in the Kembles' initial visit to Philadelphia, obviously began paying serious court to Fanny. From now on there are many references to him in the Journal. Pierce came to the riding academy every day that she rode and walked back with her and Aunt Dall to the Mansion House. At that time she never went anywhere without her father or her aunt, and apparently Pierce did not see her alone until April when they went riding outside of Boston. She cut all mention of their becoming engaged to him from the published Journal, and the exact date is not known, but there are many sentences concerning him from the first day that he came to call on her in Philadelphia in her second stay. One of them being while she is at the riding academy:

> My hair presently with the damp and the shaking became perfectly straight. As I raised my head after putting it under my cap, I beheld Pierce Butler earnestly discoursing to Dall.

And again:

> At two o'clock I dismounted. Pierce Butler walked home with us.

And on another day:

> Dall and I set off for the riding academy. We were hardly there before Pierce Butler made his appearance. I wonder what he'll do for an interest by the bye when we are gone.

And again:

Wednesday, December 26, 1832

Practiced for a short time and then went to the riding school. It was quite empty. I put on my cap and skirt and was sitting thinking of many things in the little dressing room when I heard the school door open, and Mr. Pierce Butler walked straight up to me. He told me sundry steamboat stories that made my blood curdle, such as a public brush, a public comb, and a public *toothbrush*.

Fanny does not say in her Journal who the woman is who is suggesting suitable husbands for her:

Friday, December 28

She amuses me much by her intense anxiety that I should be married. First, she wishes Pierce Butler would propose to me, then she thinks Mr. Shelton's estates in Cuba would be highly acceptable. In short, my single blessedness seems greatly to annoy her, and I believes she attributes everything evil in life to that same.

Saturday, December 29

We had a long discussion about the stage now that I am a living and breathing witness that a person may be accounted a good actor and to a certain degree deserve the title, without time or pains of any sort being expended upon the acquisition of the reputation. An actor is at best but a filler up of an outline designed by another— the expounder as it were of things which another has set down, and a fine piece of acting is at best, in my opinion, a fine translation.

At half past five went to the theatre. The play, "The Wonder." I acted only so so. When the play was over, the folks called for us, and we went on. He [Charles] made them a neat speech, and I nothing but a cross face and three curtseys. How I do hate this! 'Tis quite enough to exhibit myself to a gaping crowd when my profession requires that I should do so in a feigned semblance, but to come bobbing and genuflecting on as me myself, to be clapped and shouted at, and say, "thank ye kindly," is odious.

The Kembles played "Macbeth" on Christmas day in Philadelphia to a good house and continued their engagement to the end of the month. Pierce Butler saw Fanny nearly every day, sent bouquets to her hotel, often walked home from the riding academy with her, and went riding to Laurel Hill with her with Aunt Dall following in a carriage and bringing a picnic lunch.

On Monday, December 31, they started for Baltimore. They drove by coach to the Delaware River and took a steamer for about an hour, then disembarked to cross the narrow neck of land which divides the Delaware from the Chesapeake. "Here we got in a coach holding twelve of us to be conveyed over the railroad by one of Stevenson's engines. Neither the road nor the conveyances are comparable to those of the Liverpool and Manchester railway." It took the Kembles on the railroad one hour to go sixteen miles to Frenchtown on the Elk River where they took the steamboat, the Charles Carroll, for Baltimore, where they stayed at Barnham's Inn and acted in the Holliday Theatre. Pierce Butler met the Kembles on the Delaware River steamboat and travelled with them to Baltimore and Washington. Fanny was disconsolate at going to another city. She says repeatedly that she always hated going to new places, and she was unaware of the fact that it was New Year's Day. Of the Charles Carroll steamboat she says:

I went below for a few minutes but found as usual the atmosphere of the cabin perfectly intolerable. The ladies' cabin in winter on board one of these large steamers is a right curious sight. 'Tis generally crammed to suffocation with women *strewn* in every direction. The greater number cuddle around a stove, the heat of which alone would make the atmosphere unbreathable. Others sit lazily in a species of rocking chair—which is found wherever Americans sit down—cradling themselves backwards and forwards with a lazy, lounging, sleepy air that makes me long to make them get up and walk.

The Kembles acted in Baltimore for two weeks and then drove in "an exclusive extra coach" to Washington, where they stayed at Gadsby's Inn. They had with them letters of introduction to Henry Clay, Daniel Webster and Andrew Jackson, and Fanny describes her sightseeing.

Mon., January 14, 1833

We went first into the Senate, or upper house, because Webster was speaking, whom I especially wished to hear. The room itself is neither large nor lofty. The Senators sit in two semi-circular rows, turned towards the President in comfortable arm chairs. On the same ground, and literally sitting among the Senators, were a whole regiment of ladies, whispering, talking, laughing, and fidgeting. A gallery, level with the floor, and only divided by a low partition from the main room, ran round the apartment. This too was filled with pink, blue, and yellow bonnets, and every now and then while the business of the House was going on and Webster speaking, a tremendous bustle and waving of feathers, and rustling of silks would be heard, and in came streaming a reinforcement of political beauties, and then would commence a jumping up, a sitting down, a squeezing through, and a how-d'ye-doing, and a shaking of hands. The Senators would turn round, even Webster would hesitate as if bothered by the row, and in short the whole thing was more irregular and unbusiness-like than anyone could have imagined.

Thursday, 17th

Sat writing Journal till twelve o'clock, when we went to Mr. Bancroft's. Took him up and thence proceeded to the Presidency to be presented in due form. His Excellency, Andrew Jackson, is very tall and thin, but erect and dignified in his carriage; a good specimen of a fine old well-battered soldier. His hair is very thick and grey, his manners are perfectly simple and quiet, therefore very good, so are those of his niece, Mrs. Andrew J. Donelson, who is a very pretty person and lady of the house, Mrs. Jackson having been dead some time. He talked about South Carolina and entered his protest against scribbling ladies, assuring us that the whole of the present southern disturbances had their origin in no larger a source than the nib of the pen of a lady. Truly, if this be true, the lady must have scribbled to some purpose. We sat a little more than a quarter of an hour.

Now comes an episode which Fanny reports with candor. It is an example of her extreme tactlessness. Though it reflects discredit upon the young man who repeated and magnified a lighthearted jest, it shows the love of gossip about prominent people among the supposedly well bred in the United States. Fanny's tactlessness which she refers to as "my suddenness," was a lifelong major flaw in her character. She never overcame it, could not curb her tongue, and so helped to bring upon herself many of the grave troubles which marred her later life. Fanny was a celebrity, and it was natural that gossip about her would be spread by those who saw her briefly or knew her slightly. The public was avid for any personal news about her. She felt herself above her profession of acting, but could not grasp that as a famous star in the United States she should have been doubly careful not to say or do anything that by any stretch of the imagination could be construed against her. She was independent in thought and spirit and did not care to bow to time-established conventions.

In every city in which she acted, young men managed to be introduced to her, or went to call on her father and so formally presented themselves for his approval in order to meet her. When the Kembles were in Washington, Fanny as usual met several young men who as usual became attentive to her, and one morning Mr. Adams came as planned to take her riding but brought along Mr. Fulton (either the grandson or nephew of the Robert Fulton) whom she had never seen and who brought along an extra horse for her to ride.

Mr. Adams introduced him [Mr. Fulton] to me as very anxious to join my party. I was a little startled at this, as I did not think Mr. Adams ought to have brought anybody to ride with me without my leave. However, as I was riding his horse, I was just as well pleased that he was by, for I don't like having the responsibility of such valuable property as a private gentleman's horse to take care of. I told him this, alleging it as a reason for my preferring to ride an indifferent hack horse about which I had no such anxiety. He replied that I need have none about his. I told him laughingly that I would give him two dollars for the hire of it, and then I should feel quite happy, all of which nonsense passed as nonsense should without comment.

A few days later Fanny returned to the Inn and found her father with a strange older man. Fanny then defends herself and shows the independence and self-confidence which stood by her in many difficult situations through life. It was always a surprise to people who did not know her, particularly when she was a young girl and presumably could be easily abashed.

Sat., January 19, 1833

"Fanny," quoth my father, "something particularly disagreeable has occurred. Pray, can you call to mind anything you said during the course of your Thursday's ride which was likely to be offensive to Mr. Fulton, or anything abusive of this country?" As I have already had sundry specimens of the great talent there is for tattle in the exclusive coteries of this gossiping new world, I merely untied my bonnet and replied that I did not at that moment recollect a word that I had said during my whole ride and should certainly not give myself any trouble to do so. "Now, my dear," said my father, his own eyes flashing with indignation, "don't put yourself into a passion, compose yourself and recollect. There is a letter I have just received." He proceeded to read it, and the contents were to this effect—that during my ride with Mr. Fulton I had said I did not choose to ride an American gentleman's horse and *had offered him two dollars for the hire of his;* that moreover I had spoken most derogatorily of America and Americans, in consequence of all which, if my father did not give some explanation or make some apology to the public, I should certainly be hissed off the stage as soon as I appeared on it that evening. This was pleasant. I stated the conversation as it had passed, adding that as to any sentiments a person might express on any subject, liberty of opinion and liberty of speech were alike rights which belonged to everybody, and that with a due regard to good feeling and good breeding, they were rights which nobody ought, and I never would, forego. "For," the older man said, "not less than *fifty* members of Congress have already mentioned the matter to me." Fifty gossiping women! Why the whole thing is for all the world like a village tattle in England among half a dozen old wives round their tea pots. All Washington was in dismay, and my evil deed and evil words were the town talk —field, gaps, marshes, and all rang with them. This is an agreeable circumstance and a display of national character highly entertaining and curious. It gave me at the time, however a dreadful side ache and nervous cough.

I went to the theatre, dressed, and came on the stage in the full expectation of being hissed off it, which is a pleasant sensation, very, and made my heart full of bitterness to think I should stand, as no woman ought to stand, the mark of public insult. However, no such thing occurred. I went on and came off without any such trial ot my courage, but I had been so much annoyed and was still so indignant that I passed the intervals between my scenes in crying, which of course added greatly to the mirth and spirit of my performance of Beatrice [Much Ado About Nothing]. It were much to be desired that Americans had a little *more* national vanity or national pride. Such an unhappily sensitive community surely never existed in this world, and the vengeance with which they visit people for saying they don't admire or like them would be really terrible

Pierce Butler about 1840.

Butler Place from a sketch by Herbert Pollinger, 1911.

if the said people were but as mortally afraid of abuse as they seem to be. I would not advise either Mrs. Trollope, Basil Hall, or Captain Hamilton ever to set their feet upon this ground again, unless they are ambitious of being stoned to death. I live myself in daily expectation of martyrdom. This unhappy species of irritability is carried to such a degree here, that if you express an unfavorable opinion of anything, the people are absolutely astonished at your temerity. I remember to my no little amusement a lady saying to me once, "I hear you are going to abuse us dreadfully. Of course you'll wait till you go back to England and then shower it down upon us finely." I assured her that I was not in the least afraid of staying where I was and saying what I thought at the same time.

The Kembles returned to Philadelphia after a successful engagement in Washington and resumed acting there on the 30th of January. They were acting in the Walnut Street Theatre, at 9th and Walnut Sts. for the first time. They did not realize that the trouble caused by Mr. Fulton had followed them.

Went to the theatre at half past five. It poured rain, in spite of which the house was very good. The play was "Fazio." When I came on in my fine dress at the beginning of the second act, the people hailed me with such a tremendous burst of applause and prolonged it so much that I was greatly puzzled to imagine what on earth possessed them.

Fanny did not know what had caused the unusual applause until the intermission when she was sitting in the dressing room with Aunt Dall. She heard her father addressing the audience before the curtain. She then learned that handbills had been printed retelling the incident in Washington about Mr. Fulton's horse, saying that she had also abused the United States and that she should be hissed off the stage. The distribution of these handbills turned what they were printed for, to start a demonstration against her, into a demonstration for her, and the loud enthusiasm was the result.

At the end the people shouted and shrieked for us. He [Charles Kemble] went on and made them a speech, and I went on and made them a curtsey, and certainly they do deserve the civillest of speeches and lowest curtsies from us, for they have behaved most kindly and courteously to us, and for mine own good part, I love the whole city of Philadelphia from this time forth for ever more.

Mr. Pierce Butler came round to the stage door to bid us good-night, and as we drove off, a whole parcel of folk who had gathered round the door to see us depart, set up a universal hurrah! How strange a thing it is, that popular shout. After all, Pitt or Canning could get no more for the finest oratory that human lips ever uttered, or the wisest policy that human brain ever devised. Praise is so sweet to me that I would have it lasting. Above all, I would wish to feel that I deserved it. I must do so if I am to value it a straw, and acting, even the best that ever was seen is to my mind but a poor claim to approbation.

Now Fanny at twenty-three speaks out about the conditions under which women of her class existed in England in her day. She refers to men as "our earthly disposers." She did not know that fundamentally her life-long contest with the world into which she was born was rooted in the limited spheres allotted to women, and she was a life-long rebel. Her intellectual stature and physical stamina could not be shared with American women and set her apart from the average of her sex. It was only cultivated women and men of pronounced talent who interested her. At the time she wrote the next entry in her Journal, she had had success only as an actress and with the publication of her plays, "Francis I" and "The Star of Seville"; the tremendous range of her mind was not apparent. She was not like other well known women of her time and bore no resemblance to Madame de Stael with her success as a novelist, political meddling, and devourer of men. Fanny was never possessed by a need for masculine conquest. Fanny was self-supporting, striving somehow to give up the stage, thinking of marriage, having forgotten her early introspective forebodings that she was not suited to be a wife.

I wonder how long it will be before men begin to consider the rational education of the mothers of their children a matter of some little moment. How much longer are we to lead existences burdensome to ourselves and useless to others under the influence of every species of ill training that can be imagined? How much longer are the physical evils under which our nature labors to be increased by effeminate, slothful, careless, unwholesome habits? How much longer are our minds, naturally weakened by the action of a highly sensitive nervous construction, to be abandoned, or rather devoted to studies the least likely to strengthen and ennoble them and render them independent in some measure of the infirmities of our bodies? Surely it were generous in those who are our earthly disposers to do something to raise us from the state of half-improvement in which we are suffered to linger. If our capacities are inferior to those of men, which I believe as much as I believe our bodies to be inferior to theirs in strength, let us not be overwhelmed with all the additional shackles that foolish and vain bringing up can add. Let us at least be made as strong in body and mind as we can.

The Kembles went from Philadelphia to New York in February, 1833 by boat and coach. There a visit of lasting importance was paid to Fanny by the novelist, Miss Catherine M. Sedgwick, one of the Boston Sedgwicks and sister of Theodore and Henry Dwight Sedgwick, who was living in New York with another brother, Robert. Miss Sedgwick introduced Fanny to her sister-in-law, Mrs. Charles Sedgwick and the latter's daughter Kate, both of whom became Fanny's dearest and most intimate life-long friends in the United States. It was in the Charles Sedgwick's house in Lenox, Massachusetts, that Fanny took refuge during her marital troubles. She wrote and dedicated her Georgia Plantation Journal to Mrs. Charles Sedgwick, and only to her and her daughter confided the innermost facts of her private life. Miss Sedgwick wrote to Mrs. Frank Channing on February 12, 1833:

> We are just now in the full flush of excitement about Fanny Kemble. She is the most captivating creature, stepped to the very lips in genius. You will not see her till the middle of April. Do not if you can bear unmixed tragedy fail to see her Belvidera. I have never seen any woman on the stage to be compared with her, nor ever an actor that delighted me so much. She is most effective in a true woman's character; fearful, tender, and true. On the stage she is beautiful, far more than beautiful; her face is the mirror of her soul. I have been to see her. She is a quiet gentlewoman in her deportment.

In a letter to Mrs. Watson on February 20, 1833, Miss Sedgwick wrote:

We have been very gay of late and excited by the enchantress, Fanny Kemble. I owe her some delightful hours. There is no sensation more delicious than that you experience from the mastery of genius, that restores for a moment the flexibility of youth and melts you at will. She is a most gifted and accomplished creature and very graceful and attractive in her manners. She resembles E, and at first you would not think her handsome, but her face has the whole range of human expression.

After that engagement in New York they went in April, 1833, by boat to Providence and drove to Boston by stage coach where they stayed at the Tremont House and acted in the Tremont Theatre.

Here we are in a new place! How desolate and cheerless this constant changing of homes is.

Despite being depressed on her arrival, she at once found Boston to her liking.

Monday, April 15, 1833

Besides the advantages of possessing the very prettiest collection of actresses I ever saw, the theatre at Boston has decidedly the best company I have ever played with *anywhere* out of London.

The managers have committed the greatest piece of mismanagement imaginable—they advertise my father alone in "Hamlet" tonight, and instead of making me play alone tomorrow night and so securing our attraction singly before we act together, we are both to act tomorrow in "Fazio," which circumstance, of course, kept the house thin tonight. My father's "Hamlet" is very beautiful. 'Tis curious that when I see him act I have none of the absolute feeling of contempt for the profession that I have while acting myself. What he does appears indeed like the work of an artist, and though I always lament that he loves it as he does and has devoted so much care and labour to it as he has, yet I certainly respect acting more while I am seeing him act than at any other time.

Wed., April 17, 1833

It is quite comical to see the people in the morning at the box office. Our window is opposite to it, and 'tis a matter of the greatest amusement to me to watch them. They collect in crowds for upwards of an hour before the doors open, and when the bolts are withdrawn there is a yelling and shouting as though the town were on fire. In they rush, thumping and pummelling one another, and not one comes out without rubbing his head, or his back, or showing a piteous rent in his clothes. I was surprised to see men of a very low order pressing foremost to obtain boxes, but I find that they sell them again at an enormous increase to others who have not been able to obtain any, and the better to carry on their traffic, these worthies smear their clothes with molasses and sugar etc. in order to prevent any person of more decent appearance, or whose clothes are worth a cent, from coming near the box office. This is ingenious and deserves a reward.

While acting and also being entertained, she was seeing Pierce Butler every day and writes of one of the many horse-back rides they took. It is impossible to determine why she was sad, but then perhaps she was making up her mind to marry him, and it made her introspective.

We rode along the chiming beach, talking gravely of many matters, temporal and spiritual, and when we reached the pines I dismounted, entreated for a scrap of paper, and in the miserable little parlor of this miserable little mansion, sat down and scribbled some miserable doggerel to ease my heart.

Bostonians who so delighted Fanny Kemble were also delighted by her and were more articulate than the citizens of any other American city. Newspapers as a whole at that time did not have any drama critics and often confined themselves to a brief sentence or two about the Kembles. The *Advertiser and Patriot* went so far on April 17, 1833 as to say of Charles Kemble's appearance in "Hamlet": "His acting is chaste and dignified and made a strong impression on his audience last evening."

In a letter to the *Advertiser* that same week a correspondent who only signed himself A.Z. had this to say about the Kembles: "Their visit to this city I consider as a public advantage. It temporarily redeems one of the amusements of the people from its ordinary degradation and shows to those who have the direction of it and the public what the stage might be and ought to be—what it would be whenever the patronage of this opulent and enlightened metropolis is judiciously and liberally directed to the object." And Judge Story, professor at Harvard, said when he was asked how he could enjoy Fanny Kemble and reconcile his pleasure in her performance with his Puritanism,

"I don't try to. I only thank God that I'm alive in the same era with such a woman."

The young girls of Boston belonging to the cultivated families were enraptured by Fanny Kemble and tried their best to look like her and wore their hair in "Fanny Kemble curls." There is a contemporary diary kept by Anna Cabot Lowell Quincy who was then in her early twenties, who says of the night of Tuesday, April 17:

> We were just in time and found excellent seats. The play was "Fazio," a tragedy of the deepest kind with much stage effect, though miserably written. . . . The play was one admirably calculated to show off Miss Kemble, who entirely equalled, indeed passed my expectations. Her grace, the expression of her countenance, her shrieks, her starts, are admirable. Her voice has rather too much stage *tone,* but there are tones of it which went to my heart. Her great power, however, is in her attitudes and her expression, and her *laugh* of agony and insanity was truly horrific. The moment which I think produced most effect on the house was at the moment when Fazio is to be led off to execution in the prison. She has just been imploring the jailer to delay a few moments in the most passionate manner, when the bell tolls, the sound of which seemed to turn her into marble. She stood riveted to the spot—her eyes fixed, her cheek pale and ashen. Fazio embraces her, but she is entirely insensible of it, and he is led off the stage leaving her the solitary figure. She stood, I should think, five moments, a perfect statue, and the deathlike stillness that reigned over the crowded audience, every person seeming to hold their breath, was very striking. "She stood the bloodless image of despair" until the bell tolled again. At that sound the full sense of her wretchedness seemed to rush upon her mind and nearly to destroy it. She gave a start which everyone seemed to feel, and with one of her thrilling screams of agony, rushed from the stage.

Miss Quincy goes on to say that she cried so hard, and her friend Miss Hodgkinson cried so hard, that they were unable to stop though they were on their way to a party to meet Fanny Kemble at Mrs. Otis', and were still weeping on their arrival. Miss Quincy finally saw Fanny after the dense crowd which had crowded around her when she first came to the party parted:

> She was sitting down in a window close to the door where she en-

tered, appearing extremely modest and unassuming, and I could hardly believe that this delicate, gentle, subdued, *shadowy* creature was the Bianca who had been exhibiting such power and who had made me feel so much. Mr. Kemble is a fine looking man, very much of a gentleman and very little of the actor about him. Miss Kemble drops the character of actress entirely, and tho doubtless her manner in company is one of her fine pieces of *acting,* still she chooses her part well and plays it with good effect.

Miss Quincy was introduced to Fanny Kemble towards the end of the same evening.

I wanted to see her and was not up to *staring* without speaking. We exchanged a few commonplaces, but her voice was so low that I could hardly hear a word she said. She is not handsome off the stage. She has very fine eyes with very black eyelashes and eyebrows, and fine teeth. Her complexion is coarse, and her other features not remarkable. Her head is well shaped and hair dressed like Mrs. Cobb's, who, by the way, I think she resembles a little. She appeared like any other young lady, but had a very intelligent expression when she spoke. We were very glad to have an opportunity of seeing her off the stage and were very agreeably impressed.

Part of her great theatrical success was due to the enthusiasm of the Harvard students who walked in great numbers from Cambridge to see her perform. They came during all her Boston engagements, even walking in the ice and snow. Among them was Charles Sumner. Sumner did not meet Fanny for nearly ten years, and when he was a student was merely stagestruck by her. Professor William Russell of Cornell University who saw much of Sumner at Cambridge in 1832–33 writes: ". . . I rather think, however, that I owed a great deal of the kindness with which he treated me to the fact that I was personally acquainted, though very slightly, with Fanny Kemble, as we boys used to call her. He was, as much as any of us, infatuated by her acting, and I remember his one day stopping me on the street and drawing me out of the thoroughfare and saying, 'Come, Russell, tell me something about Fanny Kemble' with all the interest of a lover."

Amidst this professional success and between hard rides, Fanny writes of sitting between Daniel Webster and John

Quincy Adams at dinner. The Ex-President was then 66 years old.

> Last Saturday I dined at ....'s, where, for my greater happiness
> I sat between Daniel Webster and John Quincy Adams. I remember
> especially two bright things uttered, the one by the one, the other
> by the other of these worthies. Mr. Webster, speaking of Knowles'
> "Hunchback," said, "Well, after all, it's no great matter. The author
> evidently understands stage effect and dramatic situations, and so
> on, but as for the writing, it's by no means as good as Shakespeare."
> I looked at the man in amazement and suggested to him that Shake-
> speare did not grow upon every bush. Presently Mr. Adams began
> a sentence by assuring me that he was a worshipper of Shakespeare,
> and ended it by saying that "Othello" was disgusting, "King Lear"
> ludicrous, and "Romeo and Juliet" childish nonsense; whereat I
> swallowed half a pint of water and nearly my tumbler too, and re-
> mained silent,—for what could I say?

The most significant friendship Fanny made in the United States during her first year in America was with the Rev. William Ellery Channing, the most famous and influential Unitarian clergyman of his day. Though he was a Bostonian and belonged to the New England intellectuals, she actually met him in New York and was apparently introduced to him by Miss Catherine Sedgwick during her third theatrical engagement there. She had written to George Combe in 1830 that she was reading Channing's work and speaks of his essay on Napoleon. In her "Records of a Girlhood" she mentions giving her friend, Emily Fitzhugh, Channing to read when she found human beings "vile." This was his article, "The Moral Argument Against Calvinism," and how Fanny came upon it when she was twenty is not explained. It could not have been given to her by Harriet St. Leger who was an ardent Episcopalian and certainly inclined towards strict Episcopalian theology. But Fanny admired Channing's writings at once.

Channing was born in Newport, the grandson of William Ellery, a signer of the Declaration of Independence for Rhode Island, and the son of William Channing, a Calvinist clergyman. In 1833 he was 53 years old and pastor of the Federal St. Unitarian Church in Boston. He was known for his liberalism and tolerance and had an immense following. He preached in churches on the Eastern seaboard, and all his sermons were published and widely read. As a very young man he had been a tutor to a family in Virginia and had seen slavery, and in 1820 he had gone to the Bahamas before the slaves were freed. A true ascetic, he had injured his health while a Harvard student by deliberately eating too little so as not to have to exercise in order to have more time to devote to his studies. He was filled with zeal and of a truly spiritual habit of mind and had a singularly clear and melodic speaking voice. He was small and spare. He was an advocate of abolition by peaceful means, believing that the slave owners should be made to see the error of their ways, and on their own initiative free their slaves. While in Boston Fanny wrote in her Journal:

I have finished Channing's sermons which are most excellent. I think he is one of the purest English prose writers now living. I revere him greatly, yet I do not think his denial of the Trinity is consistent with the argument by which he maintains the truth of the miracles."

In New York she speaks of her first meeting with him:

I have seen Channing, who, in his outward man, bears but little token of his inward greatness. Miss Sedgwick had prepared me for an exterior over which debility and sickness had triumphed now for some years; but thought I, there must be eyes and a brow, and there the spirit will surely be seen upon its throne. But the eyes were small grey eyes, with an expression which struck me at first as more akin to shrewdness of judgment than genius, and the loftier qualities of the mind; and though the brow and forehead were those of an intellectual person, they had neither the expanse nor conformation I had imagined.

The subject of our conversation, though sufficiently natural for him to choose, addressing one of my craft, did not appear to me to be a happy one for his own powers, perhaps I thought so because I differed from him. He talked about the stage and acting in as unreal, and in my opinion, mistaken a manner, as possible. Had he expressed himself unknowingly about acting, that would not have surprised me, for he can have no means of judging of it, not having frequented the theatre for some years past, and those who have the best means of forming critical judgments upon dramatic subjects, for the most part talk arrant nonsense about them. He said he had not thought much upon the subject, but that it appeared to him feasible and highly desirable to take detached passages and scenes from the finest dramatic writers and have them well declaimed in comparatively private assemblies,—this as a wholesome substitute for the stage, of which he said he did not approve, and he thought this the best method of obtaining the intellectual pleasure and profit to be derived from dramatic works, without the illusion and excitement belonging to theatrical exhibitions. My horror was so unutterable at this proposition, and my amazement so extreme that he should make it, that I believe my replies to it were all but incoherent. What! take one of Shakespeare's plays bit by bit, break it piecemeal, in order to make recitals of it! destroy the marvelous unity of one of his magnificent works, to make patches of declamation! Channing mentioned the dagger soliloquy in Macbeth as an instance which would admit of being executed after his idea, saying that that, well read by any person in a drawing room, would have all the effect necessary or desirable.

After his first conversations with Fanny he was so interested in her outspoken views on subjects that interested him that he wanted to see her again and wrote her on November 7, 1833:

I hope Miss Kemble will do me the justice to believe that I received her letter with much pleasure, and that my delay to answer it is not to be ascribed to negligence. I should have written you at once—but you were travelling,—I knew not where you were to be found. I expected to meet you in Boston in the Autumn, but I reached this city just as you left it. I commit this letter to a friend travelling South who will see that it reaches you. I trust that I shall yet have the opportunity of renewing the conversation, I will not call it controversy, which we had at New York. It does not trouble me at all to know that I did not convince you. In truth, I spoke of a subject on which I had not thought much—it is more than possible that my opinions needed not a little modification to make them strictly true. When we meet again, we will try to understand one another better, and I hope I shall not be slow to acknowledge my error if I have adopted one. Rumor gives us reason to hope that you are not soon to leave us, and though I know how little credit is due to report, my wishes make me easy of belief in the present instance. In the Spring

I shall probably travel southward, and one of the pleasures I promise myself is an interview with you.

Believe me,
Very sincerely
Yr friend,
Wm. E. Channing

Channing did come to call on Fanny every time she acted in Boston, and she refers many times to his visits and the great pleasure they were to her. He wrote her again in February, 1834:

> Mr. Channing will thank Miss Kemble to name some hour after this day when he may have the pleasure of seeing her. He fears that should he visit her when she is receiving her numerous acquaintances, he should find little or no opportunity of continuing the conversation begun at New York or of entering on any other.

It was May when she left Boston for the first time, but in the year that she was engaged to Pierce Butler the Kembles played several more engagements in Boston. And after one of them, in the middle of the winter, Fanny in her "Records of a Girlhood" gives a dramatic account, written years later, of one of her departures from Boston without giving any date. She rode with Pierce, and was obviously engaged to him, and a Major, whose name is not given by her, went part of the way with them. The account of their midnight ride is written in a style quite different from the day-by-day entries in her "American Journal." She included it in "Records of a Girlhood" to prove a theory of hers that riding and hard exercise rested and refreshed her.

> Only once was I allowed to test my theory, and I found that the result answered my expectations entirely. I had been acting in Boston every night for a whole week, and on Saturday night had acted in two pieces and was to start at one o'clock in the morning for New York, between which and Boston there was no railroad in those days. I was not feeling well and was much exhausted by my hard work, but I was sure that if I could only begin my journey on horseback instead of in the lumbering, rolling, rocking, heavy, straw-and-leather-smelling "Exclusive Extra" (that is, private stage coach) I should get over my fatigue and the rest of the journey with some

chance of not being completely knocked up by it. After much persuasion my father consented, and after the two pieces of our farewell night to a crowded, enthusiastic house, all the excitement of which of course told upon me even more than the actual exertion of acting, I had some supper, and at one o'clock, with our friend, Major M........, and Pierce Butler, got on horseback and rode out of Boston. Major M........ rode with us only about three miles, and then turned back, leaving us to pursue our ride to Dedham, seven miles further, where the carriage with my father and aunt was to meet us.

The thermometer stood at seventeen degrees below zero. It was the middle of a Massachusetts winter, and the cold was intense. The moon was at the full, and the night as bright as day. Not a stone but was visible on the iron-hard road that rang under our horses' hoofs. The whole county was sheeted with snow, over which the moon threw great floods of yellow light, while here and there a broken ridge in the smooth, white expanse turned a sparkling, crystalline edge up to the lovely splendor. It was wonderfully beautiful and exhilarating, though so cold that my veil was all frozen over my lips, and we literally hardly dared utter a word for fear of swallowing scissors and knives in the piercing air, which, however, was perfectly still and without the slightest breath of wind. So we rode hard and fast and silently, side by side, through the bright, profound stillness of the night, and never drew rein till we reached Dedham, where the carriage with my father and aunt had not yet arrived. Not a soul was stirring, and not a sound was heard in the little New England village. The country tavern was fast shut up, not a light twinkled from any window, or thread of smoke rose from any chimney. Every house had closed its eyes and ears and gone to sleep. We had ridden the whole way as fast as we could and had kept our blood warm by the violent exercise, but there was every danger, if we sat many minutes on our saddles in the piercing cold, that we should be all the worse instead of the better for that circumstance. Pierce Butler rode along the houses looking for some possible shelter, and at last, through the chink of a shutter, spying a feeble glimmer of light, dismounted, and knocking, asked if it were possible for me to be admitted there for a few minutes till the carriage, which could not be far distant, came up. He was answered in the affirmative, and I jumped down from my saddle and ran into the friendly refuge, while he paced rapidly to and fro before the house, leading the horses to keep himself and them alike from freezing. A man was to come on the coach box with the driver to take them back to Boston. On looking round I found myself in a miserable little low room, heated almost to suffocation by an iron stove, and stifling with the peculiar smell of black dyestuffs. Here, by the light of two wretched bits of candle, two women were working with the utmost dispatch at mourning garments for a funeral which was to take place that day in a few hours. They did not speak to me after making room for me near the stove, and the only words they exchanged with each other were laconic demands for scissors, thread, etc., and so they rapidly plied their needles in silence, while I, suddenly transported from the cold brightness without into this funeral, sweltering atmosphere of what looked like a Black Hole made of crepe and bombazine, watched the lugubrious occupation of the women as if I was in a dream till the distant rumbling of wheels growing more and more distinct, I took leave of my temporary hostesses with many thanks (they were poor New England workwomen, by whom no other species of acknowledgement would have been received) and was presently fast asleep in the corner of the carriage and woke only long after to feel rested and refreshed.

This extraordinary feat of stamina and endurance in the bitter cold is typical of Fanny in her youth. She described in her American Journal during her first visit to Boston riding twenty miles before breakfast to see a stone quarry, and then back to Boston where she was acting that same night. American women were not her equal in physique, and only in New York did she ever go riding with women, while she rode with men well into middle age.

Fanny loved New England and Boston more than any city in America and said:

I visited Boston several times and mixed in society there, the tone of which appeared to me far higher than that of any I found elsewhere. A general degree of cultivation exists among its members which renders their intercourse desirable and delightful. Nor is this superior degree of education confined to Boston. The zeal and the judgment with which it is being propagated throughout that part of the country is a noble national characteristic. It is in itself a lovely place, and the country round it is charming. The people are *intellectual* and have been most abundantly goodnatured and kind to me."

Fanny wrote to George Combe on June 27, 1833:

I am quite reconciled to my surroundings—have met with nothing but success in public and the utmost kindness and cordiality in private, have had more admiration bestowed upon me than my conscientiousness knew at all what to do with—have found many things to like and few people to love—so much for a ten month's experience of North America. The peculiarities which give such offense to our Captain Hamiltons and Mrs. Trollopes are naturally enough the first to attract a stranger's notice; they are differences of customs and manners. To speak before one has had leisure to reflect as well as perceive is a great mistake and one into which I think most of the English writers upon America have fallen headlong. I plead guilty most entirely myself to having been much annoyed by the various departures from the habits of my own country which I found in this, and there are some differences to which I shall never get accustomed; to whit—spitting on the carpet and voting by ballot—but most of my other prejudices are melting away under the combined influence of use, resignation, plenty of kind treatment, and a due appreciation of my merits, all which circumstances have induced in my mind a conviction that Americans are decidely not Hottentots, and that it is possible to reside among them without one's beard and nails, either physical or mental, growing to an uncouth length.

You ask me if I have written anything—nothing worth answering *yes* to. My other occupations are too incessant and engrossing a nature to admit of my undertaking any work of length or importance. I keep a voluminous journal, and almost every other day scrawl doggerel of some sort or kind to the amount of from twenty to fifty lines, but this I do literally to ease my heart of its pressing emotions, much as a bird sings, with as little method, purpose, or trouble.

CHAPTER V

Vacation on the Hudson

The Kembles went back to New York from Boston and again acted there in the Park Theatre. They had been acting continually since September; now on June 30, 1833, they began their vacation. The first nine months of their daring venture had been a financial success. The hope of returning to London with money earned in the United States could be realized, but they had to stay a second year and fulfill their contract. The average earnings of their performances in all cities showed that they were the greatest attraction of that season on the American stage. However, it was proved that Charles could not fill a house when acting by himself. He could not tour without Fanny.

In the United States the Kembles' reputation had preceded them, and there were pictures in the shop windows of New York of John Philip and Mrs. Siddons when Charles and Fanny arrived. And soon in New York and the other cities where they played, there were copies of the Lawrence pencil drawing of Fanny on public display. Not only did Fanny have no rivals in America, there was no other combination of father and daughter of equal renown. The American theatre up to that time, as the contemporary newspapers said repeatedly, had patrons for the pit and galleries only, as the fare provided did not attract the better educated. But when the Kembles acted, cultivated men and women who were not in the habit of going to the theatre became the regular audience. Though Fanny and her father were the lesser Kembles, they were a revelation for America.

So the Kembles started on their vacation. They were on their way to Niagara Falls and were going by steamboat up the Hudson, stopping on the way, and would act in Albany and

Toronto. Pierce Butler who had become engaged to Fanny in Boston had returned to Philadelphia on business and would join them at Utica and go to Trenton Falls, New York, with them and continue to the end of the journey. They had concluded their third engagement in New York, and at the invitation of Gourvenier Kemble and his brother, William, who had claimed relationship with them, would make their first stop at Cold Springs to see the Gourvenier Kemble Iron Works.

As Fanny stepped on the steamer in New York harbor she was introduced to Edward John Trelawney, then 41 years old. Here was Fanny at twenty-three once again meeting and forming a friendship with a man who was already known in the literary world. Two years before Trelawney had published "Adventures of a Younger Son," about his roamings in India and the South Seas. He would later publish his account of finding, with Byron, Shelley's body on the shores of the Gulf of Spezia after Shelley and his small boat had vanished in a storm. Trelawney had plucked Shelley's heart from the funeral pyre on the beach, and two years later lifted the blanket from Byron's body to look at his clubbed feet. He evidently did not dwell on these, the most famous episodes of his life, but told Fanny amusing stories about Byron; as she says, "Mr. Trelawney killed us with laughing." Trelawney was an international adventurer, but he did not publish an account of his trip up the Hudson with the Kembles, and Fanny's Journal is the only record of it.

Fanny during this journey refers to Trelawney when writing of her various excursions on shore as well as reporting her conversations with him on the steamer as he became a member of their party.

I took out my work, and Mr. Trelawney sat down by us. As a nuisance which all unsought-for companionship is, he is quite the most endurable possible, for he has seen such things and known such people that it is greatly worthwhile to listen to him. Everything he says of Byron and Shelley confirms my own impression of them.

When we were in the steamboat going up to Troy, Trelawney put a letter into my hands which he told me was written by the mother of Allegra [Claire Claremont], Byron's illegitimate child. The letter was remarkable only for more straight-forwardness and conciseness

House lived in by Fanny and Pierce Butler on the Georgia Plantation 1838–39.

Cartoon, 1835. Coach with Charles Kemble's party overturns on way to Niagara.

than is usual in women's letters. I do not know whether Trelawney gave it to me to read on that account alone, or because it contained allusions to wild and interesting adventures of his own; perhaps there was a mingling of motives.

Mr. Trelawney dined with us: what a savage he is in some respects. He's a curious being; a description of him would puzzle anyone who had never seen him. A man with the proportions of a giant for strength and agility, taller, straighter, and broader than most men, yet with the most listless indolent carelessness of gait, and an uncertain wandering way of dropping his feet to the ground, as if he didn't know where he was going, and didn't much wish to go anywhere. His face is as dark as a moor's, with a wild strange look about the eyes and forehead, and a mark like a scar upon his cheek; his whole appearance giving one an idea of toil, hardship, peril and wild adventure. The expression of his mouth is remarkably mild and sweet, and his voice is extremely low and gentle. His hands are as brown as a labourer's; he never profanes them with gloves, but wears two strange magical looking rings; one of them which he showed me, is made of elephant hair.

Mr. Trelawney killed us with laughing, with an account he gave us of some of Byron's sayings and doings, which were just as whimsical and eccentric, as unamiable, but very funny. Tomorrow we start for Utica. Mr. Trelawney comes with us. I am glad of it, I like him.

Mr. Trelawney read Don Quixote to us. He reads very peculiarly; slowly, and with marked emphasis. He has a strong feeling of humour, as well of poetry; in fact they belong to each other, for Humour is but Fancy laughing, and Poetry but Fancy sad.

Trelawney was with them from the beginning. When Pierce Butler joined them, he was the only American in their party.

The weather was wonderful as they steamed up the Hudson, and Fanny, an observer and lover of nature, was singularly attracted and bewitched by running water and speaks many times in her Journal of this enthrallment. She longed to see Niagara Falls. She appears in a happy frame of mind, which indicates nothing, as she cut all matters concerning herself and Pierce Butler out of her Journal, nor does she say a word about the gulf that was separating her from her father. This party of five—the tall gray-haired Charles of noble mien, plump, kindly

Aunt Dall with her bonnet and shawl, lively Fanny whose brown curls and splendid dark eyes marked her among the passengers, the huge vagabond, Trelawney, and small, stubborn-faced Pierce Butler, were travellers together on what appeared to be a care-free expedition, but the Kembles' future was in grave doubt. Ever since April Charles had been confronted by an appalling fact: his daughter was going to marry an American. Pierce Butler had been with them since April, was going to Niagara with them, and had persuaded Fanny to become engaged to him. He was dogging their footsteps. What would become of the Kembles when Fanny gave up the stage? Charles, of course, did his utmost to prevent this. He must have been in anguish and was striving by every means to prevent her from giving up the theatre after five years of supporting her family.

Pierce Butler was born Pierce Butler Mease in Philadelphia in 1807, the son of Sarah Butler and Dr. James Mease. His grandfather was Major Pierce Butler who had come to America in 1766 from Ireland as a Major in the 29th British Regiment, and was the third son of Sir Richard Butler. In 1771 Major Butler was married to Mary ("Polly") Middleton, the daughter of Thomas Middleton of Prince William's Parish, South Carolina, founder of one of the greatest planter families in the South and builder of Middleton Place, and Major Butler became a prosperous plantation owner. He resigned from the British Army before the Revolution and became an officer in the American Army, and there is a letter from George Washington addressed to him during the Revolution, as a Major, which for years hung in the front hall of Butler Place during and after Fanny's residence there, until the house was pulled down. He was elected by the South Carolina legislature to the National Congress and later to the Constitutional Convention. He refused to sign the Declaration on the grounds that he had come to America in his Majesty's (George III's) service. He signed the Constitution for the state of South Carolina, however, and was the author of the Fugitive Slave Law, which is included in the Constitution. He became United States Senator from South Carolina. In the early 1800's he sold his South Carolina land and bought three plantations in Georgia: Woodville on the mainland, not cultivated as a plantation; Butler's Island, the rice plantation on the delta of the Altamaha River near Darien; and Hampton, or Butler Point, on the northwest point of St. Simons Island. He was one of the three biggest owners of slaves in the United States. Besides his southern holdings he owned large tracts of land in Allegheny and Wayne Counties, Pennsylvania, a house in Philadelphia where he died in 1822, on the northwest corner of 8th and Chestnut St., no longer standing, many blocks of Philadelphia city property at Second and Callowhill Streets, and two large farms six miles due north from City Hall, Philadelphia, one, Butler Place, on the west side of the "turnpike"—now York Road—and the other, York farm, opposite it on the east.

He had one son, Thomas, whose marriage had displeased him and whom he left only his holdings in Allegheny and Wayne Counties, Pennsylvania and sixty-six thousand dollars. He had three daughters, Eliza, Sarah, who married Dr. James Mease of Philadelphia, and Frances. He left Eliza and Sarah only sixty-six thousand dollars and some small legacies, but to his daughter Frances, who did not marry, he left a life interest in his southern plantations and Philadelphia properties. In his will he bequeathed his plantation and Philadelphia holdings to whichever of his Mease grandsons would change his name to Butler before he was sixteen, so that after the death of his daughter Frances, there would be a male Butler to inherit. There were three Mease grandsons, Thomas, John, and Pierce. Thomas died in boyhood. Pierce changed his name. Thus Pierce when engaged to Fanny was a young man who had never worked and was waiting for his huge inheritance. But after they were married John Mease also changed his name to Butler, and Pierce Butler signed over half the plantation inheritance to him. Major Butler had made his home in Philadelphia after 1819, and his southern plantations were run by hired managers, and the mansion that he had built on Butler's Island was allowed to fall into ruin by his daughter, Frances, who lived in Philadelphia.

Major Butler was energetic, astute, and capable, and a descendent of one of the oldest families in Ireland. They are spoken of in Winston Churchill's history and can trace their

ancestry to the thirteenth century; they sat in the English
House of Parliament. Major Butler's father had married a Percy,
one of the noblest families in England. So Fanny was marrying
a man with "old blood" on his mother's side, reaching with
distinction into Irish and British history.

Pierce Butler, always spoken of by his contemporaries as
charming and handsome, had inherited not one of his grandfather's qualities. His most outstanding characteristics were
indolence, sloth, and inertia, as well as an overmastering passion
for gambling which brought financial ruin to him and the loss
of all but an infinitesimal part of his inheritance. He was forced
to sell his half of the slaves on the Butler Plantation, the other
half belonging to his brother, John, on one of the largest slave
auctions ever held in the United States in April 1859, when 998
slaves were sold at auction on the race track in Savannah in
order to pay his debts of five hundred thousand dollars, which
he lost on the New York Stock Exchange. Such was the young
man, twenty-five years old, who was engaged to Fanny, and
who was travelling up the Hudson with her.

She gives nothing but happy accounts of this journey in her
Journal, as on Friday, July 12:

> We all breakfasted together early and immediately after breakfast
> got into an open carriage and set off for Trenton (New York state).
> Dall and my father sat beside each other, Pierce and I opposite them,
> Mr. Trelawney on the box, and so we progressed. The day was
> bright and breezy, the country was all smiling round us in rich
> beauty.

Of Trenton Falls she says:

> I can't describe it. I don't know either its height or width. I only
> know it was extremely beautiful and came pouring down like a great
> rolling heap of amber."

Fanny continues on July 16:

> Had to get up before I'd half done my sleep. At six started from
> Rochester for Murray, where we proposed breakfasting. Just as we
> were nearing the inn at this same place, our driver took it into his
> head to give us a taste of his quality. We were all earnestly engaged
> in a discussion, when suddenly I felt a tremendous sort of stunning

blow, and as soon as I opened my eyes found that the coach was overturned, lying completely on its side. I was very comfortably curled up under my father, who by heaven's mercy did not suffocate me. Opposite sat Dall, as white as a ghost, with her forehead cut open, and an awful looking stream of blood falling from it. By her stood Mr. Trelawney, also as pale as ashes. Pierce Butler was perched like a bird above us all on the edge of the doorway which was open. The first thing I did was to cry as loud as ever I could, "I'm not hurt!" which assurance I shouted sufficiently lustily to remove all anxiety from their minds. The next thing was to get my father up, in accomplishing which he trampled upon me most cruelly. As soon as I was relieved from his mountainous pressure, I got up, and saw to my dismay two men carrying Mr. Trelawney into the house. We were all convinced that some of his limbs were broken. I ran after as quickly as I could, and presently the house was like a hospital. They carried him into an upper room and laid him on a bed. Here too they brought Dall, all white and bleeding. Our hand-baskets and bags were ransacked for salts and eau de cologne. Cold water, hot water, towels, and pocket handkerchiefs were called into requisition, and I with my clothes all torn and one shoulder all bruised and cut, went from the one to the other in utter dismay. Presently, to my great relief, Mr. Trelawney revived and gave ample testimony of having the use of his limbs by getting up and in the most skillful manner plastering poor Dall's broken brow up. Pierce went in quest of my father who had received a violent blow on his leg and was halting about, looking after the baggage and the driver who had escaped unhurt. The chief cause of our misfortune was the economy with which the stagecoaches are constructed in this thrifty land. That is, they have but one door, and of course are obliged to be turned round much oftener than if they had two. In wheeling us therefore rapidly up to the inn, and turning the coach with the side that had a door towards the house, we swung over and fell. While the coach was being repaired, and the horses changed, we, bound up, bruised, and aching, but still very merry, sat down to breakfast. Mr. Trelawney who had been merely stunned, seized on the milk and honey and stuffed away with great zeal. Poor Dall was the most deplorable of the party, with a bloody handkerchief bound over one half of her face. I only ached a little, and I believe Pierce escaped with a scratch on his finger, so seeing it was no worse, we thanked God, and devoured. After breakfast we packed ourselves again into our vehicle and progressed. Although nobody, I believe, ever travelled a hundred miles by land in this country without being over-turned, the drivers deserve infinite credit for the *rare occurrence* of accidents. How they can carry a coach at all over some of their roads is miraculous, and high praise is due to them, both for care and skill, that anybody in any part of this country ever arrives at the end of a land journey at all. I do not ever remember to have seen six-in-hand driving except in New England where it is common, and where the stage drivers are great adepts in their mystery.

The overturning of the stagecoach proved a year later fatal to Aunt Dall. She had suffered what Fanny calls a "concussion of the spine," and was paralyzed below the waist before her death.

Wednesday, July 17, 1833

Arrived on the other side, i.e. Canada, there was a second pause as to how we were to get conveyed to the falls. My father, Trelawney, and Dall betook themselves to an inn by the roadside, which prom-ised information and assistance, and Pierce Butler and I clambering up the heights of Queenston, sat ourselves down under some bushes whence we looked towards Lake Ontario. I thought I perceived signs of stirring down by the inn door, so we proceeded down to the rest of the party. An uneasy-looking, rickety cart without springs was the sole conveyance we could obtain, and into this we packed ourselves. Trelawney brought me some beautiful roses which he had been stealing for me, and Pierce Butler gave me a glass of milk, with which restoratives I comforted myself, and we set forth. As we squeaked and creaked (I mean our vehicle) up the hill, I thought my father's or Trelawney's weight quite enough to have broken the whole down, but it did not happen. My mind was eagerly dwelling on what we were going to see; that sight which Trelawney said was the only one in the world which had not disappointed him. I felt ab-solutely nervous with expectation. The sound of the cataract is, they say, heard within fifteen miles when the wind sets favourably. Today, however, there was no wind. The whole air was breathless with the heat of midsummer, and though we stopped our wagon once or twice to listen as we approached, all was profoundest silence. When we were within about three miles of the falls, just before entering the village of Niagara, Pierce Butler stopped the wagon, and then we heard distinctly, though far off, the voice of the mighty cataract. Looking over the woods which appeared to overhang the course of the river, we beheld one silver cloud rising slowly into the sky—the everlasting incense of the waters. A perfect frenzy of impatience seized upon me. I could have set off and run the whole way, and when at length the carriage stopped at the door of the Niagara House, waiting neither for my father, Dall, nor Pierce Butler, I rushed through the hall and the garden, down the steep footpath cut in the rocks. I heard steps behind me. Mr. Trelawney was following me. Down, down, I sprang, and along the narrow footpath, divided only by a thicket from the tumultous rapids. I saw through the boughs the white glimmer of that sea of foam—"Go on, go on, don't stop" shouted Trelawney, and in another minute the thicket was passed. I stood upon Table Rock. Trelawney seized me by the arm, and without speaking a word, dragged me to the edge of the rapids to the brink of the abyss. I saw Niagara—Oh God! who can describe that sight!

It was Trelawney and not Pierce who followed Fanny through the underbrush and onto Table Rock and dragged her by the arm to the very edge. This episode is entirely in character for both these men. Fanny was in every way too quick for Pierce, who presumably assisted Aunt Dall out of the cart, gave her his arm, and walked with Charles and Aunt Dall in a seemly way to the brink. Fanny was, of course, better suited to be the wife of the vagabond Trelawney and roam through life with him from continent to continent, seeking and finding adventures and then writing about them, than to be the wife of Pierce Butler. She was in no way suited to settle in Philadelphia with him, a young man with no attributes except his pleasing gentlemanly ways and no intellectual attainments who had never been out of America. But there are no facts that establish Trelawney as a suitor of Fanny Kemble's, nor can it be proved that he had a romantic interest in her. He had been married three times. His Arab princess wife had died of poison. He had divorced his English wife and sent back to her brother the Greek maiden he married during his campaign in Greece with Byron. Such a man would not have been accepted by Charles Kemble as a suitor for his daughter's hand.

CHAPTER VI

A Disastrous Marriage

The Kembles' second season in the United States, 1833–34, was a repetition of their first. They acted in all the same cities and were again enthusiastically received and met with financial success. But the conflict between Fanny and her father had reached a climax. He had succeeded in persuading her to stay on the stage one more year, while Pierce Butler was still pressing her to marry him. For one whole year he travelled with the Kembles, and at times played the flute in the theatre orchestra when she was acting. Fanny did not see as a bad omen the fact that he was able to devote a year to her. She had miscast him, assuming that the heir to a vast fortune was an affluent young man of accepted leisure.

In April 1834 they were again in Boston, and Fanny wrote George Combe of Edinburgh:

April 11, 1834

My dear Sir—Our labors in this place terminated last night, and we should have been on our way to our next place of exertion at this moment, but for the dangerous illness of my poor aunt which is giving us a melancholy respite. The medical gentleman who attends upon her gives us no hope of her recovery, and our only consolation in watching the gradual decay of her strength is the certainty that she is free from pain. How sad and great a loss and an affliction this is to us you will easily believe.

Our engagements in this country are drawing to a close, and I think in the month of June we shall return to England. Circumstances such as this life is forever producing to interrupt our plans for the future have very painfully thwarted mine. I did not expect to remain on the stage after the month of May when my marriage was appointed, and I hoped to be free from a profession which has always been irksome to me, but it is otherwise. I shall return to

England with my father in June and continue my labors for another twelve months either there or here. As I have seen good cause to adopt this determination, I shall not say anything more about it, for 'tis very vain to sit lamenting over a line of action which one had deliberately chosen as the most fitting to pursue.

In this same long letter Fanny speaks of Dr. William Ellery Channing:

I have seen Dr. Channing several times. In spite of a very feeble state of health, he has been kind enough to come and see me once or twice each time we have been in Boston, and you will readily believe how much I have valued the privilege of intercourse with such a mind. He is indeed very admirable, so enlarged and benevolent in all his views, so temperate in all his feelings and opinions, so refined and cultivated in his intellect.

As to my poor head, it is merely running to waste. My time is spent in travelling from place to place, unpacking and packing, rehearsing and acting, dressing and undressing, receiving and returning visits. My studies and the few accomplishments I possessed are alike getting rusty from disuse. My chief time for reading is at night while brushing my hair before I go to bed, and as you may suppose, but little profit and pleasure can be derived from such mere sips at the well of knowledge. 'Tis a great privation to me, for my desire for information increases instead of diminishing, and I look forward with great anxiety to the time when I can improve my poor neglected mind and learn some of the few exhaustless store of things which I wish to know. The only habit to which I have resolutely adhered, and with which I suffer nothing to interfere, is that of daily exercise. On horseback or on foot I am out during some part of almost every day. My health is one of God's best gifts, and for all possible reasons I endeavor to preserve it, at least by this means. I am fond of Boston. I prefer it to all the rest of America that I have seen. The lower orders of people are *true* in their speech and honest in their deeds.

Aunt Dall died a few days after this letter, and on hearing of her death Trelawney wrote to Fanny:

Charleston, S.C
May 15, 1834

Dear Miss Kemble,
Many times I have been on the point of writing to Dall to ask

questions about you and your father, but something—or nothing—
the fear of being thought of being intrusively troublesome and an
undefined feeling of mingled emotions has held my hand. All this
was vain and foolish, particularly as regarded Dall—a being that
never gave harm to anything living until she died; the kindest and
least selfish of all human kind, and now where is she—

> "Winter is come and gone
> But grief returns with the revolving year
> The airs and streams renew their joyous tone;
> The ants, the bees, the swallow reappear;"

Alas! Where is poor dear Dall—so sudden, so unexpected a
blow. If it has been felt so heavily by one at this distance—that
knew her scarce a month—accustomed too as I have been from my
youth to see friends fall around me—what a shock must it have been
to you and your father. I will not mock my feelings by attempting to
express them in words.

Rumor that like the branded liar is not believed, even when
speaking truth, says you return to England in June and that your
father has been swindled by the Yankees; and that your lovely sister
is to appear on the stage—God forbid. It is torture to behold those
we love so placed—and to her (as she has been described to me)
it must be a fiery martyrdom—but who can control their fate.

My present intention is to penetrate on horseback the western
country then to cruise in the Gulf of Mexico and thence to Europe
if I live so long. The retrospection of the time passed with you and
your family would be unmingled pleasure but that my memory is
haunted by a malignant devil that points eternally with his horrid
claw to the only unkind sentence written in your Log Book—colossal
tho' it be, "we cannot like those who *force* themselves upon us!!! The
worst of this is its truth. This weighs heavier on my conscience than
many greater offences. To relieve me from this dead weight would
be charity—perhaps, to relieve my horse (as you love those noble
brutes) from this additional weight you will erase those leaden
words.

> "That runs molten still in memory's mould
> And will not cool in Lethe's pool?"

Am I not now—who knows—deepening my offences in again
thrusting myself in a new shape upon your notice, when you were
congratulating yourself that you had shaken me off forever.

When I was in Switzerland in 1820 a fiendish review of a poem of Shelley's fell into my hands. The next morning I mounted my horse—crossed the Alps—galloped over the laughing plains of Lombardy—toiled along the ridges of the Appenines—and entered the gorgeous valley of the Arno. There I found the Poet harmonizing with the beautiful scenery around him. I told him I had ridden a thousand miles to do him homage, so great is my admiration for genius. We became fast friends until death separated us. From some real or imagined resemblance in person or mind, or both, you recalled his image so vividly to my mind that I was forced to admire you on the instant—and every day my admiration augmented.

Will you do me the favor to say to your father that if I had thought he had been coming on to the South, I should have written him such information as I considered might have been useful— that not being the case I was loath to give him trouble. Yet I hope that he will allow me to renew my acquaintance (on my part, friendship) whenever and whereever we may meet, from which I received nothing but pleasure.

> I have the honor to be, dear Miss Kemble,
>   With the most perfect esteem and admiration,
>
>   Your,
>
>   Edward Trelawney

Trelawney did not meet Shelley until 1822 and did not ride 1,000 miles in a frenzy to "do him homage," but drove in his own Swiss carriage at leisure to Pisa where Shelley was living. It was in character for him to give a bravura flourish to the merely prosaic, but although he strayed from the facts in the accounts of his distant adventures and was not known for veracity, he had nothing to gain by writing Fanny that she reminded him of Shelley. And it is to be hoped that she received his astonishing concept of her in the spirit in which it was given. Fanny, surely, among all the women Trelawney had known intimately or admired from afar, was the only one who could have correctly evaluated this thought, and it was the highest compliment that he could have paid her. Trelawney had written of Shelley, "his head was very small—and his features were expressive of great sensibility and decidedly feminine." Trelawney aptly put to use the four lines quoted from the eighteen stanza of Shelley's "Adonais." He would not have included anything of the poet's in a letter to a person he considered unworthy of Shelley.

Trelawney shows that he either had a charmed pen or was in fact a man whose feelings graced a page because of his felicitous use of his pen. The truth of the depth of his regard for Fanny cannot be proved, nor is it known how Fanny felt about the letter, but she softened the lines in her Journal about which he spoke to read, "as a nuisance which all unsought-for companionship is, he is quite the most endurable possible."

After the death of Aunt Dall Fanny made a momentous decision. She was going to marry at once. Only in two letters, written on the same day and recently come to light, does she speak of it. She had written to George Combe in April 1834, saying that she would act for one more year, but in May she wrote to Miss Sarah Paine Perkins and Miss Katherine Sedgwick, the niece of Miss Sedgwick, the novelist. These two Boston girls became her life-long, dear friends, and the letters to them were not edited for publication by Fanny as were the letters to Harriet St. Leger but stand complete. They both kept all her letters.

To Miss Sarah Paine Perkins:

May 31, 1834

Dear little Saadi, [Miss Paine]

I am indeed sorry that we shall not see each other before I cross the great salt water. I will now tell you a piece of news which I think may perhaps be of some interest to you. I am going to be married next Saturday, and after then you are not to imagine me in your mind's eye as Fanny Kemble racing along (Chekie) beach or dipping her feet into Jamaica Pond, but sober *Mrs. Pierce Butler* with a ring on her third finger (bells on her toes, I suppose), all the grave cares of matrimony in her mind and visage.

I am not in very good spirits, tho' my health is much better and my looks greatly improved since I left Boston. I had a week's holiday at West Point a short time ago which did me a great deal of good, but I am now working very hard again and scarcely expect to repair either my strength or health but by the sea voyage which is a marvelous remedy for thinness and debility arising from fatigue. Good bye dear Saadi: the gold ring "forget me not" is always on my finger, and the many fragrant gifts with which you used to adorn my room will remain fresh in my recollection forever. God bless you dear little girl. I am very truly your friend.

Fanny Kemble

This letter to Miss Katherine Sedgwick:

May 31, 1834

A good creature going to New York offers to take this for me, and tho' I have but two minutes I must tell you how bright a ray of sunshine is parting my stormy sky. Pierce has behaved *most* nobly, and my Father most kindly—surely it is most noble to confess an error to a person that you do not like and whom you feel has committed an injustice towards you. We are together again nearly the whole day long, and on Saturday next before sailing for New York *we shall be married* so that you will never see *her, Fanny Kemble,* again.

Pierce has promised me that this shall not interfere with my departure or the discharge of my duties to my father, and relying implicitly as I do on his word, I could not resist his earnest entreaties to be his wife before I gave myself up to those chances which perhaps might never have suffered him to call me by that name. I cannot tell exactly whether I have done for the very best in this, because he implored me so that I do not believe I had much power of thought at the time, but I think now that it will be better that he should feel that I am his, fast for life, tho' at a distance, and I shall have reason without appeal for resisting any further claim which might hereafter be made upon me. Besides, tho' you seem to have thought me harsh, which indeed I was not, I *have* some compassion for him and for myself too, and I think seventeen happy days snatched on the very brink of bitterness and parting not to be denied to one who has followed my footsteps for a whole year with a hope which he now beholds defeated.

I have neither time nor head to write more. Kiss dear Kate for me. Give my love to all that are so kind as to care for me in Warren Street, [the New York home of Miss Catherine Sedgwick] and believe me most affectionately yours,

Fanny Kemble

I don't think I shall ever make out to sign anything but that!

Fanny missed the comfort and counsel of Aunt Dall, and the promise to stay on the stage after her marriage may have been given to Charles in consequence of both Dall's and his beseechings. Fanny says years later that William Hodgkinson who

sailed to America on the "Pacific" with them tried to warn her
father and aunt about Pierce.

> Mr. Hodgkinson was I think very fond of me and showed his re-
> gard by endeavoring to make my aunt and father aware of Mr.
> Butler's character when first that gentleman paid his addresses to
> me—but of course Mr. Hodgkinson spoke guardedly and generally,
> tho' I suppose he knew much of Mr. Butler's early career of pro-
> fligacy, but I was in 'love and pleased with him' and paid little heed
> to his (Mr. Hodgkinson's) cautions which reached me at second
> hand through my aunt. Very soon after my marriage I saw him and
> remember him saying to me with great earnestness, 'Since you have
> married that man there must be something good in him'.

The Kembles were foreigners in the United States, travelling
from city to city; Charles had no intimate friends, and it is not
likely that anyone would have talked to him about Pierce Butler,
who meanwhile was living on his expectations and would on the
death of Miss Butler inherit an enormous estate. His parents
were of moderate means and were not speculators on the stock
market, for which amusement Pierce was biding his time.

The death of Aunt Dall stunned Fanny, and she says that
never in her life had she cried so hard as when "my father and
I packed up our theatrical things with Aunt Dall lying dead in
her coffin." Then Fanny must have felt a revulsion for the
theatre, greater than her distaste for it, when tragedy itself was
at hand.

So Fanny, after writing to Sarah and Katherine and still acting in Philadelphia, awaited her marriage. Her full heart, eager
like Juliet's, held no reservations. She longed to give her being
and the great vitality of her mind and health into the safekeep-
ing of the beguiling Pierce Butler. She was oblivious of his
weaknesses and aimlessness, glad to exchange her wandering
life of make-believe for a husband, home and family, and enter
a new world conceived in her imagination, in which hard reality,
mastered by her in her youth, now played no part.

Fanny alludes only once to the struggle between Pierce and
her father. She says to Kate Sedgwick, "after seventeen happy
days snatched on the very brink of bitterness and parting not to
be denied to one who has followed my footsteps for a whole

year," she would return to England with her father and go back on the stage.

Pierce Butler and Fanny Kemble were married on a Saturday, June 7, 1834 in Christ Church, Philadelphia. That night a crowd gathered around the hotel where they were staying and serenaded them. In the eyes of the world the marriage was considered for her a brilliant one. Pierce was a great catch, fashionably born, and one of the largest fortunes in America awaited him. Fine things might have been expected of him. And here was Fanny, the granddaughter of strolling players, now the subject of newspaper stories, snatching this prize from many an eager Philadelphia girl. She had been less than two years in the United States.

But Quaker Philadelphia most certainly disapproved of such a frivolous union, bringing into its midst a girl whose profession was not countenanced by them.

There is a contemporary newspaper report of her wedding in the *Atlas*:

Philadelphia, June 7

Miss Frances Kemble is no more. Last night was her last appearance. Between eight and nine o'clock (this morning) carriages were observed coursing through Chestnut St. with unusual speed for so early an hour, and little herds of persons were collected at corners, apparently interchanging communications of deep and absorbing interest. Soon the current evidently set down the street, and finally in Second, between Market and Arch Streets, the populace gathered themselves into a dense crowd. An inquisitive friend of mine bent his steps towards Christ Church, and on approaching the door found his way impeded by a well dressed serving man with white gloves nicely drawn over his tawny hands. His ready wit supplied the means of entrance, and he was allowed to pass and quickly hied to that portion of the gallery which gave him a full view of the altar. But now stretching his piercing gaze farther into the space before him, he beheld the venerable Bishop. The book was opened to the marriage service, and the Bishop's voice broke the silence which had thus far been maintained. The Bridegroom uttered distinctly all the marriage vows, but so inaudible was the fair lady's voice that low bent the bishop his whitened locks to catch the sound as she essayed to follow the words he read to her. When he closed the book the feelings which she in vain had tried to curb, burst forth in a torrent of hot tears, and leaning her head on her new sister's shoulder, she fainted. Fans and a little patience soon restored the lady's senses, and she then embraced the ladies whom now she claims as relatives. So Miss Kemble vanished, and in her stead appeared a lovely bride in purest white arrayed, her head encircled with a marriage wreath, and over her fair face and form in graceful folds a blond lace veil. At half past ten the bride and groom were seen embarking in a steamboat for New York, whither she goes to take her passage thence in the next packet for her native land.

Contrary to rumor and published statements, the Pierce Butlers did not sail for England with Charles Kemble. They went by boat to New York on Sunday, the day after they were married, and starting on Monday Fanny acted for one week at the Park Theatre with her father and then stayed in America with her husband. Charles sailed back without her, taking the money she had earned on their tour with him. There would have been no use in his leaving any of it for her, as married women had no property rights and the money would have belonged to Pierce.

There is no record of the final scene after the wedding between Charles, Pierce, and Fanny, accounting for her change of plan. But scene there must have been, beyond all drama that the Kembles had ever played together. Charles was defeated in his expectation that his daughter would continue supporting Covent Garden. It must have been in weary bitterness that he parted from her, knowing that he now faced singlehanded the burden of his future.

There is a total silence without one letter to anyone or even the slightest reference by Fanny in explanation as to when or why she broke her promise to her father. Charles believed he had reached a compromise with Pierce and Fanny believed when she wrote the letters that a daughterly obligation obliged her to continue the struggle for her parents. The contract with the Park Theatre had been signed, and she never considered breaking it and thus depriving her father of his last week's earnings in America, in order to depart on her wedding trip.

While single she was under the jurisdiction of her father. Once she was married, Pierce controlled her. So Pierce, in order at last to marry her, had promised Charles that Fanny after seventeen days would go back to London. Charles believed him, and Fanny acquiesed.

Was Fanny overcome by love of Pierce and at the same time torn between that love and the love of her father? Did she believe when she wrote those letters that she was morally obliged to go on working? Had she truly loved the stage the way Mrs. Siddons had, it would be conceivable that she hoped to eat her cake and have it too. But she was not like her aunt. Why then did she promise her father that she would return with him? Did he tell her that he would refuse to allow her to marry unless she did promise? Did she believe that Pierce would let her go to England? If Charles had forbidden the marriage, she could have eloped with Pierce, but she was an obedient daughter; there was no Aunt Dall to fall back on for advice, and she lent herself to a plan that was fundamentally absurd. Fanny seems to have been emotionally exhausted by the tug of war between these two men and gave in, so she thought, to both of them.

When one considers the commanding position of a father in a British household of that day, and the fact that all the Roger Kemble children acted in their parents' troupe, Charles does not appear as an evil natured tyrant, nor does there seem to be any tinge of the unnatural in the relationship between Charles and Fanny. He shared his daughter's labors; by inheritance they were in the same profession, and per force they had been constant companions for five years and together faced the risks and withstood the hardships of their mutual adventures. In her childhood he had not made a pet of Fanny, but sent her at seven to boarding school for a year in Boulogne, and from thirteen to sixteen she was in school in Paris without returning home. She was in Edinburgh with Mrs. Henry Siddons for almost a year before she went on the stage. She had offered to earn her living as a governess at the time her family asked her to play Juliet.

Fanny had had a dazzling success and been the darling of the theatregoing public on both sides of the Atlantic. Since 1829 her existence had been one of startling contrasts. She delighted her audiences at night without being truly absorbed in her work, and by day weighed and balanced her longing for a creative and philosophical life. She found scope for her intellect and widened her horizon by conversing with men established in the literary world, and her interest in all aspects of human endeavor was insatiable. Her nature, combining moral convictions, prowess in acquiring knowledge, and high emotions would be hard to credit were she not so articulate in her Journals. She was in no way prepared or in any way suited to be the wife of a mere dawdler and to settle in a provincial city.

Fanny broke her promise to her father and stayed in America. She was unlike any other young woman who had married into a well-established American family. She was English, famous, and had given up a profession. There was not another girl in the city in polite circles who had earned her living. Pierce from the very start did not behave like the average husband, and at once provide a suitable dwelling for her. He obviously had very little money, and his circumstances could not have been accurately made clear to Charles. He was one of five children and had not inherited his fortune. Meanwhile he had little to live on, and they moved into his brother John Butler's house in Philadelphia where Fanny was not the lady of the house.

What did Pierce have to offer Fanny in Philadelphia? The town was much the same as two years before when she and her father first saw it. She had liked its appearance better than New York, but only the Nicholas Biddles had invited the Kembles to dinner, and now, apparently, the Pierce Butlers were not invited anywhere. As Fanny so often says, there was no Society in American cities, owing to the women's entanglement with their children and housekeeping, and the men toiling all day in "the counting house." But there was also no Court to set the tone in elegance, and Fanny had lived in London. There was no brilliance in hospitality or dress, no Tennyson and Thackeray to come to dinner, no Sir Walter Scott to have breakfast with, nor young Mendelssohn to be introduced to and to play the piano in the drawing room. It was the great Lord Melbourne, then Home Secretary and later Prime Minister, who asked to be presented to Fanny at Lady Dacre's reception during Fanny's first winter on the stage. In Philadelphia she could not share her physical stamina and joy in exercise with anyone, and there were neither men nor women of her worldly experience or mental caliber, and so from the beginning she was an outcast. Now she was to spend the rest of her life in Quaker, arid Philadelphia, absorbed with its commercial transactions, with the drama of the Revolution well over. It was a setting into which she could neither sink to obscurity nor rise to a place worthy of herself. There were only prim, narrow-minded women in traditional "plan clothes" who had never seen a play or heard a concert for her to associate with, or worthy matrons unaware of the world in which Fanny had been an ornament and had retrieved the fortunes of the Kembles.

The Pierce Butlers spent the first summer of their marriage at a series of watering places which are never named by either of them, and a dull, aimless winter confronted Fanny. It was the first time of leisure that she had known since her debut at Covent Garden, and she at once began preparing her Journal, kept by her during her American tour, for the press. She had written it with a view to publication, and the money she hoped to make from it had been intended by her for Aunt Dall who had not a penny of her own. After Dall's death Fanny decided to give the money to Dall's sister, Victoire Decamp, then working as a governess. Pierce forbade her to bring it out. He says in his "Statement," privately printed in defense of her accusations against him during their divorce, that he did his utmost to prevent Fanny from publishing the Journal, but that she had signed a contract with a publisher before her marriage. Pierce could not foresee that her lively Journal would be of historic importance. He only saw that Fanny had a cool eye towards manners and customs he believed sacrosanct, and that no Philadelphia matron should voice opinion on matters not in a woman's sphere and beyond her judgment. He attempted to edit the Journal, and according to him, she would only give in in small ways. How much he diluted the Journal cannot now be seen. Fanny saw no logic in Pierce Butler's command. Her mother published plays after she was married, her family had always encouraged Fanny to write, and her first play went through seven editions.

At this time Fanny was three months pregnant with her first child, but nevertheless quit the John Butler house and in anger left a note for Pierce saying that she would sail back to England. After several hours of wandering through the streets, as she did not know the neighborhood, and looking for a hotel, having packed up her belongings, she realized that she would not find lodgings and returned. This was the first of her many sudden departures from Pierce in their stormy marriage.

The Journal was printed not only in Philadelphia, but shortly in London and Paris. But before the Journal came out Charles received a letter from Edward Everett, U. S. Representative from Massachusetts, later Governor of Massachusetts and Minister to the Court of St. James, and a famous, wordy orator, which contained this passage:

> I see it announced in the papers that Miss Kemble's Journal of her residence in this country is in the press at Philadelphia. I look forward with eagerness to the appearance of a work which cannot but prove in the highest degree interesting to us in this country, particularly to those who have had the pleasure of knowing the amiable and accomplished authoress. My brother, the Editor of the North American Review, as you well know, will need no incitement from me to have Mrs. B's Journal immediately noticed on its appearance. You must know I have an especial reason for looking forward to it with interest. Shortly after your return to Philadelphia, after your first visit to Washington, a friend wrote me from Philadelphia that someone had seen my name in Miss K's Journal and that I was mentioned there in "a ridiculous light." I need not say that I repelled this idea as a part of the floating gossip of the day, ill naturedly repeated to me, and not entitled to cause me a moment's uneasiness.

The Journal became a controversial and sensational success, the cause of additional rancor in the Butler household. Edgar Allan Poe when reviewing it for the *Southern Literary Messenger* took Fanny to task for using words like "dawdled," "gulped," "pottering," "grumpily," and "doldrumish," and quotes the phrase, "When the gentlemen joined us they were all more or less 'how com'd you so indeed'," to illustrate her coarseness. "For a female to speak thus confidently," he says, "is indelicate." Another reviewer said, "the authoress has unsexed herself." Within the year two anonymous burlesques of the Journal were published, showing the notoriety it achieved. They are

"Fanny Kemble in America or Journal of an Actress with Remarks on the State of Society in America and England by an English Lady Four Years Resident in the United States" and "My Conscience! Fanny Thimble Cutler's Journal of a Residence in America Whilst Performing a Profitable Theatrical Engagement: Beating the Nonsensical Fanny Kemble Journal all Hollow."

So Fanny's marriage began in discord from which it never recovered, but she learned that she could sell what she wrote, and it gave her confidence, knowing that she possessed ability for which there was public demand. She also learned that she and Pierce did not see eye to eye on any questions important to her, and a temperamental clash began. He made no attempt to make her happy while they lived those first months with his brother. He did not entertain for her or introduce her to people who might become her friends and she felt herself isolated in a strange city. After this first reconciliation Pierce decided that Fanny would be happier in the country, and they moved to Butler Place, the large farm six miles north of Philadelphia's City Hall, part of his grandfather's Philadelphia holdings then belonging to his aunt, Miss Frances Butler.

Butler family tradition, handed down for three generations, is that Butler Place was bought by Major Butler in 1810 and had been built by a Frenchman, Boullange, in 1791. The house in which Pierce and Fanny lived and which is continually referred to by both of them as a farm was in reality a gentleman owner's dignified mansion with two square high ceilinged rooms on the ground floor with a narrow hall between them, and two rooms of the same size above them.

The Regency details in the fluted molding around the ceilings and the fluted chair rails around the walls four feet above the floor in the two downstairs rooms, and the Greek design of all four mantlepieces prove that the main body of the house shared its design with the typical American houses built at the end of the eighteenth century. The two-story porch with pillars, the third floor with dormer windows, and many rooms of varying dimensions were added through the years, and there is no record of their date. It is doubtful that Major Butler ever lived there.

Miss Frances Butler must have lived there before lending it to Pierce and Fanny, as they did not feel at liberty to make any changes in the furnishings. After Miss Butler's death in 1838 Fanny and Pierce never really settled for more than a few months at a time at Butler Place, although she spent several unhappy winters there alone while he was in the South before his fortune dwindled.

There were tenant farmers in the four small two-story stone houses within sight of the main house. There was a large stone barn with haylofts forming two sides of the square which were joined by a high stone wall making a characteristic Pennsylvania barnyard. The tenant farmer kept his cows and work horses in the barn, and his chickens and ducks in the barnyard. Across the then-called "turnpike," later York Road, was York Farm, also the property of Major Butler and hence his unmarried daughter's.

Butler Place had not been lived in for several years when Fanny and Pierce were lent it by his aunt. Fanny found that she was totally isolated and horribly lonely at Butler Place. Being the mistress of a household in the outskirts of Philadelphia did not invoke the duties of an English lady on her country estate and bore no resemblance to the life Fanny had tasted while visiting landed gentry in Britain. Fanny was slow in grasping this cardinal fact of her new existence. She made many blunders in her dealings with the tenant farmers, at first thinking they were employed by Pierce on the farm.

She at once set about trying to make Butler Place look like an English country estate. She had the fields around the house mowed for lawn, flower beds dug, and she planted a double avenue of maple trees from the main entrance on Thorpe's Lane on the south boundary through which the carriage drive approached the house, ending in a circle, and she planted out the turnpike with a thick row of evergreens.

She tried to postpone for herself the realization of the disaster that engulfed her in her marriage, and in the coming ten years alternated between despair, violent scenes with Pierce, and heroic feats of adaptation and physical endurance. The Pierce Butlers shared only a blind physical attraction for each other before their marriage, and for him the pursuit of courtship, when consummated, concluded all husbandly affection and respect. And she, finding no stimulation for her boundless intellectual vitality, and no longer faced with the daily necessity of earning her living, sank into homesickness and self-pity. Pierce was seldom at home and must have been gambling and idling at cards in town. She says in her *Records of Later Life:*

> I live alone—much alone bodily, more alone mentally. I have no intimates, no society, no intellectual intercourse whatever, and I give myself up, as I never did in my life before, to mere musing, reverie, and speculation. I cannot dignify the process by the title of thought or contemplation.

George Combe had married Fanny's cousin, Cecilia Siddons, only surviving daughter of Mrs. Siddons, on September 25, 1833. Combe wrote Fanny a letter of congratulation on her marriage on December 6, 1834 in which he calls her "Mrs. Butler," saying: "Cecy is to me a treasure of the highest price, and she is pleased to say that I have added in no little degree to her happiness. Our minds harmonize admirably." In the face of the great happiness of her cousin Fanny felt obliged to try to answer them in kind, wanting to put a good face on her marriage. Also, Fanny longed for news from home which Harriet St. Leger, living in Ireland, could not give her. Cecilia might occasionally relay news to her, and so Fanny was keeping up a correspondence with the Combes. On March 20, 1835 she wrote Mr. Combe:

> My dear Sir,
> All that I have to tell you of myself is comprised in three words, I am well—should I add further, and *tolerably happy,* perhaps you would not be so apt to exclaim in amusement as a friend of mine here, to whom, being questioned, I made the same reply. I know I am of a very unhopeful nature, and for anyone upon this earth to live one hour *entirely happily,* I should conceive they must for that hour forego altogether the faculty of thinking.
> Philadelphia, I lament to say, is a most unliterary city. However, in this respect as in *all* others, Boston and the New England portion of America are vastly superior to all the rest of it that I have seen.

However, as it is, myself and my husband act as mental moderators to each other. He is nothing if not mathematical, and in every subject whatsoever that comes under his contemplation, from the traditions of history, to the hypotheses of astronomical speculations, truth, reality, *fact* is the end upon which he fastens, and without a most palpable and solid body of fact there is no satisfying him. We are fortunately different in temper. He is cheerful and contented, exceedingly calm and self-possessed, and has abundance of patience with my more morbid mental construction, without, however, quite understanding it. I shall leave the bottom of this page to him that he may answer all your kind mention of him himself. I am going to write one word to Cecy—so good bye.

There now follows a piece of the letter in Pierce Butler's own hand.

The space left me is small to express my thanks for the many kind wishes for our happiness contained in your letter to my wife of December last, and to thank Mrs. Combe for her kind invitation to be your guests should we visit Edinburgh. It will not be in our power to leave home this year, but I trust that we shall pass the summer of 1836 on the other side of the Atlantic. Of course we shall visit your city, of which Fanny has such pleasing and happy recollections, and I look forward with no little pleasure to seeing and making the acquaintances of all her very good friends in Edinburgh. I have only space to offer you my warmest thanks for your kindness and to write myself, yours very sincerely,

Pierce Butler

Fanny writes Mrs. Combe:

Dear Cecy,

I shall neither see Scotland nor any of my friends this year. My confinement will not take place till the beginning of June, and that will leave us no time before the winter. I have written twice to my father and once to my mother since he left the country but have heard from no one and know nothing of any of my family but dear Henry who writes me from the West Indies, and whom I have had the happiness of seeing since my marriage.

I am living in the country, six miles from Philadelphia. By this time I am carrying housekeeping tolerably easily, but an American household, to an Englishwoman, is a fertile source of wonder, fortitude, and long suffering.

The New Englanders are in every way the noblest race here—the southerners I should imagine upon the whole the lowest. I have visited none of the slave states, but the results of that great curse are infallible. The South is made up of a handful of gentleman proprietors, and a *land* full of their slaves. The intermediate classes, or rather, class, is a horrible compound of ignorance and tyranny. They are generally agents, slave brokers, slave raisers, or overseers. New York and Philadelphia are *commercial* and nothing else. Boston is much more. I should have been glad to have lived there. The West is yet a wilderness, and the southern slave states are eaten away by that very property.

It is strange that there is no record of Fanny awaiting apprehensively the publication of her Journal, after overriding Pierce, and knowing the temper of newspapers and magazines towards English authors who voiced their opinions on American customs. But had she been absorbed by this coming major event she would have confided to George Combe or Harriet. Nor does awaiting her first child absorb or content her. Instead she speaks of slavery.

Why did neither of her parents write to her? Were they so embittered by her leaving the stage that they would not forgive her? Or were they merely so harassed and worried about their own affairs that they gave her no thought?

Less than a year after her marriage Fanny writes to Miss Sarah Perkins congratulating her on her engagement to Henry Cleveland, and when she says "Saadi, Saadi, it's always determined characters who make the greatest fools," it may well be that she is referring to herself and her marriage.

I have but one piece of counsel to give you. I hope your own judgment may approve it a good one, and that you may be willing and able to follow it. Persuade your lover to embrace a profession. To be idle, objectless, useless, becomes neither man or woman. An idle man of pleasure is everywhere a sad specimen of *waste* in its worst shape. But in this country such a one is more to be pitied and disapproved of, I believe, I mean despised, than in any other in the world. In my own country there is a large class of them, but the peculiar form of government and vast landed wealth furnishes them with high interest and duties. This is not the case *here*. An idle man is positively a drone here. His associates, pleasures, and pursuits must all be of an unworthy class, for the intelligent and cultivated are also here the laboring and idleness in this country can in no way be dignified, graceful, or respectable.

Fanny's first child, Sarah, was born at Butler Place on May 28, 1835. On June 11, 1835 she again writes Miss Perkins, advising her about marriage, and it is strange to see that she believes that women, owing to their upbringing, are incapable of choosing a husband, when she had one whole year of companionship with Pierce Butler and yet failed to see what sort of a man he was.

My dear little Saadi,

Marriage quite as much as death seems to be the way of all flesh, so I have nothing to say to you or any other poor creature whose "time is come" but to bless you and grant that you may have thrown yourself into good hands. The manner in which women are brought up renders their exercising any degree of judgment and reason in the choice of a husband so very unlikely (I might say so *impossible*) that it appears to me the merest chance in the world whether their existence after marriage is happy or miserable. In the cares and interests and absorbing affections of maternity a woman finds, however, a safe and for some time at least happy channel for all those feelings which are too often miserably disappointed in the partner of her inconsiderate choice—and thus *some* degree of happiness is attained, tho' I believe far far less than that which was intended and might be found in the intimate relationship and companionship of marriage.

I am running to a disquisition instead of telling you my news. I have a little girl, now two weeks old today. A very fine, strong, healthy baby, with dark *blue* eyes and a luxuriant head of hair. (no teeth tho', which is a pity!) I am myself perfectly well and up and about as if nothing had happened. My health and strength seem to amaze everybody here. I thank God for both and steadfastly determine to lose neither by coddling, which I find is very fashionable among your countrywomen to do on these occasions.

When marriage is what it ought to be, it is indeed the very happiest condition of existence. That it may be such to you, dear, is the prayer of your very true friend.

Fanny Butler

Pierce Butler and his parents, Dr. and Mrs. James Mease,

were Unitarians and parishoners of the Reverend William Henry Furness of the First Unitarian Church, Philadelphia. When Fanny and Pierce first lived in town with his brother, she attended the Unitarian Church, and the Reverend Furness and his wife became her life-long and dear friends. In the summer the Furnesses lived in Germantown not far from Butler Place and were among the very few people who Fanny saw. The Reverend Furness was born and educated in Boston and was a disciple of Channing, who came to stay with him frequently in Philadelphia. And so Channing saw Fanny after her marriage. In 1835 he published his book *Slavery,* which was surely read by Fanny, and perhaps even given to her by the author. At this time the Reverend Furness was searching his conscience to determine whether he would preach abolition, which he did for the first time three years later with Pierce in the front pew. Fanny says in her *Records of Later Life:*

> I wrote a long and vehement treatise against negro slavery which I wanted to publish with my Journal, but was obliged to refrain from doing so lest our fellow-citizens should tear our house down and make a bonfire of our furniture—a favorite mode of remonstrance in these parts with those who advocate the rights of the unhappy blacks.

Fanny wrote Mrs. George Combe on November 8, 1835:

> My husband, my child, and myself are all well—the second being at this moment busily engaged in a game of romps with her nurse to the small confusion of my ideas and proportionate incoherency of this my epistle. She is a pretty child, and having had the advantage of a very lively nurse, she is remarkably brisk and gay—laughing a great deal and taking a great deal of notice of everything. Further than this I have no particular brag to make about her, and indeed you are at liberty to score off as much from this as you think due to maternal partiality in general and my philoprogenitiveness (which I believe is not large) in particular.
>
> I am glad to hear that there is even a remote possibility of your visiting America—glad of course in the first place because I shall have the pleasure of seeing you. I should think too that Mr. Combe would derive much pleasure from seeing the operation of those

principles of government of which I believe he approves above all
other. It appears to me that the *theory* of the American government
is perfect, as perfect perhaps as any human theory can possibly be,
but its present success is by no means so. Disorders and riots have
prevailed lately in many parts of the country from various causes
without, however, materially disturbing it. This country is so vast
that one half might eat the other half and the third half be none
the worse.

There is, however, a question now arising which will surely never
again be suffered to rest, which in the opinions of the wise here-
abouts threatens the union far more closely than any previous one
that has yet arisen. I speak of the slavery in the South, against which
the people in the North are beginning to protest most violently. The
evils of this system are horrible; not the positive evils endured by the
wretched blacks alone, but the demoralization and degradation
which exists wherever they exist, and which extends from the souls
of men downward to their intellect, their body, and the very soil
they cultivate. The white population of the slave states are, I should
think, almost the most depraved of their species.

In Pennsylvania there exists no slavery, but they (negroes) are
much employed as house servants, and frequently servants thus hired
are afterwards claimed as runaway slaves, taken from the house of
their master, and carried back to the hateful existence from which
they had vainly endeavored to escape. 'Tis impossible to conceive a
greater anomaly or one more shocking to one's sense of justice than
the existence of this infinite evil in a country where "Liberty" comes
with every other word out of every man's mouth. Dear Cecy, you
bid me give you practical information about this country. I do not
know whether a disquisition upon slavery comes under that head, but
I'll tell you what does—if you abuse it in the Northern states, they
will agree with you—in the middle ones they will cut you, and in
the Southern ones they will *lynch,* i.e. hang, you without a judge or
jury.

Oh, Cecy how I wish I was in blessed England or Scotland where
I could have a household of decent servants. If you could but conceive a tithe of the misery I endure with my Americans—don't
know what to call them—for dependents, servants, or *helps* they
certainly are not. Our household consists of six, and it requires all
the energy I possess and a great deal more knowledge than I possess
to keep them to the proper fulfillment of their duty. However, I
won't write you storeroom and kitchen details across the Atlantic,

but if ever you come here, you will find few things more singular than the result of the institutions of the country upon the serving classes. The fact is that under the system which exists here, the duties of masters to their servants more imperatively require fulfilling than anywhere else. In Europe by the intervention of an agent, a housekeeper, people contrive to keep themselves removed from the inconveniences of personal communication with ignorant and vulgar minds. The consequence *morally* speaking is bad—the lower class remains unimproved—the higher one is wrapt in selfishness. Here there is but *one* way of being well served—you must deal with your servants as your *equals;* that is as conscientious and rational beings having duties and responsibilities to fulfill towards you as you towards them. Nothing but this and a good deal of firmness and withal constant attention will keep them in order. I have myself to superintend every detail of my household economy—sometimes I am inclined to think this a terrible hardship—perhaps, however, it is not so. The plague of all is that you cannot hope to attach a servant here or retain them beyond a few months in your service. They all look to bettering themselves and remain with you only until they can find a more advantageous situation. They then without quarrel or disagreement whatsoever, and whatever kindness they may have received at your hands, give you warning and leave you. But why do I write you all this? Come and see.

Although Pierce had not yet inherited his grandfather's fortune, in the winter of 1836 he went with his brother to the Georgia plantations, leaving Fanny at home, in order to report to his aunt on conditions, there. Fanny wrote to Mrs. Follen:

My husband, my baby, and myself are well and happy. What have I to say more—oh, of our southern plans. I am not going to Georgia, I am not to accompany my husband in his expedition, I am not to open his mind to the evils of slavery, I am not to ameliorate the condition and enlighten the minds of those whose labor feeds me, nor am I to be l*ynched;* alas! all of which I had so fondly anticipated. Dear Mrs. Follen I need not tell you what a disappointment it is to me not to be allowed to accompany my husband, but there is no house on our estate, and though I have offered, nay entreated, to be permitted to share any and every inconvenience to which Pierce might be subjected, and *even* to leave my child behind, the better to do so, he has deemed it expedient to determine otherwise, and I have no resource but to submit. I had hoped to have been the means of good, and am sorry that I may not so be used. The good will come and instruments will be chosen for its furtherance, though I may not be one of them. I pray God who is with each of us to do far better for my dear husband than I could have done might I but have followed him. This being the case, and my prospect being that of a dismal winter separated from Pierce who alone is *home* to me in this country, my thoughts and wishes have turned to my natural England, and I have half obtained leave to pass the period of our separation with my own friends. How seldom do our happinesses come complete and perfect; how *never* I should have said. I who have been longing with inexpressible desire for the last two years to be once more in England am now indeed going thither, but without my husband in whose companionship lies the best half of every pleasure. . . .

Pierce went to the plantations, and Fanny sailed for England in October, 1836 with her baby and nurse. She had a happy winter with her parents and saw her mother, who died two years later, for the last time. She saw all her old friends, and much was made of her. There is no reference in her letters to her sister, Adelaide, who was seven years younger and who may have been in school in Italy since she was studying to become an opera singer. She had written George Combe saying, "I fully propose visiting Edinburgh before I return to America," but on January 6, 1837 she wrote him saying:

I have just received a letter from my husband in which he tells me that we must return to America by the beginning of May. This shortens the period of my stay a good deal and will allow him, I am sorry to say, little more than three weeks to spend in England, which for the first visit is indeed too little.

I shall delight to show Edinburgh to him and to make him known to you. His qualities are those which you would esteem and appreciate, for though a person of no brilliancy of intellect, his moral faculties are strong and excellent.

My father as the newspapers will I suppose have informed you has left his profession for the exercise of the office of Licenser. I rather fear the reaction which generally follows upon leaving a life of such over-seasoned excitement as an actor's but sincerely hope that his new occupation may have sufficient attraction in some measure to break the fall from publicity to the stillness and comparative monotony of private life."

Fanny was ten months in England, and Pierce joined her and stayed only three weeks. They returned to America so that he could attend the Pennsylvania Constitutional Convention in October. It is the only time that he is known to have participated in anything but his own pleasure. Fanny writes to George Combe from Harrisburg:

I want to know how the dear doctor does. Tell him that he has induced the people of this country to wash themselves [Mr. Combe had written a book on health]. The consititution of the American women is ruined by unwholesome diet, insufficient exercise, unhealthy atmosphere, and irregular hours, before they are twelve years old. After that period they finish the work begun by their parents themselves by tight lacing, tight shoeing, added to all the above pernicious habits which they persevere in most laudably. I wish I could show you my little child. She is uncommonly stout, healthy, and active. Robust health I positively *never* see, and I am myself considered as a species of miracle woman whose frame must be different from that of all others simply because my physical existence is what God intended it should be, one of pleasure rather than of pain.

Fanny tried to explain to George Combe the differences between Boston, New York, and Philadelphia:

I am, however, perhaps no very adequate judge of the two latter (New York and Philadelphia) because it is now a considerable time since I made any stay in New York, and with regard to Philadelphia, altho' I live within six miles of it, I have not six intimates within its walls.

On May 28, 1838, the third birthday of her daughter, Sarah, her second daughter and namesake was born, and in October Fanny writes to Saadi:

The penalties of being a woman to which you profess yourself unreconciled hitherto are in my opinion very severe, but there are some physical compensations for these physical sufferings, which if a woman is healthy almost atone for her seasons of tribulation. Nursing a child, I mean suckling it, is an unspeakable delight, and tho' you will never again feel your heart light in your bosom after the birth of your child, the very weight that will be there is a joyful one, the weight of very precious treasure.

I took exercise on horseback daily when I was seven months gone with child and know several Englishwomen who do the same.

As for me I am about to depart into slavery; Mr. Butler, the children, and myself being bound for Georgia on the twentieth of next month. There whether I shall die of a yellow fever or the jaundice, whether I shall be shot at from behind a tree for my Abolitionism, or swallowed horse and all by an Altamaha alligator are matters yet folded within the unopened chambers of time. Should none of these accidents interfere to prevent it, I expect to be back in white land at the beginning of April.

Fanny wrote Saadi again on December 4, 1838:

Here I am still departing and not departed yet, in that most uncomfortable state of suspense, for assuredly of all earthy conditions uncertainty is the most unblest, and because it is peculiarly irksome to me, it seems to be my appointed trial; indecision and procrastination entering largely into the composition of the disposer of my present destinies, Mr. Butler. I do not even now know when we go, but presume that after languishing through a week or ten days more of doubt and darkness, I shall suddenly be startled as by a trumpet call to get up and be going, which is the species of abrupt summons which invariably terminates these seasons of weary waiting with my husband.

By all I hear, civilization of any kind does not abound in the region to which I am bound, and I am *fitting out* as folks do who go into savage lands.

The Pierce Butlers actually started for Georgia in the middle of December and stopped in Savannah where Fanny wrote to Mrs. Cleveland. The letter is dated in another hand, December 29, 1838, presumably by Mrs. Cleveland, and must have taken about one week to reach New Jersey:

I am fatigued and out of spirits, and under these circumstances it might perhaps be kinder to you to defer epistlizing till tomorrow, but to write to you soon has been my intention ever since I left Philadelphia. Here we are at length near our journey's end, for which as you may suppose I am not a little thankful, for dragging two young children from railroad to steam boat and from steam boat to railroad at this season of the year over eight hundred miles and more of weary journeying is no sinecure. We have come the greater part of our way by a yet unfinished railroad which will accomplish the distance between Baltimore and Charleston as quickly and more safely than the boats, and I should think be preferred by everybody. I cannot say that I am particularly charmed with what I have seen of the South or its ways and manners hitherto. Charleston itself was agreeable to me from its resemblance to an old European town, and the small item of bituminous coal being the combustible chiefly used there added greatly to its English appearance. It has, however, a melancholy and ruinous look; the largest and finest houses being miserably out of repair and appearing as tho' they were abandoned to decay and neglect. Nevertheless the city is by far the most picturesque I have seen in this country, and its old tumble down mansions, kindly screened in their raggedness by beautiful ever-greens which seem as old as the buildings themselves, appeared pre-ferable in my eyes to those execrable brick and marble perpetra-tions which distinguish Philadelphia in particular and most of the northern cities in general. The people appear to me to be nothing but indolent, at least hitherto that is the only impression they have made upon my mind, nor is this confined to the free lords and ladies of the land. They are imitated of course in this by their slaves, and such another *dawdling pottering* lazy lounging listless set of black and white folks I never saw. They talk of the luxurious mode of living in the South, because if you please you may have a slave to tie each of your shoes, but when all's said and done, you would have draped yourself from head to foot before your shoes were tied, and I should go mad if I was so well "waited upon."

As we have travelled without intermission night and day, I have not of course seen much and have little to tell you. One of our ad-ventures, however, was rather funny. Arriving at sundown after a hard day's journey over horrible roads at a place in the midst of a pine wilderness where we were to take the railroad to our next stopping place, we found that the cars had not come on and sat patiently waiting while the twilight came down and the bitter cold day grew into colder night in a place that seemed really the very outside and selvage of all creation. At length the gentlemen fear-ing lest we should have to pass the night in the woods with no better protection than the cold, ill-fastened stage coaches we were sitting in, piled us, the women and children (baggage properly so called) upon an open luggage car which stood on the railroad. Here we crouched among the trunks with our babies, and a score of stout negroes who were enlisted on the spot pushed the car along the railroad for about a mile to the residence of one Colonel Slocum, one of the most substantial gentlemen of that part of North Carolina at whose house it was thought we might obtain shelter for the night. After struggling through some dark fields and a nest of negro huts we arrive at an old discolored frame house into which I rushed at the head of the female rout and found the Colonel sitting by the light of a roaring pine wood fire in a large unplastered room hung round with all sorts of queer odd articles with a wooden table and chairs and a large coarse but comfortable looking bed for all furniture. The Colonel, a stout hale hearty old man with a red face and snow white hair, made us very welcome, bade us be seated and warmed, and seemed well prepared to house us for the night. He made us drink his homemade wine, pressed us even if the locomotive arrived (which it presently did) to stay and sup with him and wound up my enthusiasm to the very highest pitch by informing Pierce that he was one of the soldiers of the Revolution. Well we waited till far into the night for this supper which when it was forthcoming proved to be some tea very like dish water, half baked bread, and bad cheese, for which the Colonel *accepted half a dollar apiece from the whole company*. Furthermore, three of the black people who were trotting about among the rest of his slaves were the Colonel's own children, with which touch I will leave the Colonel's picture to your admiration.

Goodby dearest Saadi. I have written myself into something like good spirits, and being now come on board the steamboat which is to take us to Darien will go and lie down, because I have not slept for the last two nights.

After a torturous journey of eight days the Pierce Butlers, their two baby girls and Irish nurse arrived at Butler's Island. Fanny was nursing her nine months old baby, and often on the way from Philadelphia there had been no meal of any kind on their stopping for the night at some vile roadside inn. Occasionally there would be greasy dough and mangled greens for supper and then no breakfast, or "unnatural looking things." Fanny often sat up all night on stagecoach or train with the baby in her arms, and they changed three times onto steamers.

Before going south Fanny had promised Elizabeth Sedgwick (Mrs. Charles) to whom *A Residence on a Georgian Plantation* is dedicated that she would keep a journal on the plantation and record day by day what she did and saw. It is the only first-hand account by the wife of a slave holder of the negroes' lives on a plantation. It brings an Englishwoman's fresh perspective to the then-accepted custom of slavery and the never-to-end degradation of the slaves. Fanny describes their arrival on the plantation in this journal. Their last stop at a city was Savannah from where they took the steamer "Ocmulgee" to Darien.

On Sunday morning the day broke most brilliantly over those southern waters, and as the sun rose the atmosphere became clear and warm. At the mouth of the Altamaha is a small cluster of houses, scarce deserving the name of a village, called Doboy. At the wharf lay two trading vessels; the one with the harp of Ireland waving on her flag; the other with the Union Jack flying at her mast. I felt vehemently stirred to hail the beloved symbol, but upon reflection forbore outward demonstrations of the affectionate yearnings of my heart towards the flag of England, and so we boiled by them into this vast volume of turbid waters, whose noble width and rapid rolling current seem appropriately called by that most sonorous of indian names, the Altamaha. On either side lay the low, reedy swamps; yellow, withered Lilliputian forests, rattling their brittle canes in the morning breeze. Through these dreary banks we wound a most sinuous course for a long time. At length the irregular buildings of the little town of Darien appeared, and as we grazed the side of the wharf, it seemed to me as if we had touched the outer bound of civilized creation. As soon as we showed ourselves on the deck we were hailed by a shout from the men in two pretty boats which had pulled alongside of us, and the vociferations of "oh, massa! how you do, massa? Oh, missis! oh! lily missis! me too glad to see you!" accompanied with certain interjectional shrieks, whoops, whistles, and grunts, that could only be written down in negro language, made me aware of our vicinity to our journey's end. The strangeness of the whole scene, its wildness (for now beyond the broad river and the low swamp lands the savage-looking woods arose to meet the horizon) the rapid retrospect which my mind hurried through of the past few years of my life, the singular contrasts which they presented to my memory, the affectionate shouts of welcome the poor people, who seemed to hail us as descending divinities, affected me so much that I burst into tears and could hardly answer their demonstrations of delight. We were presently transferred into the larger boat and, the smaller one being freighted with our luggage, we pulled off from Darien, not, however, without a sage remark from Margery

that though we seemed to have travelled to the very end of the
world, here yet were people and houses, ships, and even steamboats,
in which evidences that we were not to be plunged into the deepest
abysses of savageness she seemed to take no small comfort.

We crossed the river and entered a small arm of it which presently became still narrower and more straight, assuming the appearance of an artificial cut or canal, which indeed it is, having been dug
by General Oglethorpe's men. The banks of this little canal were
mere dykes, guarding rice swamps, and presented no species of
beauty, but in the little creek from which we entered it I was
charmed with the beauty and variety of the evergreens growing in
thick and luxuriant underwood beneath giant, straggling cypress
trees whose branches were almost covered with the pendant wreaths
of gray moss peculiar to those southern woods. Of all parasitical
plants it assuredly is the most melancholy and dismal.

After emerging from the cut we crossed another arm of the
Altamaha—I should rather, perhaps, call them mouths, for this is
near its confluence with the sea, and these various branches are
formed by numerous sisterhood of small islands which divide this
noble river into three or four streams, each of them wider than
England's widest, the Thames. We now approached the low, reedy
banks of Butler's Island and passed the rice mill and buildings surrounding it, all of which, it being Sunday, were closed. As we
neared the bank the steersman took up a huge conch, and in the
barbaric fashion of early times in the Highlands, sounded out our
approach. A pretty schooner which carries the produce of the estate
to Charleston was crowded with negroes, jumping, dancing, shouting, laughing, and clapping their hands (a usual expression of delight
with savages and children) and using the most extravagant and
ludicrous gesticulations to express their ecstasy at our arrival.

On our landing from the boat, the crowd thronged about us like
a swarm of bees. We were seized, pulled, pushed, carried, dragged,
and all but lifted in the air by the clamorous multitude. I was afraid
my children would be smothered. Fortunately Mr. O——— the
overseer, and the captain of the little craft above-mentioned, came
to our assistance, and by their good offices the babies and nurse
were protected through the crowd. They seized our clothes, kissed
them, and then our hands, and almost wrung them off. One tall,
gaunt negress flew to us, parting the throng on either side, and embraced us in her arms. I believe I was almost frightened, and it was
not until we were safely housed, and the door shut upon our riotous

escort that we indulged in a fit of laughing, quite as full, on my part, of nervousness as amusement. Later in the day I attempted to take some exercise, and thought I had escaped observation, but before I had proceeded a quarter of a mile, I was again enveloped in a cloud of these dingy dependents who gathered round me, clamoring welcome, staring at me, stroking my velvet pelisse, and exhibiting at once the wildest delight and the most savage curiosity. I was obliged to relinquish my proposed walk and return home. Nor was the door of the room where I sat, and which was purposely left open, one moment free from crowds of eager faces, watching every movement of myself and the children until evening caused our audience to disperse. This zeal in behalf of an utter stranger merely because she stood to them in the relation of a mistress caused me not a little speculation. These poor people, however, have a very distinct notion of the duties which ownership should entail upon their proprietors, however these latter may regard their obligation towards their dependents, and as to their vehement professions of regard and affection for me, they reminded me of the saying of the satirist that "gratitude is a lively sense of benefits to come."

Nowhere on the three plantations was there a civilized dwelling for them. Miss Butler had allowed Major Butler's mansion to crumble into ruins, and none of the family had lived, except temporarily, on the plantation for nineteen years. Fanny and her family moved into the overseer's house, and he continued to sleep in a small room on the ground floor. Despite Pierce's great fortune, he did not consider building even a modest home for his family. Fanny had seen that the large houses in Charleston were dilapidated and that inertia and slackness were enveloping the South, but it was neverthe-less an anomaly that the Pierce Butlers should be living in an overseer's five room sleezy cottage. There was no other landed family in Georgia, the third generation of slave proprietors, living in such a fashion.

The heyday of slavery was on the wane when Pierce in-herited his grandfather's holdings. Major Butler's three plan-tations had been famous and self-sustaining. His long-stapled cotton was shipped directly to Liverpool in schooners owned by him. Nothing was bought; all food was grown and raised, simple agricultural tools were forged in the blacksmith shop, and even the machines for baling cotton were made on the plantation. However, these economic triumphs no longer could sustain the increasing negro population and provide the large profits of the past, and the struggle for gain became less easy.

Fanny took in her stride the appalling, primitive conditions which faced her as a housewife, and Pierce seemed complacent and utterly oblivious of them. While throughout the South the ladies on the plantations were living in pampered ease, high ceilinged, columned mansions lending shaded dignity to their idleness, Fanny was addressing herself to tasks not only considered beneath a white woman, but held as dangerous by contributing to the undermining of white supremacy. Fanny describes them, her house on the plantation, and her first sight of Butler's Island to Mrs. Henry Cleveland, and again the letter is dated in another hand:

January 15, 1839

I promised your husband that I would write to you as soon as I arrived at the end of my journey, and the time which has intervened since my reaching this place being no more than a reasonable interval for the drawing of my breath and looking around me, I proceed to inform you of our safe descent upon Butler's Island, which is quite the most amphibious piece of creation that I have yet had the happiness of beholding. It would be difficult to define it truly by either the name of land or water, for 'tis neither liquid nor solid but a kind of mud sponge floating on the bosom of the Altamaha, of whose sandy sediment it is chiefly formed and into whose turbid, brimming waters it looks as if it was again about to dissolve. The produce of this delectable spot is rice—oranges, negroes, fleas, mosquitoes, various beautiful evergreens, sundry sort of snakes, alligators, and bull rushes enough to have made cradles not for Moses alone but the whole Israelitish host besides.

Now for our abode—it is as luxurious as its site (upon the edge of a ditch) is desirable. We have a whitewashed apartment fifteen feet by sixteen which serves us for dining room, drawing room, and library. Next to this is a rather smaller room where Pierce and I sleep, beyond this a small place where he dresses and transacts business with the negroes, and above our parlour and under the roof, a room where Margery and the two children are stowed. Our furniture is scanty in quantity and most primitive in quality; some of our wash-hand stands being made of unpainted wood. Then we have exceedingly dirty negroes in abundance to wait upon us whose want of cleanliness and profound ignorance made it infinitely less troublesome to wait upon oneself. My occupations in this Paradise of delights are various—from washing dirty little negro babies in the hospital to transplanting evergreens out of the swamps to the rice banks in the immediate vicinity of the house. For exercise I scramble along the said rice banks which are full of holes and overnetted with briars about three feet wide, with sometimes the river on one hand and a ditch on the other, and sometimes a pestilential looking swamp on either side. Of course riding is out of the question, but I have taken to rowing as we have beautiful little boats and a river of magnificent width.

You will be glad to hear that Pierce seems better and that the children are both well. The climate is so warm that Sarah is out from morning till night with bare head, neck, and arms. Indeed to me it is as debilitating as your northern summer, and I should infinitely prefer the weather of Vermont just now to that which we have here.

Though Fanny had at once felt the injustice of slavery when first she was told about it in America, and though she had many times discussed the question with the Reverend Channing and the Reverend Furness, Pierce, when she married him, was not the legal owner of slaves but merely his grandfather's designated heir. She was going to live in Philadelphia, and the question was not immediate. Despite writing to the Combes about slavery, it could not have been a reality to her until she arrived at the plantation. Then she found herself imprisoned among eight hundred negroes, her presence countenancing what she had declared herself against. It would have been expedient and wiser for her to eat her words and in silence bear that which she could not change. But Pierce had been wrong when he assumed that she was made of the same stuff as the women of his narrow acquaintance.

On her arrival at the plantation, Fanny, ignoring southern tradition, went into the slave cabin used as a hospital where there was neither a doctor nor nurse, and the negroes lay on the earthen floor dying in their filth. They were the old as well as the newborn. Fanny, unafraid, was not paralyzed by what she saw, nor did she faint from what she smelled, but bathed the infants and administered to the utmost of her ability to the sick. She never dwells in her letters or Journal on her fortitude but says once, "you must admit I have a strong stomach."

In her months on the plantation she devoted herself to the slaves' welfare. She was the first wife of an owner to teach a negro to read, which was forbidden by law, and to labor for the slaves, thus reversing tenets of an established tradition as old as slavery in America. This set her apart, and she was hated by the Southerners even before she had published any anti-slavery articles. She showed then to her husband and the whole South that she held her conscience above worldly compromise. To her the slave was a human being, as worthy as herself of a place in the world, who must be given freedom, religion, and education. She worked, fearless of disease, heedless that she was causing bitter resentment and anger among other slaveholders and restlessness among the negroes who looked upon her as a benefactress and worshipped her. To them she was a symbol of hope as well as a means, by playing on her feelings, of escaping their mandatory duties.

She was at first unable to grasp the fact that her husband, merely part of an economic system, could not control the inhuman but accepted practices of the South. She besought him on her knees to give up age-old standard brutal customs and was stunned to find that she could achieve nothing for the slaves of true value. He told her that the plantation would not pay if he gave in to her childish meddling, and her pleadings led to marital scenes. Pierce Butler was living with her, and on the plantation he saw her only as aggravatingly tearful and wrongfully sentimental about his concerns. No woman should intervene in what was not her province and so hinder her husband's interests. As a wife, mute acceptance and obedience in all things must be her role. Her feelings and attitude towards the slaves were beyond his comprehension. It was a far, far cry for his young wife from the stage of Covent Garden to the Georgian plantation. One night in anger and hysteria she rowed alone from Butler's Island to Darien on the mainland, but finding no steamer, returned. This may have been the result of her pleading with Pierce in a particular instance for a woman slave who had been forced to return to the cotton fields immediately after a miscarriage, or it may have been the discovery that he was living with a negress. Fanny gives no account of this episode, but Pierce attributes it to her unreasonable temper. He could not foresee that in twenty-three years the North would answer her prayers and go to war.

After this winter of severe emotional stress in Georgia with repeated major quarrels, the Butlers returned to Butler Place in March, 1839. Fanny had made the most of the outdoor life possible on the plantation. She had learned to row a boat, gone fishing, transplanted blooming shrubs from marshy banks of the many inlets and jungle-like stretches of drier land to add fragrance to the surroundings of the overseer's cottage. She had lived both on Butler's Island and St. Simon's Island in cottages of equal disrepair, and she had written her Journal.

Though loneliness and isolation engulfed Fanny when she moved to Butler Place, and the six miles of muddy or dusty road to Philadelphia certainly cut her off from the to-her-minor festivities of that city, she occasionally went to parties. She never bothered to describe or mention them because to her they were small potatoes, and she did not make an effort to seek friendship among the women. This was typically British. The Sedgwick family of Boston, introduced to her by Miss Catherine Sedgwick the diarist who had at once recognized Fanny as a gifted human being, was sensitive and cultivated, of broader outlook than the Philadelphians whom she met, and Philadelphia had no Dr. Channing to come to call. But there was Sidney George Fisher, a well born articulate Philadelphian who was one year older than Fanny and who kept a diary in which the current activities of society and happenings in the city and countryside were recorded. He writes of seeing Fanny at parties where Pierce must have taken her, although Fisher only once mentions him. Fanny is included in his various entries beginning in 1837. Sometimes he writes several admiring sentences and sometimes merely gives her name among the guests. He never speaks of her as being stiff, aloof, or of looking down on her surroundings or making uncomplimentary statements about her new life. No one found Fanny conceited. Fanny never speaks of the public displeasure with her *American Journal* which had come out only two years previously, nor does Fisher give an opinion of it, so it did not mark her at parties as either one to be shunned or made much of. Fisher never writes of entertainments at Butler Place and had there been any he would have been among the guests. When the Butlers first moved to Butler Place Pierce was living on his expectations, but by 1839 he had inherited his grandfather's fortune, had not had time to squander it, and why they did not undertake to return accepted hospitality is impossible to understand. The following are the longest entries in Fisher's diary, but he speaks of having seen her three or four other times:

October 24, 1839

Weather today warm and sultry. At 11 drove with Fisher [Joshua Francis] and his wife in Harrison's [George] carriage out to Mrs. Pierce Butler's, a visit we have projected for some time. First time I ever called there, tho I ought to have done so years ago, as I knew her when Fanny Kemble, and since her marriage have met her often. She is a very gifted person, and her qualities of heart and character are as excellent as those of her intellect. We staid an hour, had some animated talk, and a warm discussion on the nature of true art. We had a very pleasant visit. They were very gracious. They are very rich and live in handsome style. The place tho it possesses no advantages of situation, is surrounded by fine trees and the grounds are admirably kept.

April 19, 1840

Stopped at Wakefield. Mrs. Fanny Butler was there, on horseback and alone. She is very independent and rides about constantly unattended. Had some agreeable talk and accompanied her home. Never saw her look so well. Her costume was becoming and peculiar. A green cloth riding habit with rolling collar and open in front, under it a *man's* waistcoat with rolling collar, yellow and gilt buttons, a calico shirt collar and breast, blue striped and turned over and a black silk cravat tied sailor fashion, with a man's hat and a veil. She was mounted on a beautiful horse highly groomed. Rode with her up to the house but did not go in, as I was in a hurry to get to town. Their place looked very well. It has no natural beauties, but is kept in admirable order, and is surrounded by many and fine trees. The avenue of maples and the hedges are things not often seen here and add greatly to its attractions. When we went in, there were five or six men employed about the grounds.

On January 2, 1840 Fisher mentioned seeing Fanny at a supper party at Dr. Randolph's (probably Dr. Jacob), and on January 28, 1840 he "went to a musical party at Mrs. Nick Biddle's. Mrs. Pierce Butler played on the piano."

In the autumn of 1839, Pierce, after a long rheumatic illness during which for no good reason the Pierce Butlers again moved in with the John Butlers, finally recovered and with his brother went south without Fanny. He was afraid to take her back on account of the unrest she had caused among the negroes and the animosity towards her among the neighboring plantation owners. After Pierce's departure she went back to Butler Place with the two little girls. That summer she hoped to visit Mrs. Henry Cleveland and writes to her on Tuesday, June 2, 1840, and for the first time makes clear to her friend that she and her husband are not happy. Fanny begins by making plans for a visit, but there are complications.

All this, however, depends entirely on Mr. Butler's movements. Should he alter his mind about going to Virginia or imagine by accident that my society and that of his children would be desirable, then it will not be possible for me to come to you. I do not, however, anticipate any such events.

I should dearly love to see Boston again and all the haunts made happy in my memory by their association with the season of my courtship, for which golden time of my existence I have a most melancholy and reverential affection.

Fanny at about this time wrote to Kate Sedgwick who was travelling in Germany and not yet married.

> June 20, 1840
> [in another hand]

But do you know, Kate, that external material objects, provided that they are as God has for the most part made them, fair, satisfy me wonderfully? As I held these first violets in my hand it seemed to me that I liked them better than husband or child, and I have felt a positive thrill in watching shadow and sunshine in hill country which nothing but some moral beauty should cause. I am sure I am half pixie or brownie or gnome or elf and shall evaporate when I die; I mean that portion of me which most resembles spirit into mere matter—water, light, etc.

The source from whence people are to draw their happiness depends infinitely on their education and habits. If the intellect and the taste have been cultivated, I may say pampered, and the healthy affections of our nature starved and suffered to diminish, the individual thus educated should certainly not in the hope of finding happiness place themselves in a situation where their *only* enjoyments must be those of the affections. To this point I can speak above all living, in whom a violent passion which has scarce grown into anything deserving a calmer name for the man I married. A fortunate portion in point of worldly matters and the blessing of two precious children have yet failed to destroy the painful recollection of all that ministered to the intellect, the taste, the imagination in my former existence—all of ideal, refined, noble, beautiful and grand in society, in art and nature in those lands where I was born and nurtured. Now, putting aside my attachment for Pierce and my love for my children, there are besides the elements in my character which cause me to regret Europe, others which help me to appreciate, honor, admire, and even love America.

In November, 1840 Fanny received word that her father was seriously ill, and she and Pierce and the children sailed for England on December first.

CHAPTER VII

The Pierce Butlers In London

The Pierce Butlers stayed for three years in London. On their arrival Fanny was in poor health as a result of a terrible December crossing and in poor spirits because the situation between Pierce and herself did not improve.

Pierce Butler immersed himself in London society. It was only because of Fanny that they were invited to stay at the great country houses of her titled friends and were included in large dinner parties and balls. It is likely that he gambled at cards, although there is no mention of this by Fanny now or at any other time, but for three years he was totally idle in London, living on the pleasures that did not exist in the United States. Pierce was invited out to dinner by Trelawney on his arrival, and according to Fanny, owing to the rich food of London had to consult a surgeon about his stomach.

Pierce, Fanny, Charles Kemble, and her younger sister, Adelaide, all went to the Duke of Wellington's ball given in honor of the King of Prussia. Fanny was introduced to the Duke whom she had only seen in 1830 in Liverpool when he was in the car ahead of her at the official opening of the Stephenson railroad.

Among the house parties they attended was one at Belvoir, the castle of the Duke of Rutland, of which she says, "The whole mode of life is stately and splendid." Fanny found "the society very easy and free from stiffness or constraint of any sort." On this same house party were the Duke and Duchess of Bedford, the Duchess of Richmond, and Lord and Lady Winchelsea. Fanny says in *Records of Later Life,* "Every morning the Duke's band marched around the castle playing all sorts of sprightly music to summon us to breakfast, and we had the same agreeable warning that dinner was ready."

It was at Belvoir that Fanny was first introduced to afternoon tea, which the Duchess served to the women guests of the castle in her own room, using her own tea kettle.

Fanny wrote to Cecy Combe on July 16, 1841:

> I think you will not be sorry to hear from me if it is only on account of the excellent report I can make of my father. He now seems entirely recovered, cheerful and free from pain and wonderfully active considering the utter prostration from which he is only so lately restored. Our prima donna [her sister Adelaide] has come back to us not *like* my mother only, but literally my mother herself. Her plans for the winter are at present undecided. My husband continues to amuse himself here, and I think it extremely possible now that we shall spend the winter in Europe, very probably in Paris. My children thrive and flourish, and I am of course in no particular hurry to cross the Atlantic again while they are well and my husband well satisfied. Since my beginning this letter to you my sister's plans have so far assumed a more definite shape that she has determined to make her debut at Covent Garden this winter where she has accepted a short engagement upon very advantageous terms.

Fanny kept up her letters to Kate Sedgwick, who was her age, and on August 4, 1841 wrote her from London:

> The season for my return to America grows more and more indefinite. My husband himself does not know, having I am very sure, made up no mind whatever upon the subject. I am sure that you will be glad to hear from me that we are all going together to Germany in about a month. My sister is not inclined to pass the whole summer without employing her talents rather more profitably than merely amusing her friends as she has been doing ever since her return from Italy. She will probably go leisurely down the Rhine giving concerts wherever it may suit her purpose to do so. Liszt, the great pianist, has advised her to do this and will probably join her in the professional part of her tour. As for Pierce and myself, we are too glad to have such a motive as accompanying her, to see the Rhine and all that may come in our way of the picturesque or interesting.
>
> My father is now completely recovered. He will, however, require all his physical faculties in all their strength, for I fear he will be obliged to resume his profession at least occasionally; the little property that he had realized being lodged in the United States Bank,

where in common with the worldly dependence of hundreds of others, it has suffered irretrievable shipwreck.

Charles Kemble had put part of his earnings from his American tour in the United States Bank in Philadelphia. This was a private bank owned by Mr. Nicholas Biddle which failed.

The Butlers went by boat up the Rhine with Adelaide in the early autumn of 1841. Charles Kemble was with them for only a few days as he was again manager of Covent Garden, but there were several friends who joined them temporarily, among them Fanny's brother, Henry, and Mary Anne Thackeray, sister of the novelist, and Henry Chorley, music critic of the Athenaeum.

Fanny, in her published letters to Harriet in *Records of Later Life* goes into many flowery, lengthy, and rhapsodic descriptions of cathedrals, towns, and scenery that she saw during the Rhine tour, as she was trying as always to amuse, instruct and divert Harriet. Fanny did not keep a journal after her *Journal of a Residence on a Georgian Plantation,* and it was forty years later that she says in *Records of Later Life,* "Our whole expedition partook more of the character of a party of pleasure than a business speculation, and though Liszt's and my sister's musical performances were professional exhibitions of the highest order, the relations of our whole party were those of the friendliest and merriest tourists and compagnons de voyage."

The most important person in their compagnie de voyage was Franz Liszt. He was 31 years old, a giant in the music world, and at the height of his career as a performer. From the keyboard in never before heard tones he proclaimed his unrestrained masculine prowess. He was creating a new horizon for the pianoforte and liberating it from the pedantic. He stirred his audiences to frenzy. His flights beyond tradition overcame female decorum. Women, old, young, single, and married were making hysterical fools of themselves about him, swooning at his feet and dying for love of him the way they had for Lord Byron. The Kemble sisters did not fling themselves at any man and were not victims of the famed charms of the flamboyant genius in their midst. Fanny, out of love with Pierce and steeped in anguish, had no thought of furtive romantic dalliance. No more fortunate beginning to Adelaide's career as a prima donna could have been wished for her than to sing on the same program as Liszt. Crowded houses were assured, and her merit established by his sharing concerts with her.

What was described to Harriet as a leisurely, idyllic, sun-spangled interlude in Fanny's emotionally tattered existence was in reality filled with such discord between the Butlers that the journey only glossed over the continuing disunity of their marriage. Liszt's presence and the many times she heard him play did not dispel for Fanny her deep woe. She did not speak of Liszt at first hand in her letters to her friends the way she had spoken of Trelawney in her *American Journal* on the trip up the Hudson. She took for granted that all those she wrote to knew all about Liszt and did not pause in her letters to report conversations or describe immediate happenings. Not until 1870 in Munich did she see Liszt again when at the opera with her daughter, Sarah, and son-in-law, Dr. Owen Jones Wister, and then wrote of him, describing him on the Rhine tour: "Liszt was at this time a young man, in the very perfection of his extraordinary talent, and at the height of his great celebrity. He was extremely handsome; his features were finely chiselled, and the expression of his face, especially when under the inspiration of playing, strikingly grand and commanding."

Fanny wrote Kate Sedgwick on October 22, 1841:

Here we are in our new home [a house rented at 81 Harley Street] just returned from our German trip. We went a large party together, and this which is a source of pleasure is also a possible one of pains. Our children were with us whose little inconveniences I am by no means philosophical about, and a due consideration of all these circumstances made me reasonable enough in my anticipation of enjoyment. There were events, however, which took place during our stay abroad of so painful a nature as to render even the recollection of one part of our pilgrimage most unwelcome.

We did not join my sister till we got to Frankfort after which we continued with her nearly all the time. She sang and acted at Frankfort, at Mayents, at Wiesbaden, at Cologne, at Aix La Chapelle, and

Liege with very great success, generally beginning by appearing at a concert with Liszt, the great pianist, and then singing the Norma and the Somnambula. She is now most busily preparing for her debut at Covent Garden which takes place on Monday week when she will sing the Norma in English.

Pierce has such a nervous horror of his health being discussed that I almost feel I ought not to mention it. He is better just now than during the latter part of our stay in Germany. The fact is that I believe his stomach is the seat of almost all his disorders, for the unwholesome cooking there affected him as he believes unfavorably, and he thinks he perceives a change for the better even in these few days return to our extremely plain English mode of living. It is singular enough too, but this climate appears to agree very well with him. The damp does not affect him as I should have supposed it might.

I wish I were at home, dear Kate; the wish is a strong conviction of what I think would be best that expresses itself like a desire. I do not wish you to imagine that I am longing for the farm, but I cannot but think it would have been better had we been there—I may be mistaken however.

When Fanny writes of "events of a painful nature" she must be referring to unpleasant scenes between herself and Pierce, but there is no clue as to the cause. Perhaps he saw some woman who attracted him and began paying attentions to her which were remarked by their fellow passengers or by hotel guests. There could have been no opportunity for gambling on a large scale, and surely, marital difficulties which Fanny did not allude to were the reason that she did not fully enjoy what should have been a delightful excursion.

Despite these laments to Kate and the increasing quarrels and misunderstandings between Pierce and Fanny, she often enjoyed herself during these three years in England. In May, 1842, Pierce is going, apparently regularly, to the Prince Consort's Levees, and the Duke of Rutland told Fanny that Queen Victoria had asked him why she had not been presented at Court. Fanny makes light of this invitation, saying that it is surely only the Queen's curiosity which prompted her to speak to the Duke. Fanny had overspent her dress allowance; this is the only time that she ever speaks of extravagance, and she had to ask Pierce if he would allow her to rent a diamond necklace. Pierce gave his consent, and she ordered, as she calls them, "my tail and my top, train and feathers" and went. Fanny says, "I suffered agonies of nervousness." That was because Fanny, although experienced as an actress, had the humble British veneration for her sovereign, and the occasion was no pleasure to her. Again she says, "a cat may look at a King, it is said, but how about looking at *the* Queen." This, of course, was the peak of her social success as a married woman.

The Butlers continued with their festive life except when Fanny was in such bad spirits that he went out without her. The following spring when Pierce had at last made up his mind to return to America the Butlers gave "our first grand party of the season" attended by nearly 200 people, with Irish jack o'lanterns as decoration; both Adelaide and Fanny sang to the guests, and there were six policemen at the door. This was followed by another large evening party of not quite such elegance. Then in a few days Fanny went to a party at Henry Chorley's house. At the party was "dear Mendelssohn" who played, and Fanny read some scenes from "Much Ado About Nothing." This is the first time that Fanny ever speaks of reading, and she was doing what she so vehemently disagreed about with Channing in their initial conversation ten years before, reading part of a Shakespearean play.

Adelaide had a great success at her debut in London, creating the role of Norma for Covent Garden, and the Duke of Wellington came to call and gave her a bracelet. For a time Adelaide, Fanny's father, and his sister-in-law, Victoire Decamp, lived with the Butlers.

Pierce says scornfully in his "Statement," published privately by him in his defense against Fanny Kemble in the divorce, that living with her family around her did not content Fanny. In order to follow their crumbling marriage, exerpts from his "Statement" must now be included to illustrate the abyss which separated the Butlers. The statement is an attractive, slim volume of 183 pages bound in red leather which he presented to his friends.

The first major clash between them was caused by her insistence on publishing her *American Journal*. She spent eight months in 1836 with the baby in London visiting her parents. The winter in Georgia was one of terrible scenes between Fanny and Pierce; it was the second major crisis. The following winter he spent in Georgia without her, and she was alone at Butler Place. In the spring of 1840 he went alone to the Virginia Hot Springs for his rheumatism, and she visited the Sedgwicks. Their seven years of marriage were years of constant strife.

In his "Statement" he declared his conception of marriage, from which he was incapable of yielding an inch. Fanny's conception of marriage was the antithesis of his. Pierce writes, "one reason, and perhaps the fundamental one, for the ill success which attended my marriage, will readily be found in the peculiar views which were entertained by Mrs. Butler on the subject of marriage and her unwillingness to abide by the express and inculcated obligations of that contract. She held that marriage should be companionship on equal terms—partnership, in which if both partners agree, it is well, but if they do not, neither is bound to yield—and that at no time has one partner a right to control the other." It was the misfortune meted out to Fanny by Providence that her husband should hold these views as well as being an unsuccessful gambler at cards and on the stock market.

Pierce's "Statement" continues: "One painful subject of difference between us was that of negro slavery. Although we resided in Pennsylvania where slavery does not exist, the greater part of my property lies in the state of Georgia and consists of plantations and negroes. Mrs. Butler, after our marriage, not before, declared herself to be in principle an abolitionist and her opinions were frequently expressed in a violent and offensive manner. This was grievous enough to bear; however, I seldom opposed or combatted them, but when it came to the point of publishing her sentiments, I offered the most unqualified opposition to it."

It was in London during Adelaide's triumphs that the third terrible disagreement between the Butlers took place. Pierce says:

An occurence took place during my second visit to England when I was residing with my family in London, 1841. A lady [Mrs. John Child], editing an anti-slavery paper in New York, wrote to Mrs. Butler and asked as a contribution, for some portions of a Journal which it was understood she had kept while in Georgia. Again I used entreaty and remonstrance to induce her to disregard this request or to refuse it, but as on the former occasion, it was to no purpose. This lady was a stranger to her, except by name, yet she immediately assented to her wishes and wrote her the following letter:

81 Harley St.
Tuesday, November 2, 1841

My dear Madam,

That part of my southern journal which was written on my husband's slave estates would be, I suppose, at once the most interesting and the most useful to the publication for which you request me to furnish you matter, but I do not feel at liberty to give that to the public, or I should have done so long ago. It is possible, however, that what I wrote on my way to Mr. Butler's plantation may be of use or interest to you, and that I should be very happy to place at your disposal. This would consist of about four or five longish letters containing the account of my journey from Philadelphia to Georgia, in the course of which some observations on the effects of slavery as they were apparent wherever I went necessarily occur. I am sorry that it is not in my power to do more than this, and only hope that what I offer may prove of the least use to you. Pray let me know, if you accept this, how I shall get it conveyed to you.

I am, my dear Madam
Yours truly,
Fanny Butler

The above was the first of many letters to Mrs. Child and others that Pierce printed in his "Statement." "This letter, together with several others, was given to me by Mrs. Butler for the purpose of being sealed and forwarded as was her custom. I intentionally omitted sending it and threw it into a drawer of my writing table where it was found by her after a lapse of some weeks. When she understood that I had purposely kept it back, she evinced anger." Pierce did not tell Fanny that he would not mail the letter to Mrs. Child. Fearing a scene, he hid it, so allowing Mrs. Child to believe that Fanny would not answer her. How did he know what was in the letter? He read it of course.

Then why did he say "she immediately assented to her wishes," when Fanny, as the letter proves, had told Mrs. Child that she would not send her the diary she kept on the Georgian plantation, but instead offered her some letters like the letter she wrote to Mrs. Cleveland describing her journey to Georgia with only a few generalizations about the slaves she had seen during her journey. Why did Pierce keep a copy of the letter for seven years and include it in his "Statement" at the time of his divorce? He offers no explanation. The result of this surreptitious and dishonorable action by Pierce in hiding her letter and not telling her led to a major crisis in the Butlers' marriage.

All of this was going on between Pierce and Fanny while Adelaide was making her successful debut at Covent Garden, and Fanny was attending the performances. It was common knowledge in Fanny's circle in London that she and Pierce were quarreling. She says in her letters that often for days at a time she hardly saw him and that he was amusing himself. Surely her father must have heard from her and also seen that there was grave trouble between them.

Pierce Butler continues in his "Statement" to say that Fanny without any explanation fled the house and went to Liverpool, taking their oldest child with her. This was because the serious trouble about the letter to Mrs. Child was still hanging over her, and Pierce often went out without her, and they had many bitter scenes. Pierce continues in his "Statement," referring to a second letter which Fanny had written to Mrs. Child, and which he was afraid would be published: "I scarcely knew what to do but resolved on an effort to prevent the catastrophe. I accordingly wrote to a lady in this country [U.S.A.], Mrs. MacIntosh, [Mary Appleton, sister of Mrs. Longfellow] a friend of Mrs. Butler's and an acquaintance, as I believed, of the editress. I detailed the circumstances and asked her to request the editress not to publish Mrs. Butler's communication, or at least not to do so without an express sanction from Mrs. Butler. I begged her to write to Mrs. Butler, strongly urging her not to allow the letter to be printed and advising her against contributing to the paper."

After the clash about the letter to Mrs. Child Fanny wrote to Katherine Sedgwick, now the wife of William Minot:

Wednesday, March 2, 1842

As to my coming home, my dear Kate, as you so affectionately [word missing] it is long since I have given up all idea of doing so at any given time. Mr. Butler keeps me in the most profound ignorance of his mind upon all subjects. I think it more than probable that he has no definite idea at all of returning at any particular season, and I am sad to see how well content he is for the sake of present amusement to leave country and kindred for so long a time.

My dear friend, you may remember the affection I long ago expressed for the beautiful slope that rises from the north side of the Mountain Mirror up to the road that heads the lake. I want you to find out for me what a piece of land going straight down from that road to the margin of the lake and of about three acres breadth would cost. I never passed that spot without thinking that were I to choose my place of residence at a future time, it would be there, both on account of the loveliness of the place itself and its near proximity to your family, who in America are my dearest friends.

I do not wish either you or Lizzie to imagine worse things with regard to me than are really true. My case at present is this—having found a letter of mine to Mrs. Child (the abolitionist) together with one I had written long ago to Lizzy, both lying in Mr. Butler's secretary, I took them and put them into the post, resolving at the same time never to entrust my letters to him again. Upon my informing him, however, that I had put these letters into the post, he replied that my sending that letter to Mrs. Child put an end to our living together and that henceforth we were parted as man and wife. Of course I cannot be maintained by a man who casts me off from him as wife, neither can I under *any circumstances of misery whatever* give my conscience into the keeping of another human being or submit the actions dictated by my conscience to their will. Therefore at present the only prospect before me is to return to the stage for a year, in which time I can earn an abundant competence for the rest of my life in Berkshire where I think I have a better chance of building out of the fragments of my happiness a fabric at least of peace and repose. Therefore, find out for me, I beg my dear friend, what such a plot of land would cost in that situation. Tell me too what would be the utmost cost of erecting a house of about the same dimension as your own, and tell me after that what yearly sum would feed me and a couple of servants a year in that place. All this I have to know as accurately and with as much detail as you can give it to me. It may be too that in my husband's mind may come enlightenment to the perception of justice, the holiness of moral freedom, and the sacredness of conscientious action. God bless you all—Keep this, I beg, to yourself.

A short time later Fanny wrote to Mrs. Child:

> 81 Harley St.
> Friday, April 1, 1842
>
> Madam,
> I must request that you will have the kindness not to publish the letter which I wrote you about a short time ago, and at the same time must inform you that I intend to break my promise with regard to the papers which I promised to furnish you for publication upon the subject of my southern journey. I can add nothing to this but the assurance that however great your contempt may be for my want of purpose, or your indignation for this proceeding, it cannot possibly exceed my own.
>
> I am, Madam
> Yours truly,
> Fanny Butler

So Fanny gave in to Pierce and sent nothing to Mrs. Child for her magazine. The months following this altercation were dreadful ones for Fanny. When the lease expired on the house on Harley Street, Pierce Butler, unwilling to return to America, moved into the Clarendon Hotel. In July Fanny wrote to Kate Minot:

> I have nothing to tell you, my dear Kate, that can interest or amuse you. I am declining all invitations into society, for my spirits are bad and my heart heavy, and I do not feel inclined to make the effort necessary to conceal this fact.

The following winter Charles Greville, the noted diarist and man-about-town in London who had followed Fanny's career from the beginning, wrote:

> December 8, 1842 . . . I have been seeing lately a great deal of Mrs. Butler, whose history is a melancholy one, a domestic tragedy without any tragical events. She went to America ten years ago in

the high tide of her popularity and when she was making a fortune. There, Pierce Butler fell in love with her, and she fell in love with him. She gave up her earnings (£6000) to her father, left the stage, married, and settled in America. And now, after wasting the best years of her life in something very like solitude near Philadelphia with two children, whom she is passionately fond of, what is her situation? She has discovered that she has married a weak, dawdling, ignorant, violent tempered man, who is utterly unsuited to her, and she to him, and she is aware that she has outlived his liking, as he has outlived her esteem and respect. With all her prodigious talents, her fine feelings, noble sentiments, and lively imagination, she has no tact, no judgment, no discretion. She has acted like a fool, and he is now become a brute. The consequence is she is supremely and hopelessly wretched. She sees her husband brutal and unkind to her, ruining himself and their children by his lazy, stupid management of his affairs and she lives in perpetual terror lest her alienation should at last mount to such a height that their living together may become impossible, and that then she shall be separated from her children for whom alone she desires to exist. Among the most prominent causes of their disunion is her violent and undisguised detestation of slavery while he is a great slave proprietor. She has evinced the feeling (laudable in itself) without a particle of discretion, and it has given him deep offense. . . .

In April, 1843, Pierce says in his "Statement" that he wrote her the following in a letter, of which he must have kept a copy:

On my soul and conscience I have done everything in my power to make you happy and contented as my wife. I have not succeeded, God knows, but if I have not, at least I can console myself with the knowledge of having done all that I could, and the firm conviction that the fault is not with me. The fault has been entirely your own. If you will govern your irritable temper, and if you can consent to submit your will to mine, we may be reconciled and may be happy. I firmly believe that husband and wife cannot live happily together unless upon a clear understanding of the conditions I propose, and a full determination to abide by them."

Fanny would not be controlled. She was not an underling and could not change her nature any more than he could change his. She fled the apartment in the Clarendon Hotel and took refuge with her sister, Adelaide, who gave up the operatic stage after one year and had married Edward John

Sartoris early in 1843. She wrote Pierce, "Save yourself and me, Pierce, and our darling children from a ruin worse than any worldly beggary, from self-condemnation of each other, from a daily and hourly departure further and further from all noble and holy influences." These resounding sentences echo her early years in Covent Garden and the contemporary tragedies the Kembles had played for four generations. She continues in the same letter, "Having loved you, you can never be to me like any other being. It is utterly impossible that I should ever regard you with indifference. My whole existence, having had you for its sole object, and all its thoughts, hopes, affections and passions having in their full harvest been yours, as you well know they were, it is utterly impossible I should forget this. Such love as mine has been for you might in evil hearts and by evil means be turned to hatred, but be sure it never can become hatred."

Pierce says that it was in April that he wrote her the letter about her being controlled by him, but it must have been during the winter because Fanny wrote to Kate Minot:

26 Upper Grosvenor St.
February 3, 1843

I am happy to tell you that I am just now in better plight than I have been now for many months, chiefly thro' the instrumentality of Mary MacIntosh. The terrible and long-enduring difference between my husband and myself has been adjusted, and for the first time for many a day I am possessing my soul in peace and breathing an atmosphere of affection and happiness. Mary herself whose ministry in this has certainly been most blessed has I fear gone thro' some most bitter experiences of a similar kind.

My father about whom we have suffered much alarm and anxiety this winter is recovering wonderfully and bids fair to regain for perhaps some years a state of health which will admit of his enjoying his existence in very tolerable comfort. My sister is going on prosperously in her new home and with her new husband. They have both of them sweet dispositions and are at present very happy.

Our departure from England is now fixed at the middle of April. The house we are now in will then be claimed by its rightful owners who let it only while they are out of town, but experience has taught me that while that most commodious hostelry, the Clarendon, is above ground, our leaving our house is no earthly reason why we should leave England. . . . . .

CHAPTER VIII

Separation and Divorce

In May 1843 the Butlers returned to America to live in a boarding house in Philadelphia. It was cheaper than trying to run Butler Place which was then rented, and Pierce's fortune was diminishing rapidly. Their reconciliation in London, the result of Mrs. MacIntosh reasoning with them, did not last long. Pierce in the divorce case says they "resumed marital relations and were happier together than they had been in years." In the summer Pierce sent Fanny and the children to Yellow Springs, about thirty miles from Philadelphia. Then he ordered them back to town in the extreme heat. Fanny wanted to go to visit the Sedgwick family at Lenox but could not leave the children as they both had been sick.

After this brief interlude, there was nothing but discord between the Butlers. In November, 1844 she wrote to Mrs. Cleveland who was in Rome:

> I take blame to myself for not sooner having answered your affectionate letter from St. Goar. It is very true I am sure that you care to hear from me, and yet it seems almost like bringing the dim darkness and narrow bounds and noisome atmosphere of a prison across your present free, bright and beautiful existence to conjure up before you my image struggling with injustice and wickedness in all the petty details of little vexations and malice as well as the more cruel anguish they have inflicted upon me in my separation from my children. They and I have, as I suppose you know, left the wretched house where you last saw me. They to take up their abode in their father's house, and I to establish myself in the nearest boarding house that I could find in their neighborhood where they visit me for an hour every day, and this is the purpose and sole object of my existence—to retain this wretched portion of intercourse allowed me with my children. Mr. Butler having exacted that I should *not* go to New-

port by threatening if I did so to keep the children all the summer in Philadelphia, I was obliged to give up the lodgings I had been retaining there for two whole months in the vain expectation of being with my children, and when they had left town I went up to Lenox. Here, dear Saadi, I enjoyed peace and that infinite delight of existing for a while in a perfect atmosphere of love.

What shall I tell you of myself. I am very sad, my life of trial and perpetual irritation as well as deep and fatal disappointment is I think exhausting by degrees my wonderful strength and vitality. I am weak and languid, nervous and spiritless, and have a sense of weariness unspeakable, and yet I feel I must in no wise give way to this but resist it with all my might, for I suppose worse days to be in store for me than any I have yet known. I see my children but an hour a day, and every conceivable measure is resorted to to detach them from me as much as possible; all of which is merely preparatory to Mr. Butler's taking them abroad with him in the Spring of next year when I suppose I must look forward to losing them utterly unless some supreme interposition of providence should save me from a misery.

In the Spring of 1844 Fanny went riding with Mr. Sidney George Fisher who was still keeping his diary. He wrote:

Yesterday rode out with Mrs. Butler to Champlost [the home of the Fox family near Butler Place]. Got a tolerable nag from Duffy and had a pleasant ride. Mrs. B. is an agreeable companion but does not interest me. She is too prononcée, wants delicacy and refinement, and is the reverse of feminine in her manners and conversation. She is also guilty of the imprudence and bad taste of alluding constantly to her domestic troubles, which I believe are brought about by her own want of tact and temper. She has talent, however, and converses well. She has seen the best English society, and her descriptions of men and manners are very interesting. What a different and superior existence do they exhibit to anything here, or anything that can possibly exist here for many a long and troublous year.

While staying with the Sedgwicks at the end of the summer Fanny again saw Charles Sumner, who as a student in Boston had admired her acting though he did not know her. A letter from him to Dr. Samuel G. Howe written from Pittsfield on September 11, 1844 speaks of Fanny:

Tomorrow I move to Lenox where I sojourn with the Wards [Samuel

Ward] and count much upon the readings of Shakespeare, the conversation and society of Fanny Kemble, who has promised to ride with me and introduce me to the beautiful lanes and wild paths of these mountains. She seems a noble woman—peculiar, bold, masculine and unaccommodating, but with a burning sympathy with all that is high, true, and humane.

The day before Sumner had written to George G. Hillard, saying that he had seen Mrs. Butler with "the girls and others engaged in the sport of archery. Mrs. Butler hit the target in the golden middle," and in the same letter he says he rode home the longest way with her. This was the beginning of an enduring friendship. Sumner became an admirer of hers, but there is no indication in any letters from him or any reference by her that his interest was a romantic one.

Fisher and Sumner, two men of different backgrounds, speak of Fanny as masculine. This aspect of her is not felt in her correspondence, in her warm, outgoing sympathy with her friends who often set her on a pedestal, or in her boundless sympathy for the slaves. It is hard to reconcile with the impression created by her on the stage when she is always spoken of by critics as charming and girlish. However, fifteen years had passed since she went on the stage, and evidently her demeanor and characteristics had changed. Of course, merely riding alone through the countryside was unconventional for American women, and that alone contributed to these two American men's opinion of her.

In the winter of 1843–44, Mrs. Charles Sedgwick wrote Pierce and told him that she was siding with Fanny who was living alone in a boarding house as the children were with their father. Mr. Theodore Sedgwick came to see Pierce at that time and said that he had been engaged as Fanny's lawyer. Shortly thereafter four members of the Sedgwick family arrived in Philadelphia to reason with Pierce. They were Mr. and Mrs. Charles Sedgwick and Theodore, and apparently, Miss Catherine Sedgwick, though Pierce does not name her. It is unlikely that Kate Minot came to Philadelphia without her husband and children. Fanny wanted to move into her husband's house to be with the children, even though she did not want to live with him as his wife. The "Statement" continues, "Leagued with confederates whose double-dealing I had detected, she, (Mrs. Charles Sedgwick) and they, spread abroad imputations against me as defamatory as they were unfounded. Not only was the slang of infidelity pertinaciously reiterated, but in their zeal to injury they did not scruple to accuse me of conduct of even a more serious character, and to soil their own lips with calumnies so gross that I cannot here even allude to them."

Pierce does not say what these "calumnies" were. But the Sedgwick family, honorable and well-established, had the courage to tell Pierce what they believed to be true, and that is why he turned against them. Did they say that he was living with a negro woman on the plantation? And if they did, the custom was only in keeping with the accepted conduct of many another slave holder, which numerous mulattoes among the blacks proved. Was this the "gross calumny?" Why was Pierce so shocked? Mulattoes were tacitly understood and as much a part of a Southern gentleman's life as drinking mint juleps and gambling on horse races. But Pierce was born and had grown up in Philadelphia and so knew that his fellow townsmen should hear nothing of his plantation domestic arrangements. Northerners were not Southerners and so could only use a false yardstick to measure him by. Victorian Pierce thought to shelter himself with silence, assuming that what was too base for him to repeat in his "Statement" was also too base for his friends to see in writing, and his word must be believed. He asserted that the Sedgwicks were lying. Why did he not quote the Sedgwicks and categorically deny their accusations, furnishing proofs of his innocence? If these well-born, dignified New Englanders of flawless reputation could come from Boston to stand by Fanny and confront Pierce, he should have proved to them that they were wrong. He invalidated his case by declaring that the "calumnies" were "so gross that I cannot here even allude to them." He did not want his friends to know what the Sedgwicks said, realizing that it would certainly cause them to speculate on his morals. Nor did he want their imaginations aroused so that they would lend an ear to derogatory stories about him. He realized it was more expedient to take a noble tone, that he was above even committing to paper the Sedgwicks' accusation.

Fanny, even before engaging Mr. Theodore Sedgwick, had in October, 1843 asked Benjamin Gerhard and William Meredith for legal advice and had written Pierce asking for a separation. However, Pierce would give no heed to a legal separation and thought that if he paid her separate maintenance she might rejoin him and the children in his boarding house, although living separately, in order to see more of the children, but he stipulated that this arrangement would continue only if she conformed to three rules, namely; "not to go on the stage—not to advocate in print the abolition cause—and not to publish any writings disapproved by me."

In 1844 Pierce was doing over a house in Philadelphia for himself and the children, and Fanny learned from Dr. Furness, Rector of the First Unitarian Church, who was trying to mediate the dispute, that Pierce would not allow her to come and live in it though separately as she had done in the boarding house unless she signed "The Conditions" he had drawn up governing her behavior in the future. Fanny was in desperation. She longed to be with her girls and mistakenly thought she could bestow motherly love on them in their father's house when he was totally estranged from her. During all these months Fanny continued in a boarding house, seeing her daughters only one hour a day.

She spent the summer of 1844 in Lenox with the William Minots and the Charles Sedgwicks next door, while Pierce took the children to Newport without her.

It was not until February 24, 1845, after seven months of reasoning with herself, when Fanny at last realized that without signing "The Conditions" she would never live again with her children, that she signed them. Her sister and father in England urged her to do so. She says in her "Narrative" attached to the divorce case:

> In order to remain near my children and retain as far as possible the right of a mother over them, I fully and unconditionally agreed to certain terms referred to and insisted on by Mr. Butler in a letter to Mr. Furness on December 18, 1844. But Mr. Butler then demanded that I should copy and sign the following agreement,

stating that he considered it to contain nothing new or in any way different from the former one, with which understanding I proceeded to copy and sign it.

"The Conditions" were:

Being about to reside in Mr. Butler's house, I promise to observe the following conditions while living under his roof: I will give up all acquaintances and intercourse of whatever kind, whether by word or letter, with every member of the Sedgwick family, and hereafter I will treat them in every respect as entire strangers and as if I had never known them. I will not keep up an acquaintance with any person of whom Mr. Butler may disapprove. I will observe an entire abstinence from all reference to the past. Neither will I mention to any person any circumstance which may occur in Mr. Butler's house or family. I will neither write nor speak of Mr. Butler to anyone while I remain under his roof. I will also conform to the arrangements of his house as I shall find them on entering it, and I promise, if I find myself unable to fulfill any of the aforesaid conditions, immediately to give notice to Mr. Butler of my inability to do so and to leave his house. . . . I [Pierce Butler] require also that Mrs. Butler shall not speak of me. Neither will I mention her name to anyone, and communication that I may have to make to her shall be made in writing and shall be addressed to herself. Under no circumstance will I allow the intervention of a third person in any matter between us after she enters my family.

Before taking this hopeless step Fanny wrote two letters to Kate Minot:

> February 11, 1845
>
> Since writing this to you yesterday I have heard that Mrs. John Butler told someone that I was expected to go into Mr. Butler's house in the course of a week. It would be difficult for you to conceive the sort of sick-heart sinking with which I hear this—and when I remember that my doing so is my own and deliberate act, I have a sort of feeling of contempt for the cowardice with which my spirit shrinks from the ordeal which itself accepted. Certainly at no time did I imagine that my residence there was likely to be pleasant, but the near approach of my martyrdom for a little while filled me with dismay. However, I cannot do otherwise than I am doing. I presume I shall be cared for if I take no care for myself. God bless you, dear friend, dear chick, dear darling. Give my kind love to your husband and his father and mother who certainly are all my friends. Tell Mary Dwight

that I shall write to her not once but often, and that I remember and
think of her most affectionately. Once more, my dear child, farewell.

Fanny

Fanny again wrote to Kate on the very day of going into
Pierce Butler's house:

Monday, March 3, 1845

I am only putting off my entrance into Mr. Butler's house while I
write a few lines of farewell to you and yours. I have nothing to say,
for you know all. I am exhausted too with packing, suffering, antici-
pating—and a great deal of positive physical indisposition against
which I have struggled during the last week. God bless you my dear
child—long may your life be peaceful and serene—long may love
enrich you on all sides, and your sweet and placid temper carry you
thro' your smooth and peaceful existence, unvisited by storms and
agonies such as brasher and less disciplined dispositions are schooled
and ruled by. Once more, my dear and pleasant Kate, whose sweet
image rises now while I write like a "gracious presence" full of joy
and hope before me—God bless and keep you and yours—I am and
shall be ever the same to you.

On March 3, 1845 Fanny moved into Pierce Butler's house.
Within a month of Fanny's move, Pierce sent her a letter which
had come from Miss Sedgwick; she opened it, thinking he meant
her to have it, and when he found out, he vilified her for breaking one of the "conditions."

Pierce in his usual bombastic tones tries to put Fanny in the
wrong for reading the letter but later admitted that he could
not logically blame her for opening what he had sent her.

There is no mention in Fanny's existing letters of the duel
fought by Pierce and James Schott on May 15, 1844 in an affair of honor concerning Mrs. Schott. Schott had accused Pierce
of being her lover. Duelling was unusual at that date, and Philadelphia rang with this melodramatic event which smacks of
comic opera, with an intercepted letter, attempted stranglings,
and a pistol held to the breast of Mrs. Schott by her husband.
This series of narrow escapes from the hands of her husband
were sworn to by Mrs. Schott. James Schott calls Pierce "a
crafty knave," and both Pierce and Schott in letters to dear
friends swear that what the other says about them is untrue.

Nothing can be proved. Schott, in his published statement vindicating himself and the duel with Pierce, says that delicacy prevents him from saying what he saw when he stood in the corridor outside his wife's bedroom in a New York hotel when Pierce was one of the Schott party, and Mrs. Schott had refused to share her husband's bedroom and had requested one to herself. It was then that Schott wrote Pierce that their friendship was over and challenged him to a duel. Schott says that his suspicions of Pierce had been aroused when Pierce called on Mrs. Schott at their Philadelphia house and stayed from 11:30 to 1:30 AM when Mr. Schott was ill upstairs. After the duel Mrs. Schott divorced her husband.

Public opinion sided with Pierce Butler, though at various times he was linked in public print with several women and is referred to as "a gallant."

Fanny showed good breeding and self-restraint in not establishing Pierce's infidelity in the Schott affair. She could have induced the Schott servants and the servants in the hotel in New York to give evidence against Pierce, particularly as that is how divorce evidence was obtained in England.

In an undated letter to Mrs. Joshua Francis Fisher of Philadelphia Fanny says more about the reasons for her divorce than in any other letter extant. The date of the letter is established by her saying, "the Sedgwicks have been my firm and devoted friends ever since I came to this country, for nearly twelve years," and she was referring to her difficulties of 1845.

Dear Mrs. Fisher,

I do not wish to trouble you with a detail of my affairs, but simply to reiterate my assurance to you that neither Mrs. Charles Sedgwick nor any other member of that family ever informed me of any misconduct on the part of Mr. Butler. I have every reason to believe them utterly ignorant of his career up to the moment of my making them acquainted with some particulars of it and of my consequent determination to separate myself from him. I have acted upon no advice of theirs in my whole course of conduct since that, with one single exception; namely, the accepting during the past year of a maintenance from Mr. Butler for the sake of retaining my intercourse with my children. This which was at first exceedingly repugnant to me, Messrs. Charles and Theodore Sedgwick induced me to do, and

I am satisfied now that they were right in their advising me, and I am following their advice. This, my dear Mrs. Fisher, is the *only instance* in which I have received advice from any member of the Sedgwick family.

I will now tell you what I believe to be Mr. Butler's real motives for endeavoring to cut me off utterly from them and for stating the various falsehoods with regard to them which his family do not scruple to circulate. The Sedgwicks have been my firm and devoted friends ever since I came to this country, for nearly twelve years. They are aware of the neglect, the disappointment, the sad existence of defeated hopes and wasted affections to which I have been doomed from the earliest days of my union with Mr. Butler, and *they now,* as well as myself, possess the key to all that I have endured in the instances which have gradually and one after another been brought to light of Mr. Butler's whole career. And whereas they for years were his friends as well as mine, they now very naturally have no feeling but that of utter disapprobation for such a character. This in itself is not agreeable to Mr. Butler. They have been witnesses, the only ones, and that, too, principally through correspondence of the life of wretchedness which I have led since my marriage and, now that instead of deploring it as the consequence merely of ill-suited dispositions and uncongenial characters they perceive his profligacy and falsehood to have been the cause of all I have endured. Two of the members of that family are lawyers—able and intelligent men of business, who were it possible to serve me, would be both willing and capable of becoming my defenders. This is another most obvious reason for Mr. Butler's desire to cut me off from them, and when in addition to this I tell you that to one of these men in a moment of unguarded exasperation Mr. Butler *repeatedly* acknowledged the fact of his infidelity, adding, however, "She (myself) cannot help herself, for the letters (which would have been proof against him) she has herself returned to me, and besides, she knows no names," you will perhaps not wonder that he is anxious to break off if possible all connection between myself and people who have such good reason to despise and condemn him.

In the imprudence committed by my friend, Elizabeth, which I neither sanctioned at the time nor have ever since defended, I can only say the cause was her affection for me, her desire to spare me the aggravated misery of having my children taken from me by the man who had so long neglected and ill treated me, and the singular overture of the woman whom she questioned.

Dear Mrs. Fisher, pray forgive the infliction of this long statement. Your good opinion is of value to me, and your words carry with them the weight that belongs to character. Let me beseech you then for the sake of this truth which I know you hold sacred not to lend your countenance to reports which are as false as they are malignant and which are propagated surely to justify if possible the unjustifiable conduct of an unprincipled man. I am, dear Mrs. Fisher, very sincerely yours,

> Fanny

Fanny, after the episode of the letter from Miss Sedgwick continued this fundamentally impossible arrangement of living on the third floor of Pierce's house, and the situation deteriorated from week to week.

That summer Pierce took the children to Newport but would not let Fanny accompany them.

Charges and counter-charges contradicting each other continued between Pierce and Fanny. She wrote to Samuel Gray Ward, a prominent Boston lawyer, who was a staunch friend and admirer of hers and a friend of the Sedgwicks and Charles Sumner:

> August 21, 1845

My dear Sir,

As I hold you to be my friend, I am glad that what I propose to do seems well to you, but at any rate, in taking the most painful step in my whole life, I would fain be consoled by the good esteem of good people and not feel that besides being miserable I am blameworthy.

I think the earliest date of my coming to Lenox will be October. I shall not leave this place without making one more appeal to Mr. Butler to restore me to my maternal rights. As, however, my sister has written to him to tell him that my whole family wish and urge my return to Europe, he is less likely than ever to make any concession by which the object he has aimed at so steadily for the last three years will be defeated—I mean his getting rid of me. When, therefore, I do leave this house and this place, it will be not to return to it, and I have much to attend to before that. I think I shall be in Philadelphia, even if I go to England, till the end of September. It is extremely doubtful whether Mr. Butler, in order to carry out his scheme to its completion (which is, I believe to oblige me to go upon the stage again and then get a divorce from me) will furnish me any means whatever. My allowance, as I probably wrote you, he has withdrawn, and tho' I suppose he must be liable to the few bills which I have here in Philadelphia, it is more than likely that he will refuse to afford anything towards my maintenance in order to compel me to support myself rather than tax my father. On the other hand I have, of course, my right of dower upon his property, and all these things must be adjusted before I leave Philadelphia.

It may occur that I may be absolutely distressed for the means of carrying myself to England. When I am there my father will take care of me, and Mr. Butler reckons wrong if he supposes that I will not rather depend upon him than return to the stage. Part of my father's present income is the fruit of my former labor, and therefore however distasteful it may be to me to withdraw anything whatever from him, in living with him I shall in truth be subsisting upon my own means. I hope hereafter to be able to write, but at any rate, pensioned by Mr. Butler or not, have no anxiety for the future.

You forget in speaking of fortune's having emptied his iron quiver at me how singularly prosperous—according to the world's reckonings—my youth was. I do not, I confess, look for much keener sorrows than those I have latterly known, but I think in the health and high popularity and success which I enjoyed before my marriage, I have assuredly had my share of the good things of this world. An existence of outward repose is what I now most of all desire, together with leisure and capacity (if by working I can attain it) to do something good for something with my wits—which must be more superficial even than I fear they are if I have hitherto done them anything like justice. Farewell, my dear Sir—give my kindest regards to your wife, and believe me ever,

Yours very truly,
Fanny

In her "Narrative" Fanny obviously copied a letter she had written Samuel Ward on September 1 and included it.

I had now, however, sufficiently tested the experiment I had made in accepting "The Conditions" imposed on me by the libellant. My life had been all but intolerable in his house. My presence there had been made the means of injuring my children. They had been removed from me for two months, and I had finally been forbidden to see them. Thus my ministry towards them seemed in God's righteous dispensations either to be ended utterly, or for the present utterly suspended. My friends and family in England, whose advice I now demanded, strongly urged me for my children's sake to come away, and I perceived the necessity that I should do so.

On the sixteenth of October, 1845, I sailed for England; a friend in this country (but for whose kindness I should have been utterly penniless) having furnished me with the means of doing so. And after spending two months in England, I joined my sister and her husband in Italy and remained there a year with them.

Fanny sailed alone for England and joined her father in his lodgings at 44 Mortimer Street, Cavendish Square. It is astonishing and hard to believe that after the agony and soul-searching which led to her decision to leave her children that she had the resiliency to write cheerfully to Kate.

44 Mortimer St.
December 2, 1845

Here I am in this smoky, foggy town of my birth, and I am sorry to say there is exceeding little prospect of my removal from it towards those bright skies which I thought were beckoning me when I left America. My sister is at Rome where she has taken a house till the spring. My father has relinquished all idea of going abroad, and being *perfectly* well, stronger and active than I remember him for many years, seems to be concentrating all his energies upon sure making of money, which he is doing very rapidly and successfully by reading in every direction thro' the provinces. Under these circumstances he will certainly not leave England, and tho' he leaves me alone in his lodgings in London while he goes travelling about in every direction in the most independent manner, I cannot bring myself to propose to him to let me go and join my sister in Italy, which I am absolutely dying to do. Perhaps I shall make up my mind to do so if I find that he continues well and as much engaged out of London as he has been hitherto since my return.

I went with Harriet St. Leger, who met me at Liverpool (my father being then absent on a reading expedition in Yorkshire) immediately to Bannisters to Emily Fitzhugh and stayed a week at that lovely place in peace and quiet with them. After my return to London I went into the country in another direction to see my eldest brother who lives with his family at a pretty little place which he inherited from my mother and which he has improved extremely. My youngest brother is quartered with his regiment in Dublin, and him I have not yet seen as he cannot get away at present. All my friends here make me very welcome and seem so glad to be sure that I think it is really worth while to go away for a few years to come back to this great world of people who are dying for excitement and be so charmingly *new*. Of course this does not apply to *friends* but to society in general, which is sure to open its arms with acclamation to King Solomon's grand desideratum in the shape of a fellow creature who has been *long enough* and not *too long* (for it's a nice point) away. Tell Charles Sumner that I do nothing but laud his nation to the right and left.

She was able to withstand the abiding sorrow of the separation from her children with no certainty that she would ever live with them again. Her father urged Fanny to go to Rome to visit her sister Adelaide and her husband, Edward John Sartoris, and their two children who had asked her to visit them for a year. She journeyed by diligence and steamer to Italy and spent the winter in Rome and summer at Frascati with them. She wrote what she referred to as "trash," her description of Italian sights and festivals, and it was published the following year under the title of *A Year of Consolation*. It sold well, and Fanny says she only wrote it as she needed the money, as the allowance from Pierce Butler came only intermittently and then ceased. She wrote to Kate:

Frascati
July 2, 1846

I can hardly tell, my dearest Kate, how far as a girl the beautiful aspect of all outdoor things in this land of beauty might have rendered me insensible to the misery and degradation of its inhabitants, but the years of my residence in America would hardly, I think, have fulfilled their ministry upon me if they had not awakened in me perceptions of better good for a nation than a fertile land, a benignant climate, treasures of art, and stores of noble historical associations. You know that America has taught me to dislike living in my own country because of the oppression of the poor, and however much tendencies towards justice and humanity may have existed originally in my own mind, this proper development is undoubtedly owing to my sojourn in your most fortunate but most responsible country.

On December 8, 1846 Fanny returned to London, realizing that she must support herself and not allow her father to maintain her. Going back on the stage was the only means possible to her, as she would not read in public while her father was supporting himself by reading. This proved to be a painful and unnerving decision. She had not acted for thirteen years and refers to herself as fat and middle-aged. It meant travelling with a maid from town to town as she could not at first get an engagement in London. She had no manager and wrote to the managers of the provincial theatres asking to be engaged and made contracts with them stipulating that she must be paid by the performance only, so that if she did not fill the houses, the contract could be cancelled. She collapsed more than once in trembling tears on the floors of rented rooms and wrote Kate that she thought she had St. Vitus Dance but overcame her fear and repugnance of taking the first steps which would lead again to her first profession, goaded by the knowledge that she had to earn her living. Her first performance was on February 16, 1847 as Julia in "The Hunchback" at Manchester. As a whole her return to the stage proved a financial success but was not brilliant. She journeyed from city to city, and often good friends such as Charles and Henry Greville, who came to her opening night, would join her to see her act and give her their support.

Unknown to her, and while she was touring, Pierce wrote to his lawyer, John Cadwalader:

April 21, 1847

My dear Sir,

It is my wish and intention to seek a divorce from Mrs. Butler. She has left her home and her children, and she has no intention of returning to them. Under these circumstances I presume that I may ask for an absolute divorce as a right. When you have a little leisure to devote to this subject, I shall be glad to attend you at your office.

Yours very truly,
Pierce Butler

Fanny wrote to Kate on May 6, 1847 from London:

I have been very ill indeed and unable for some time to make even the exertion of writing. Besides the regular performances three nights a week at the theatre for which I am paid, my fine lady and gentlemen friends have thought fit to get up two amateur performances for the benefit of the starving Irish and Scotch, and these not only give me two fatiguing parts to perform, but rehearsals without end, so that on my days of rest when I do not act for pay, I have for the last week spent seven hours rehearsing. This is all pretty severe, but I am inclined to take it patiently. Much more than this I shall not be be able to do. The expectation of realizing enough to live upon in the course of a few months with which I returned to the stage has vanished away before the state of things in the theatrical world here, and indeed, in society generally.

In such a state of things as this I cannot hope to do more than support myself and lay by a *little* by degrees. But for the illness I have just come through and also lending my youngest brother some of my earnings, I should already have realized upwards of a thousand pounds which is something to start with. It is, however, owing to these two circumstances only seven hundred at present, but I am receiving fifty-four pounds a night and have several engagements which are likely to be lucrative for the provinces. I have received a large offer from New York but do not wish to leave England until I have done all that I can here. I shall not, therefore, come to America until next year, when I shall work as hard as I can in the free states and see what I can do for myself among you.

Thank you, my dearest Kate, for your husband's kind offers of service. I have at present invested my earnings in Emily Fitzhugh's name in the English funds. They are low, and it is a good time to buy into them, and tho' the interest is very little, the money is safe, and I shall keep it here until I leave the country when I will have it transferred to some Massachusetts investment. I hope by working hard and living economically to have near upon three thousand pounds in my hand when I come to America.

Mendelssohn died on November 4, 1847, and as he had been a close friend of Adelaide and Edward Sartoris and Fanny had often heard him play at their house, she felt his death keenly. Charles Kemble had been asked by Queen Victoria to read "Antigone," accompanied by Mendelssohn's music, at Buckingham Palace. Charles declined, saying that his deafness made it impossible for him to read anything with music, but he suggested Fanny do it. At this time Fanny had never read in public, and she explained that she would not be able to make her first appearance as a reader to Mendelssohn's music as she knew she would weep. No Command Performance before the Queen had ever been refused, and this brought unfortunate censure on Fanny, and her explanation was not held as valid. However, several weeks later, on hearing Mendelssohn's music for the first time since his death, Fanny could not prevent herself from weeping bitterly and says how right she was not to read for the Queen.

In February, 1848, Fanny returned to London and was engaged by Charles Macready, then the most popular actor in England, to play Shakespeare with him at the Princess Theatre. She played Desdemona, Cordelia, Ophelia, Lady Macbeth, and Queen Katherine. Macready made her engagement with him as difficult as possible. He was known for his violence, and many actresses were afraid to play Desdemona with him for fear of being really strangled in the death scene. Fanny, playing Desdemona for the first time in her life, braved this and survived with only a broken little finger. The engagement was a disappointment, lasting only three weeks, as Macready could no longer fill a house, a theatrical slump prevailing in England.

After acting with Macready Fanny was at last able to consider reading Shakespeare for her livelihood instead of acting, as her father at that time retired and was appointed theatre censor by the English government with a small salary. Her father gave her his reading copies of the plays with all his cuts, and to her dismay she found that she would have to do as he did, fitting each play into a two-hour performance with an intermission in the middle. At first she had impractically thought she could read one play through without cuts which would require an audience to come two or three evenings to hear the same play, but she soon realized that was impossible. Charles had read only the few most frequently acted plays, and when Fanny did her own cuts on her far greater repertory she found how difficult it was and how skillfully Charles had cut the ones he read. She then set a precedent which she adhered to while she remained on the platform. She read in sequence the twenty-four plays that she liked best and would never read only the ones which had the greatest public favor merely to fill the halls. She said her reading would become mechanical if she repeated them too often. She said, "the public always came in goodly numbers to hear Macbeth, Hamlet, Romeo and Juliet, and the Merchant of Venice, but to all the other plays the audiences were considerably less numerous." Fanny's managers said she was "sacrificing her interests" by adhering to this plan. Of her reading she said, "I have wished and hoped and prayed that I might be able to use my small gift dutifully; and to my own profound feeling of the virtue of these noble works have owed whatever power I found to interpret them."

Fanny upheld her artistic integrity against worldly profit in a situation when money was all-important. She read in sequence King Lear, Macbeth, Cymbeline, King John, Richard II, both parts of Henry IV, Henry V, Richard III, Henry VIII, Coriolanus, Julius Caesar, Anthony and Cleopatra, Hamlet, Othello, Romeo and Juliet, The Merchant of Venice, A Winter's Tale, Measure for Measure, Much Ado About Nothing, As You Like It, Midsummer Night's Dream, Merry Wives of Windsor, and The Tempest. She read for the first time before a small audience at Highgate on March 25, 1848 and made a short tour before opening in London with great success at Willis' Rooms, King Street, St. James, London when she read The Merchant of Venice. The public realized and she realized that reading was the profession in which she could become a great figure. She planned to read in England and then in America.

On March 29, 1848, still unknown to her, Pierce Butler filed an application for divorce in the Court of Common Pleas in Philadelphia, charging that she had deserted him on September 11, 1845.

She wrote Mrs. Charles Sedgwick on May 1, 1848:

> Adelphi Hotel
> Liverpool
>
> About the twenty-fifth of this month—May—I shall in all human probability be landing in New York. I have received a legal summons thro' a lawyer here from Mr. Butler to appear in the Courts of Common Pleas in Philadelphia on the fifth of June to encounter and resist his suit for a *divorce* upon plea of *my having deserted him! ! !* Now I have hereupon taken my passage by the Hibernia which goes direct from this place to New York and suppose if nothing unusual occurs that I shall see New York before the end of the "Merry Month of May"—a merry month truly it will prove to me. I have engagements contracted until the middle of June to the amount of four hundred and seventy pounds. These I must forego together with whatever more (probably nearly as much) I might have made from that time till the first of August when I had settled to leave England.

In short it would be difficult to conceive anything more full of loss, vexation, annoyance, and torment than this proceeding of Mr. Butler's, letting alone the miserable prospect of all the wretchedness I may be made to undergo and the very uncertain issue of any defense I can make for myself. I have written to Theodore and to Gerhard and begged them to undertake to protect me if possible from this crowning iniquity of Mr. Butler's. Of course, the divorce is not what I care to escape, but I *do* care after *all* that I have endured not to be publicly branded as a woman who has deserted her most sacred duties, and I do also care to resist if possible a decree, which if given in favor of Mr. Butler, assails my existence as a mother as well as a wife and makes the wrongful separation from my children which I now suffer, legal and formal. *The award of justice is punishment of my ill conduct.* Dearest Elizabeth, God knows how sudden and shocking this blow was to me when first it fell upon me. Now I have prepared myself to meet it, and all I can hope is that it may prove the last of the strange series of persecutions to which I have now been subjected for so long. The interruption to my exertions for my own support is very grievous, for as it is, I shall only bring with me fifteen hundred pounds to the United States, and God only knows how much of that will be wasted in this bitter process of my defense, and how much in inevitable idleness till I can begin again in September to work. All my plans are completely upset and routed by this. I have only just begun to give public readings in England. I cannot think of renouncing utterly the prospect of so profitable a field of labor. I shall, therefore, if I am free in September, begin my theatrical engagements in the United States and continue them until this time twelve months, when I will return to England for another year, as I am well assured that I cannot do better in a pecuniary point of view.

My thoughts and feelings are in a state of most painful confusion. I see nothing before me but wretchedness and trouble, and the idea of being dragged back to Philadelphia to encounter Mr. Butler and perhaps my poor children before a tribunal has given me an absolute horror of the idea of America altogether. I shall come, however, at the appointed time and go thro' this ordeal with what courage and patience I may say. I must beg, my dear Elizabeth, that you will forward immediately to Theodore my Journal and letters written during my last stay in Mr. Butler's house, also whatever letters of mine you or any members of your family have preserved, written at any period *subsequent* to my *last return* to the United States.

Mr. Butler's legal summons to me is dated the 30th of March. It only reached me on the 24th of April, and my announcement of this attack to Theodore and Gerhard will not be received by them before the 13th of May, so that they will have but a short time for preparing my defense. I have myself, dearest Lizzy, so much to do that I must conclude this letter abruptly. God bless you, dearest, 'tis an immense comfort in the midst of all this misery to think how soon I shall embrace you again.

It is hard to see why Fanny was shocked and surprised at the court summons to return to Philadelphia and defend herself against a suit for divorce. She had planned to go forward with her reading in England and even spoke of reading in America. Apparently she thought to continue indefinitely as the estranged wife of Pierce Butler and had no plan for being reunited with her children.

Sidney George Fisher who had gone riding with Fanny two years earlier when she was living separately from Pierce now speaks of her under the date of May 28, 1848 in his diary.

Mrs. Pierce Butler returned by the last steamer. She came in consequence of an application for a divorce on the part of her husband. He claims it on the ground of "willful and malicious desertion." As it is quite notorious that she was driven from his house by his own barbarous treatment, I think he can hardly succeed. It is impossible to predict, however, such is often the difference between the reality and the evidence. The position is certainly a very painful one. She is obligated to return to the stage for a support as Butler makes her no allowance. I shall be very glad to see her again.

It is difficult to hew a clear line through the charges and counter-charges of the divorce suit. Many times Pierce and Fanny contradict each other, and the chapters of their woes become tedious. As an example, she says in her "Narrative" that when she had to go back onto the stage in the autumn of 1847 she wrote to her daughters explaining that it was the necessity of earning her living that forced her to go back to her profession. From then on, she says, Pierce returned her letters to her children unopened.

Pierce had gathered to represent him in the divorce a formidable galaxy of lawyers, as at first it was thought there would be a jury trial, and Pierce was apprehensive. Pierce wrote to John Caldwalader:

Walnut St.
February 16, 1849

My dear Sir,

After anxious consideration on the subject of additional counsel, and after weighing well all the circumstances likely to affect my case when it shall come before a jury, I have come to the determination to ask you to allow me to associate with yourself and Mr. Dallas [Vice President under Jackson], Mr. Charles O'Connor and Mr. John Duer of New York. The result of this trial before a jury is so full of consequences to me, that my anxiety will not suffer me to neglect or omit a single thing which can be supposed to influence it in any degree. I believe the case may be gained, and on the issue hangs my happiness, my peace of mind, and my existence itself.

I have some reason to think the other side will desire to employ the services of Mr. Webster when they come to the knowledge that we have employed additional counsel, and that you may not have this strength to contend against, I have written to Mr. Dallas and begged him to retain Mr. Webster. I have no wish to employ Mr. Webster in the trial before the jury, but I should be sorry to have his power against me.

Your obliged friend,
Pierce Butler

When John Cadwalader learned that Daniel Webster had been engaged by Pierce, he withdrew from the case, and this alarmed Pierce, who then wrote to him:

February 27, 1849

My dear Sir,

Mr. Dallas entertains similar views with yourself as regards the employment of additional counsel. The reasons which influence you to retire from my case bear with equal weight on him. As he expressed himself, "Mr. Cadwalader and I are one in the case." This decision of yourself and Mr. Dallas, if adhered to, must be fatal to success, and my present feeling is to drop the suit if your determination cannot be changed.

Very truly and sincerely yours,
Pierce Butler

Pierce did not give up the suit, however, and Mr. Dallas remained as his counsel after Cadwalader withdrew. Fanny also had an array of lawyers. As well as the Philadelphians, Mr. William M. Meredith and Benjamin Gerhard, she had Messrs. Charles and Theodore Sedgwick of Boston, Mr. Samuel Gray Ward, and Mr. Charles Sumner whom she asked to be trustee for the settlement of a mortgage on Butler Place which her lawyers were demanding for her. Fanny wrote to Mr. Ward concerning a settlement, and later in this same letter says:

> Meantime it is now generally understood that Mr. Butler is insolvent. I felt very certain of this as soon as the first rumors of the disorder of his affairs reached me. Of course I do not know how that will affect my claim, and indeed I do not care at all. I make it because I feel bound to endeavor if possible to save that much of his property for his children.
>
> I have today written to William Minot to beg him to adjourn Frank Parker to himself in any legal steps necessary to be taken in my behalf. Mr. Parker came to see us before we left Boston, and I think he will be willing to serve me if he can, and I know hardly anybody but himself who seems to me able to encounter the species of glamour with which everything connected with Mr. Butler seems enveloped here—a sort of hallucination so strange that I think if I remain here much longer, I shall come to perceive that he is a paragon of every earthly excellence and myself a monster of all iniquity.

Fanny also asked advice of the husband of her dearest friend, Kate Sedgwick Minot and wrote him in September, 1848:

> La Pierre House
Philadelphia
>
> Dear Mr. Minot,
>
> I have had a long interview with one of Mr. Butler's assignees and could only wonder while listening to the incredible tale of ruin which he told me in talking of Mr. Butler's affairs that there should remain any doubt on the mind of any human being of his unsoundness of mind. In England if it had been anybody's interest to do so, a statute of lunacy would have been taken out against him and his property led from utter devastation by that means. He gave in to his assignees as the amount of his debts *five hundred thousand dollars,* but his estimate is *below* the truth, and they are daily finding new claims upon the estate, the southern property is mortgaged, he has cheated his sisters each of a large sum of money—and I believe *all* that will remain to my children of the large fortune they had a right to expect will be the forty thousand dollars which will be reserved for

them by my claim. So disastrous a story of mad havoc of property I never heard. The poor children bear their loss of fortune and what is probably a greater trial to them, the great discomfort of their present mode of life, with great sweetness and cheerfulness and an affectionate loyalty to their father beyond all praise. Give my affectionate regards to all your home circle, and believe me always, dear sir,

Your truly obliged,
Fanny Kemble

Pierce's gambling on the stock exchange and at poker was reaching staggering proportions. Fanny did not know the immensity of his losses until Pierce's lawyers told her lawyers. There is no date of an episode referred to in the *New York Herald* twelve years later of Pierce once losing $24,000 at one hand of poker when he held four deuces against four kings, and this may not have taken place at the time of the divorce, while it is an extreme example of the recklessness in money matters which was taking possession of Pierce. It may not be a fact, but it bears out the reputation he was acquiring before the eventual ruin which forced him to sell his slaves to pay his debts.

The divorce dragged on for many months, and Fanny demanded and was finally given a mortgage on Butler Place. She knew that Pierce's fortune was being swept away, and she wanted to own a piece of land as security on which he would pay her the interest. Had it not been for her foresight, her girls would have had nothing after his financial ruin. She left in her will Butler Place to her daughters, and it was lived in by her descendents for three generations.

At the beginning of the divorce Fanny had asked for a trial by jury, expecting to vindicate her having left Pierce by citing his treatment of her, but the case was postponed from April to September, 1849, and without further struggle she agreed to let Pierce divorce her in exchange for having the children for two months each summer and the interest of the mortgage on Butler Place as an allowance. The divorce was granted to Pierce on September 22, 1849 and made it legal for either of them to marry again, but neither Fanny nor Pierce did.

Many facts and details of her marriage to Pierce are missing because Fanny many years later wrote to Kate Minot asking her to cut from the letters Fanny had written to the Sedgwick family all revelations accounting for the personal difficulties between herself and Pierce. Fanny wrote that she knew Kate would agree with her "in thinking no such account of past misconduct and misery should be preserved to grieve the hearts of those who remain after us. I have so dreaded wounding my children's hearts by these painful revelations that I have effaced from the MSS of my memoirs that I made for Sarah every expression of my bitter heartsick yearning for her and her sister during my years of separation from them that when I am gone they may not grieve over my past agony." The Sedgwicks did as Fanny wished and cut out with scissors many parts of the letters and also destroyed some letters completely.

CHAPTER IX

Independence as a Reader of Shakespeare

After fifteen years of marriage Fanny was once more a single woman. She did not crumble or throw herself on the mercy of others or allow anyone to assume her financial maintenance. She at once began her second profession as a reader of Shakespeare and brought his plays in this manner for the first time to many an American city. She was welcomed into the literary hierarchy of New England and says of herself, "During the time that I spent in Boston the persons I knew best and saw most frequently there were Dr. Channing, Prescott, Motley, the historians; Felton, the learned Greek professor; Agassiz, Holmes, Lowell and Longfellow . . . I had the honor, pleasure, and privilege of the acquaintance and friendship of all these distinguished men and was received by them with the utmost courteous kindness in their homes and families . . ."

She read for the first time in America in the winter before her divorce was final, and it was in Boston at Masonic Hall, with Charles Sumner leading her to the platform and introducing her, that she read "The Merchant of Venice" on January 26, 1849. She established the custom that evening from which she never varied. She made a curtsey, sat down behind a table which in America had a cover hanging to the floor, opened her book, said, "I have the honor to read . .", named the play, read the cast of characters, and began at once. She was always beautifully dressed in a dress that she considered suitable for the subject made especially for each play. She wore white satin for Romeo and Juliet, soft green for A Winter's Tale, and wine red for Hamlet, and her dresses were always spoken of with admiration.

Henry James wrote in his essay on Fanny Kemble:

> I have mentioned that Henry V was the last play I heard her read
> in public, and I remember a declaration of hers that it was the play
> she loved best to read, better even than those that yielded poetry
> more various. It was gallant and martial and intensely English, and
> she was certainly on such evenings the 'Anglaise des Anglaises' she
> professed to be. Her splendid tones and her face lighted like that of
> a war-goddess, seemed to fill the performance with the hurry of
> armies and the sound of battle; as in her rendering of "A Mid-
> summer Night's Dream," so the illusion was that of a multitude and
> a pageant.

Her reading which she began in England briefly, using her
father's marked copies, now proved a tremendous success. She
had one rebuff, a very painful one. She wrote to Mr. Ward while
the divorce was pending:

> My friend, Mr. Wister [William R. Wister] (a young lawyer to
> whom I gave a pair of spurs when he was twelve years old, son of
> old Germantown friends and neighbors of mine) took me to the
> lecture rooms of the Pennsylvania University. . . . [Fanny was
> hoping to give a reading, but the application was "respectfully de-
> clined"]. I was a good deal surprised and shocked, but what was to
> be done—nothing, of course, but pocket the affront. I think, how-
> ever, that settles the question of my reading here.

Fanny did, however, read in Philadelphia on October 5, 1849,
at Sansom St. Hall where Sidney George Fisher heard her:

> On Monday evening went to hear Mrs. Butler, or rather, Mrs. Kem-
> ble, as she is now called, read *As You Like It*. It was admirable,
> much better than I expected, notwithstanding all that has been said
> about these performances elsewhere. I anticipated more of theatrical
> display, but of this there was very little. The piece, in fact, does not
> admit of it, and I fancy in some of the tragedies she acts too much.
>
> I called to see her on Wednesday. She looks well but older. Had
> a long talk with her. She agreed with me that tragedies and plays of
> much passion were not suited to these readings, and that all of
> Shakespeare's, *The Tempest, Midsummer Night's Dream,* and
> *Merchant of Venice* were the best for the purpose, as neither
> admitting nor requiring much dramatic effect, yet remarkable for
> eloquent and beautiful poetry. She said she intended to read *The
> Tempest* here and the *Dream* in Balti.

Fanny read for a whole month in Boston and was later introduced by Longfellow, and in New York she earned $8,000 in one month that same winter. Eventually she travelled to Chicago and Indianapolis, and her fame as a reader was unrivalled in England and America for two decades. Defrauded by fate of a consuming and encompassing passion for her husband, the study, love, and worship of Shakespeare and reading in public provided the ballast essential for her future, and for the coming twenty years ruled her life. Of these years Fanny says:

> My greatest reward has been passing a large portion of my life in familiar intercourse with that greatest and best English mind and heart and living almost daily in that world above the world into which he lifted me.

With her earnings Fanny soon bought a cottage, "The Perch" on what is now Kemble Street in Lenox, and so the wish expressed eight years earlier in a letter from London to Kate was realized. She owned a house of her own near the Charles Sedgwicks and their daughter, now Mrs. William Minot, and it was to "The Perch" that her daughters came to visit her every summer for two months. Among her neighbors, and with whom she was on agreeable terms, was Nathaniel Hawthorne, living two miles away, and within riding distance was Herman Melville at "Arrowhead," and she often stopped to see him when passing his farm on her rides.

Her third profession, that of a diarist and writer of memoirs, casually begun with no thought of enduring fame, brought her international attention in 1863 when she at last published her *Journal of a Residence on a Georgian Plantation,* the journal she had kept daily for Elizabeth Sedgwick while living on her husband's plantations in the winter of 1838–1839. Fanny was living and reading in England in 1863 and found that many of her friends were siding with the South and were unaware of the never-to-end degradation of the slaves. She wanted them to know what she had seen. After publication, parts of Fanny Kemble's Journal were read aloud in the English House of Commons, and the cotton spinning factories of Manchester, learning for the first time about the lives of slaves, stopped buying cotton from the South and thus hastened the financial ruin of the Confederacy. The Journal's publication brought her recognition in the literary world, a lasting fame, and veneration among abolitionists who saw her book as a monument to their cause, filling a place in the history of slavery attempted by no other writer. It was the high water mark of her third career.

There was a lapse of twenty-four years between the writing and the publishing of the Plantation Journal. Why did Fanny wait so long? It is obvious that it was forebearance. For ten years after she wrote it she was still the wife of Pierce Butler. She had written the editress of the anti-slavery newspaper in 1841 from London that she did not feel "at liberty" to send her the manuscript of her Plantation Journal. She was then the wife of a slave holder. She would not publish her experiences on her husband's plantation, but she had declared herself before going to Georgia as an abolitionist.

After the divorce she was thinking of her daughters who were in the care of Pierce. She did not add to their emotionally scarred childhood the burden of a mother who decried their father's way of life in a volume for all the world to read which would bring new sorrow to them and a fresh cause for anger against her by their father. The indignation aroused by such a Journal in the South might have harmed them. It would have been a heavy blow to Sarah and young Fanny had the book been published during those years. They were obliged to explain almost daily to schoolmates and acquaintances the fact of having a living mother but a home without both parents. Divorce was not usual in Philadelphia, and their plight marked the Butler sisters and cast a haze of pity and unwholesome curiosity over them.

In 1863 the Civil War had been raging for two years. The North was fighting for the views Fanny had expressed in 1832. Fanny's daughter, Sarah, was married to Dr. Owen Jones Wister, living in Germantown, the outskirts of Philadelphia, and was an avowed abolitionist. She fostered the cause of the North and sold her autograph book with many famous signatures at the Sanitary Fair in Philadelphia. Since she had been grown she had refused to go South with her father. Young Fanny was a confederate sympathiser, but even if the South had won, she would never had been an owner of slaves, as her father had been obliged to sell his slaves four years before. She was old enough to understand that her mother voiced the feelings of many people, and the success of *A Residence on a Georgian Plantation* did not mar their relationship.

Pierce, in 1861, was confined for five weeks in the Federal Prison, Fort LaFayette, on Staten Island. He had been arrested and accused of smuggling arms into Georgia. But he had been born, grown up, and spent more than half his life in the state on whose battleground Lincoln would stand to give the Gettysburgh Address.

Abolition was not the governing factor of Fanny's existence. She reported a great wrong as she saw it but did not dedicate her life to preaching anti-slavery. As an Englishwoman it would have been presumptuous of her to join the militant abolitionists and make a profession of exposing from the platform what she had seen in Georgia. Once the Civil War began her Journal could be legitimately published, adding her narrative of the hopelessness of the slaves' lives to the Northern cause. Before going to the plantation she had conceived a plan for freeing the slaves about which she wrote to Harriet: the owners should educate the slaves, and the slaves, according to their merit and industry, should gradually be given freedom. This design, as outlined to Pierce and her in-laws, horrified the Butlers. Later she refers to it, saying, "They must have considered me a meddlesome madwoman."

From 1849 Pierce had been in increasingly straitened circumstances. He did not mend his ways but continued to gamble and speculate, even after the forced sale of his slaves. It was a disgrace for a plantation owner of his magnitude to have to pay his debts by such a means. Butler Place had to be rented many times.

In the Spring of 1867 Pierce was alone on the plantation with only a handful of his former slaves, now free of their new owners, who had made their way back to Butler Island in the hope of existing without work on the place of their birth. Pierce, the procrastinator, knew that malaria came with the

hot weather and that all owners took refuge in the piney woods
of Alabama for the summer. He had always gone North but
now lingered on and got malaria and died.

In 1874 Fanny, who had not lived in Philadelphia since the
divorce, settled at York Farm in a small house across the turnpike from Butler Place. Her daughter, Sarah, son-in-law, and
their son, Owen had moved into Butler Place after the death
of Pierce, and it became their home. York Farm was part of
Butler Place, and its farm house was done over for Fanny, and a
conservatory built onto it; she settled there with her English cook, her maid, Margaret, who postponed her marriage
two years to serve her adored mistress, an American gardener,
and an American housemaid. Fanny had no carriage and depended on Sarah to take her to pay calls, and once Sarah over-
turned the sleigh with painful injuries to both of them.

Fanny was sixty-five and had given up her nomadic, strenuous
life of reading in England and America. She had never owned
a house except "The Perch" and preferred to live near Sarah
and have young Fanny and her English husband, the Reverend
James Wentworth Leigh, whom she had married on June 29,
1871, come and stay with her in the summer. The Leighs were
attempting but did not succeed in trying to run the plantation
with at first twenty Irishmen whom they imported and then
with a remnant of the former slaves by sharing crops with them
and later as paid workers. At York Farm Fanny could see more
of her daughters than if she lived at Lenox, and she finally
sold "The Perch" and merely visited the Sedgwicks for a few
weeks each year. In the summer of 1875 she writes of meeting
Bret Harte:

> He was staying in the same hotel with us and did us the favor of
> spending an evening with us. He told us of one of his striking ex-
> periences, and his telling it made it singularly impressive. He had
> arrived at night at a solitary house of call on his way, absolutely
> isolated and far distant from any other dwelling—a sort of rough
> roadside tavern, known and resorted to by the wanderers in that
> region. Here he was to pass the night. The master of the house, to
> whom he was known, answered his question as to whether anyone
> else was there by giving the name of a notorious desperado, who had
> committed some recent outrage, and in search of whom the wild

justices—the lynchers of the wilderness—were scouring the district. This guest, the landlord said, was in hiding in the house, and was to leave it (if he was still alive) the next day. Bret Harte, accustomed to rough company, went quietly to bed and to sleep, but was aroused in the middle of the night by the arrival of a party of horsemen, who called up the master of the house and inquired if the man they were in pursuit of was with him. Upon receiving his repeated positive assurance that he was not, they remounted their horses and resumed their search.

At break of day Bret Harte took his departure, finding that for the first part of his journey he was to have the hiding hero of the night (thief or murderer probably) for his companion, to whom, on his departure, the master of the house gave the detailed and minute directions as to the only road by which it would be possible that he could escape his pursuers, Bret Harte meanwhile listening to these directions as if they were addressed to himself. They rode silently for a short time, and then the fugitive began to talk—not about his escape, not about the danger of the past night, not about the crime he had committed, but about Dicken's last story, in which he expressed such an eager and enthusiastic interest, that he would have passed the turning in the road by which he was to have made his escape if Bret Harte had not pointed it out to him, saying, "That is your way."

Couched in her nineteenth-century language and stamped with her point of view and lack of knowledge of the West, this typical Bret Harte story takes on the flavor of Fanny Kemble's writing. It would be unrecognizable when told by Harte.

Fanny needed money, as she could not live in comfort in America on her past earnings. In the Spring of 1875 Mr. Bentley, editor of the *Atlantic Monthly,* wrote to her and asked her for any articles about herself that she would allow them to publish. Fanny was delighted as this meant a new source of income, and her wonderful energy enabled her to start her memoirs, largely composed of the thousands of letters she had written to Harriet in the course of forty years, Harriet having returned them all to her.

She describes her life at York Farm to Harriet, and at the age of sixty-five kept a rigid daily routine and refers to it by saying, "I do nothing," but she arose at seven o'clock and took a four-mile walk, then wrote and edited for several hours, using a "little printing machine" that her son-in-law, Dr. Owen J. Wister, had given her, and which, she says, was a boon to the typesetters of the *Atlantic Monthly* as her handwriting was so difficult. In the winter she attended to the conservatory, and on Sundays let her canary fly in it as a weekly treat. She always went to the Episcopal Church with her daughter, Sarah, had a few callers, and visitors for the night. In the evenings she played duets with her grandson, Owen, when he was on vacation from school, or embroidered, sending her maid to bed at ten o'clock, as she said she could undo her own dresses, and went to bed at midnight. And so, her third profession maintained her in her old age.

She complained to Harriet of the dullness and loneliness of her existence on York Farm, and when young Fanny's husband accepted a living in a church in Staffordshire, England, in 1876, Fanny followed them on January 20, 1877, and from then on lived in a series of rented houses in London, once more taking up her life of visiting and receiving callers and continuing with her memoirs.

The most rewarding friendship of her later life was with Henry James, who was introduced to her by her daughter in Rome in early January, 1873. Dr. and Mrs. Wister were living in Rome, and James rode horseback with them almost daily on the Campagna. Fanny was thirty-four years older than James, but he not only came to call frequently in London but took her to the theatre and spent Christmas week of 1873 with the James Leighs at Alverston Manor House in Stratford-on-Avon where Fanny was staying and trimmed the Christmas tree. On several occasions he spent a whole week with her in Switzerland. Fanny had loved Switzerland all her life. In the very opening paragraph of *Records of a Girlhood* she says she believes this love was inherited from her mother who was born in Switzerland. The Swiss mountains, as she says, had a fascination for her, and this enthrallment became stronger as she grew older. As a young woman she had walked up the mountains or gone on muleback; later she was driven up the mountains behind a team of horses, then she was carried up in a chair by four men, and at last she sat on a hotel porch and looked at them. She spent every summer in Switzerland when she was in Europe after her divorce, and from 1877 onwards spent every summer from June to September in her favorite mountains until she was too old to travel.

On January 18, 1879 Henry James wrote to his mother:

Mrs. Kemble has returned to town for the winter—an event in which I always take pleasure, as she is certainly one of the women I know whom I like best. I confess I find people in general very vulgar-minded and superficial—and it is only by a pious fiction, to keep myself going, and keep on the social harness, that I succeed in postulating them as anything else or better. It is therefore a kind of rest and refreshment to see a woman who (extremely annoying as she sometimes is) gives one a positive sense of having a deep, rich, human nature and having cast off all vulgarities. The people of this world seem to me for the most part nothing but surface, and some-times—oh ye gods! such desperately poor surface. Mrs. Kemble has no organized surface at all; she is like a straight deep cistern with-out a cover, or even, sometimes, a bucket into which, as a mode of intercourse, one must tumble with a splash.

Henry James in his essay on Fanny after her death said that "her talk reflected a thousand vanished and present things. It swarmed with people and with criticism of people, with the ghosts of a dead society. She had, in two hemispheres, seen everyone and known everyone, had assisted at the social com-edy of her age."

In London Fanny continued writing her memoirs, and in 1878 the *Atlantic Monthly* published in three volumes her *Records of a Girlhood,* and she followed it by two more volumes, *Records of Later Life* in 1882, and *Further Records* in 1891.

For the last years of her life Fanny lived with the Leighs. Fanny had always longed for a sudden death, and in the Leighs' house on Gloucester Place, Portman Square, London, she died suddenly in the arms of her devoted maid, at eighty-three, on January 15, 1893, and was buried in Kensel Green Cemetery. Both her daughters were in the United States, but Henry James, being on intimate terms with them and their mother, wrote to Sarah on January 20, 1893:

34 DeVere Gardens

Dear Mrs. Wister,

I have just written to Mrs. Leigh, and she may send you my letter—but I must speak to you a direct, and a very old friend's word. I stood by your mother's grave this morning—a soft, kind, balmy day, with your brother-in-law and tall pale handsome Alice, and a few of those of her friends who have survived her and were in town and were not ill. The number is inevitably small for of all her generation she is the last and she made no new friends, naturally, for these last years. She was laid in the same earth as her father—and buried under a mound of flowers—which I don't like—but which many people, most people do. It was all bright somehow and public and slightly pompous. I thought of you and Mrs. Leigh "far away on the billow" as it were—and hoped you felt with us here, the great beneficent and good fortune of your mother's instantaneous and painless extinction. Everything of conditions at the last, that she longed for was there—and nothing that she had dreaded was. And the devotion of her old restored maid, Mrs. Brianzoni, appears to have been absolute—of every moment and of every hour. Your mother looked, after death, extraordinarily like her sister. I mention these things—to bring everything a little nearer to you as I am conscious of a strange bareness and a kind of evening chill as it were in the air, as if some great object that had filled it for long had left an emptiness—from displacement—to all the senses. It seemed quite like the end of some reign or the fall of some empire. But she wanted to go—and she went when she could, at last, without a pang. She was very touching in her infirmity all these last months—and yet with her wonderful air of smouldering embers under ashes. She leaves a great image—a great memory. Please receive, dear Mrs. Wister, all my sympathy—all my participation, which though far is not faint, in everything which touches you closely—and believe me when I say that I hope you will look upon me ever as your constant old friend.

Henry James

Epilogue

When Pierce Butler married Fanny Kemble, he took for granted that being his wife would be enough. She would sink into domesticity and renounce all that still for her within her, and the creative force he had seen in her acting and published plays would henceforth be dispelled. He was in love with a glowing personality but wanted only a colorless, submissive woman as a wife. He assumed that her driving talents would be compensated for by establishing her among the stiff-necked Quaker tenant farmers at Butler Place, and the malnourished, grovelling, soapless negroes on the plantation. He was too limited a man to see that he could not stem with rigid commands the tide of her overflowing emotions, which since her girlhood she had expressed on paper, or stop her publishing the keen observations and multi-hued experiences of her American tour.

It is hard to visualize the man she should have married. She did not find a husband in London. In America she might have been happy had she married a Bostonian with a taste for strenuous exercise, who could rejoice with her in the wonders of nature, share her abhorrence of slavery, delight in the range of her mind, and applaud her talents. But even an overmastering and enduring love for so unlikely and extraordinary a man would not have resolved the contradictions or welded together the many facets of her nature. Had she married such a man, she would have written only her *American Journal*. It was unhappiness and necessity that made her a writer.

Of course, her abhorrence of slavery was eventually mingled with her abhorrence of Pierce. But it must be remembered that the first sign of her love of humanity was voiced by her when she was taken as a young girl to Newgate Prison to see the women criminals and hear the discourse preached to them by Mrs. Fry. She was mortified by the tone of Mrs. Fry's lecture and said,

217

had she been alone, she would have gone and sat among the
prisoners. She was made ill, as she put it, by the very first accounts of slavery told to her in New York by Ogden Hoffman,
and in Philadelphia by Dr. Charles Mifflin before she met Pierce.
So she was aware before her marriage of human suffering.

At twenty-three in ther *American Journal,* Fanny lamented
the education and position of women of her day and referred
to men as "our earthly disposers." She had to include herself
with her whole sex, and not for fifteen years did she achieve
independence. It was impossible for her to evaluate herself
separately from her era. She did not ever realize that fundamentally she was waging a life-long contest with the accepted
station of women of the nineteenth century. In 1834 when she
married, women were allowed no choice of action or beliefs
such as Fanny insisted on. No other husband-wife relationship
had ever been envisioned.

What was Fanny's inheritance? Her mother, Maria Theresa
Decamp, was afflicted with hysteria, and Fanny had many of
her traits. Among them was an ability to play comedy lacking
in Mrs. Siddons. Fanny's father, Charles, seems a bloodless
figure when compared to his wife and daughter, though he wept
when he said goodbye to his wife before sailing from Liverpool
and voiced despair in London over the threatened loss of Covent
Garden. As a whole he did not give in to his emotions, and like
all the well-known Kembles showed valor and industry matched
by stoic behavior. But Fanny's brilliance of mind, physical and
moral courage, and granite fortitude are not seen in her fore-
bears.

Fanny was born introspective and given in her youth to lone
wanderings in the country, rhapsodising over nature. She asserted in her Journal her belief in an all-powerful Deity as was
the custom of many poets of the nineteenth century. She indulged in mental self-castigation in her early letters to Harriet
St. Leger, a habit Fanny shared with famous living writers on
the continent and England, and she often exploited in her letters her determination not to let the "unwholesome excitement
of acting" have a debasing effect on her. Despite being well
bolstered by the hard-headed methodical example of her uncle,

John Philip Kemble, and Mrs. Siddons towards the stage, Fanny knew that she was not like them and was all but defeated by fright when playing new parts during her first year in the theatre. It was essential for her to describe this torment and explain over and over again to someone who was not a Kemble that she could not feel about her work as they did. The inconceivable number of her letters to Harriet prove them to be the sustaining factor in an outwardly triumphant opening to her career. Fortunately, she only leaned on Harriet in them, eventually achieved self-reliance, and outgrew her Goethe-like self-absorption. So while writing almost daily of her longing for solitude and a life of contemplation, she was participating in arduous, gruelling reality, but none-the-less relishing the worldly fruits of her efforts. She became "a little lion," was in raptures over the "shoals of partners" at balls, and wanted her parents to let her stay longer. She often wrote in her letters that she only liked dancing parties and was entranced by the beauty of her titled hostesses at receptions and described them minutely. She enjoyed being a guest in large country houses and developed a taste for elegance in living, but ease did not soften her boundless, driving energy. Fanny learned in Scotland at seventeen that mental exercise with educated, thoughtful men and women was essential to her, and she made several life-long friends in fashionable London circles whose minds were stimulating. Acting brought her these well-earned mundane rewards and intellectual gratifications. Sir Walter Scott stopped her on the street in Edinburgh when she was riding and invited her to breakfast. He had admired her performance, and like other famous men, then found her worth knowing. After her marriage, alone at Butler Place or on the plantation, there was no dual world for her of opulent living and creative vigor.

The greatest fault in Fanny's character was her uncontrolled outspokenness. She referred to this trait as "my suddenness," and only her admiring friends could overlook it. This "suddenness" caused serious difficulties for her always. The greatest weakness in her character was being unable to control her temper in her marriage, but her temper is never referred to, except by Pierce, and evidently did not mar her relationship with others. Pierce expected her to swallow slavery and all his shortcomings without a murmur, and scathingly in his "Statement" quoted her when she wrote him that she put her "conscience above all." Fanny was saying that never would she lend herself to what in her eyes was wrong. She had written this to Katherine Sedgwick in March 1842: "I cannot give my conscience into the keeping of another human being or submit the actions dictated by my conscience to their will." She held her integrity beyond the governing interference of her husband. While nineteenth-century women as a rule, from training and expedience, let their husbands hold sway, she would not give in, and the conflict between them was fundamental.

Not a weakness or a flaw but merely an often amusing divergence was her disregard of small convention. She never accomodated herself to her times, never deliberately flaunting, but merely giving no thought to customs which were to her without merit. She walked, fully clad, into a mountain stream in Switzerland, as she had always found running water irrestible. She remounted the donkey being led by a guide, and when her friends protested, said that passers-by would only exclaim, "Ah, cette pauvre dame qui est tombee dans l'eau."

She shocked the neighborhood of Lenox, Massachusetts, in the 1850's by going fishing with Mrs. Charles Sedgwick, who was dressed in a long skirt with bustle, leg-o-mutton sleeves, tight high-boned collar, and bonnet, while Fanny wore trousers, a man's shirt, and hat. They returned from their expedition with Fanny's costume in good order, while Mrs. Sedgwick's skirt was torn and splashed with mud.

The wellspring of her being was her fluent pen. First it was a solace, soon became a necessity, and later, a temptation. Words flowed from it with astonishing ease. When facing her divorce, she wrote to her friends, enumerating her woes, in rolling Shakespearean sentences. Her accusations against Pierce, attached to the court records, could be declaimed from a stage and ring out in the manner of Queen Katherine addressing Cardinal Wolsey. When defending herself or begging Pierce to take her back, she frequently exaggerated the facts, but convinced herself that what she wrote was true. There could, however, be no exaggeration in the fact of the contrast of their characters. From youth onward, using a pen became a mounting daily habit.

The pillar of her intellect was her life-long study and veneration of Shakespeare. It made her a very great reader. With the traditions of the Kembles back of her, and her researches and judgment, she was able to bring to the platform a perfection in interpretation that set her alone in this field. In 1882 Fanny published a volume, *Notes Upon Some of Shakespeare's Plays,* giving her well-reasoned scholarly views on the way certain parts should be acted and lines spoken and restoring words in Shakespeare's text that had been wrongfully changed from earlier editions. In her preface she did not hesitate to disagree with Mrs. Siddons' essay on Lady Macbeth. Her aunt, Fanny stated, played the role by instinct, and Mrs. Siddons' reasoning in her essay was false. In this volume Fanny's mastery of her vast subject is made plain.

The core of her nature was love and respect for the lowly and down-trodden. God made them, and honor and compassion were due all her fellow creatures. The Pierce Butlers did not hold this conviction in common. Thus, the accord between herself and Reverend William Ellery Channing was fundamental. She discussed and disputed with him his belief in the Trinity, but shared his views on slavery. This was also true of her relationship with the Reverend William Furness, who preached abolition, and was one of the reasons he felt her to be a better person than her husband.

In Fanny Kemble's turbulent existence there was more drama than was ever played in Covent Garden, and surely her nascent associations with the theatre were reflected in her unchecked scenes of anger and anguish with Pierce. The pattern of her life in all other respects shows the most iron self-command, and though she gave way many times to hysteria and lay on the floor in tears, she always realigned her emotions and accomplished the essential task before her. At nineteen she mastered herself to play Juliet. When her marriage ended she carved success out of ruin, achieved independence with her reading and a second fame. Her pen, which never failed her, gave her at last a third profession. She wove together her journals, letters, and remembrances, published in several volumes, making the story of her life. Fortune had bestowed on her a talent for the use of words which served her well. She recounted her arduous youth in the manner both of a diarist and autobiographer, and her letters reveal her philosophy of independence and her troubled spirit. *A Residence on a Georgian Plantation* makes clear her sorrow for the slaves and has stature as social history, and through all her writing glows her often tormented heart. She must not be defined as an author with the single theme of slavery, so limiting and falsely relegating her to narrow bounds. She wrote vividly on many themes and thus fulfilled her life of three careers, actress, reader of Shakespeare, and author.

INDEX

Index